CHASING FAE

The Upper Realm

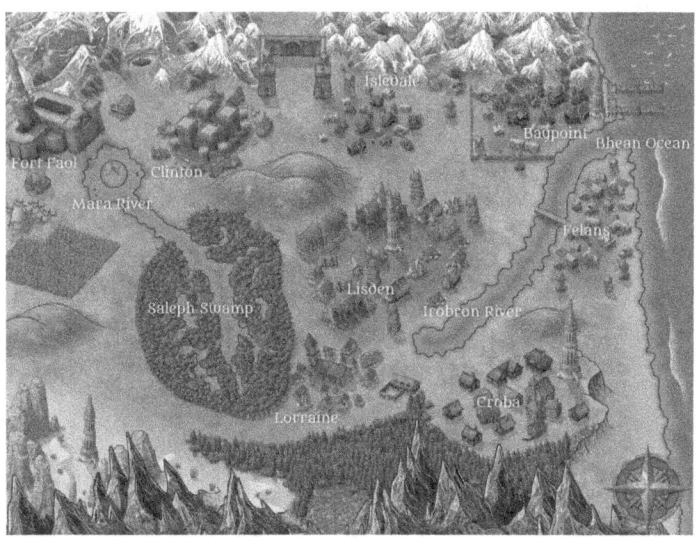

The Middle Realm

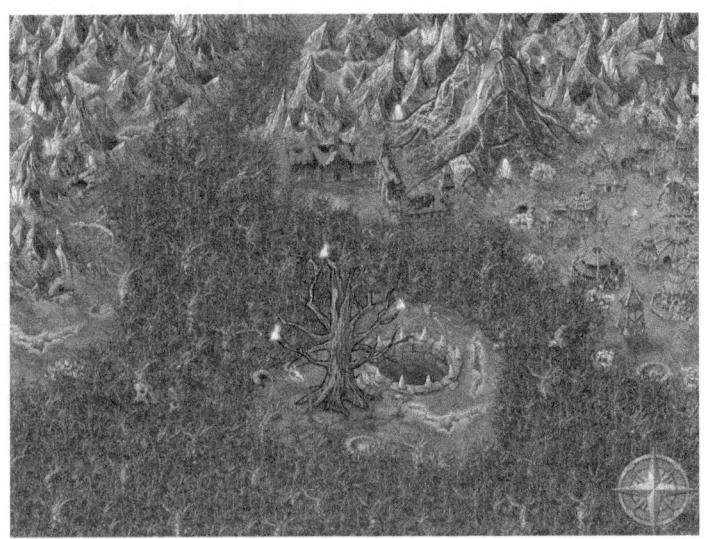

The Lower Realm

CHASING FAE

CADY HAMMER

NEW DEGREE PRESS
COPYRIGHT © 2020 CADY HAMMER
All rights reserved.

CHASING FAE

ISBN   978-1-64137-917-5   *Paperback*
978-1-64137-679-2   *Kindle Ebook*
978-1-64137-681-5   *Ebook*

*For my mom and my dad who taught me
how to go for what I wanted.*

For my sister, Morgan, my biggest fan and my greatest friend.

For Daniel, my love and my heart.

CONTENTS

AUTHOR'S NOTE	11
CHAPTER ONE	15
CHAPTER TWO	21
CHAPTER THREE	27
CHAPTER FOUR	37
CHAPTER FIVE	47
CHAPTER SIX	55
CHAPTER SEVEN	67
CHAPTER EIGHT	75
CHAPTER NINE	85
CHAPTER TEN	93
CHAPTER ELEVEN	103
CHAPTER TWELVE	115
CHAPTER THIRTEEN	123
CHAPTER FOURTEEN	133
CHAPTER FIFTEEN	143
CHAPTER SIXTEEN	151
CHAPTER SEVENTEEN	159
CHAPTER EIGHTEEN	167
CHAPTER NINETEEN	177
CHAPTER TWENTY	183
CHAPTER TWENTY-ONE	191
CHAPTER TWENTY-TWO	199
CHAPTER TWENTY-THREE	207
CHAPTER TWENTY-FOUR	217
CHAPTER TWENTY-FIVE	223
CHAPTER TWENTY-SIX	229

CHAPTER TWENTY-SEVEN	235
CHAPTER TWENTY-EIGHT	247
CHAPTER TWENTY-NINE	253
CHAPTER THIRTY	259
CHAPTER THIRTY-ONE	267
CHAPTER THIRTY-TWO	277
CHAPTER THIRTY-THREE	287
CHAPTER THIRTY-FOUR	293
CHAPTER THIRTY-FIVE	299
CHAPTER THIRTY-SIX	305
CHAPTER THIRTY-SEVEN	313
CHAPTER THIRTY-EIGHT	321
ACKNOWLEDGMENTS	331
AUTHOR BIO	335

AUTHOR'S NOTE

TEN REASONS TO READ CHASING FAE

This is for the reader who wants to fall into a story and never climb out.
I have been an avid reader my entire life. I started reading when I was three years old, and by kindergarten, I was already reading chapter books. I couldn't get enough of stories.

Fantasy has always been my favorite genre. The world draws you in and makes you chase the characters through the book, never wanting to take your eyes off for a second in fear you might miss something. The characters are vivid and passionate and flawed and *real*. You want to join them. You want to *be* them.

And the magic! You can't forget the magic. It captivates and swirls around you as you turn the pages and wonder what trouble it's going to cause next.

I wanted to write that kind of book, and I hope that you, the readers, believe I have created that book.

This is for the introverts who dream of being leaders in their own way. This is for the quiet and the bold.
How many of you reading this identify with introverts? How many of you have been waiting to read something with an introverted main character who seizes her own destiny while staying true to the woman she is?

My main character, Grace, is a passionate young woman who is perfectly content to recharge on her own and keep to herself. But she is a leader in her own right; when faced with a challenge, she attacks it head-on with a stubborn fierceness that will inspire. In my experience, introverts do not get enough credit for their leadership skills, particularly if they are quiet. I promise you will see Grace take charge and blow everyone else away.

This is for the adventurous.
In *Chasing Fae,* the reader is going to be taken along for a high-stakes adventure with new surprises and secrets hiding around every corner. You will be kept on your toes as Grace navigates her way through the ever-changing Fae world she is thrust into. Prepare yourself for the rush of hiding from soldiers, traveling between realms, and running from those who would do you harm.

This is for those who have loved and lost.
This book is for those who have experienced loss in their life, whether it be death, the breaking apart of a family, or breaking of contact with a friend. *Chasing Fae* is about loss and grieving after that loss.

Grace loses her brother to mysterious circumstances, and she will stop at nothing to find out how and why. She is determined not to waver from her goal, which causes her walls to go up whenever someone pokes a hole in her plan. She will be forced to adapt, and in that, you will see her raw emotions start to peek through the cracks.

This is for the romantics who like to see things fall apart before they get put back together.
I. Love. 'Ships. One of the best parts of any story is watching relationships build up and crash, get back together, and fall apart again. Something about the ups and downs of being in love and falling in love makes characters feel more real, more vulnerable. Keep an eye out.

This is for readers who want to scream at a book every time there's a new twist.
I want readers flipping pages at 2 a.m. when they have to get ready for class the next morning, but they *just can't put it down*.

This is for readers who love to get attached to their Harry Potter house.
The Fae's world, the Upper Realm, is made up of Twelve Noble Houses, each with their own distinct culture. They are as follows: House of the Sun, House of the Moon, House of the Day, House of the Evening, House of Light, House of Darkness, House of Water, House of Fire, House of Earth, House of Wind, House of Peace, and House of War. As the book unfolds, and as the entire trilogy unfolds, you will have a chance to step into each one of these lands and catch a glimpse of life there. I am hoping there will be a fantastic split over which House is the best. I know I've got my favorite.

This is for the good girls who want to be just a little bit dangerous.
Don't let anyone put you in a box. You have so much potential inside of you, it is staggering. Believe me, I know a thing or two about what it is like to feel trapped in your identity and unsure of where you fit into the world. Grace is going through this very situation, and she is going to shatter all expectations. I hope she inspires you to do the same.

This is for those who keep getting back up despite the odds.
I love strong female characters. I love how they talk. I love how they go after what they want. But I also like to see their vulnerability. I want to see how they react to heartbreak, struggle, and everything being thrown at them at once. That is the test of a true legend—someone who can get hit with everything in the book, take it all in, and while feeling all of the emotions that come with the challenge, stand back up and live to fight another day. I want readers to know they have it in them. Just like Grace.

Finally, this is for all of the young writers out there who need a little extra push to start that manuscript. To take that leap of faith. I did it. I want to see the rest of you join me.

CHAPTER ONE

Everyone's time runs out eventually. Sometimes it comes quietly in the middle of the night at the end of a long life. Other times, death cuts across your timeline without warning.

Today just happens to be my time.

No, I'm not dead. But this is the end for me.

It's a week before the Winter Solstice, which has always been one of my favorite times of the year. A full feast on the table, as large as money can buy, music pouring out of the windows of every building in Lisden and family to spend the day with. Mom's been accumulating canned vegetables for weeks and recently ventured into the market to bring home the best of the fresh fruits in a small bag. My mouth waters just thinking about the *blackberries*. We never get blackberries in this part of the Middle Realm outside of solstice-time. They're one of my favorite treats. My older brother Leo is due to be home any day now. He's been gone for six months off on another of his mercenary expeditions.

One more assignment, he said, and then he would be home for the Winter Solstice. Just one more assignment and he'd bring me back something nice for the celebration. Just one more assignment.

I was lying in bed when it happened. It was late morning: not late enough to be noon, but not early enough to have time to get things done. I had been awake for hours, but I liked to lie in bed and just think. Sometimes, I'd read, but today, I couldn't get myself to focus. Leo was due home in a week, and I was expecting a letter from him soon. He hadn't written in a few days. I figured the letters must be backed up—communication in between realms is rare and therefore not always speedy—but I had an awful sense of foreboding.

When Leo decided to become a soldier, my mother and I were both terrified. She tried to respectfully talk him out of it whereas I threw a fit and stormed out. I was just scared. Anything could happen out on the roads in this realm. He could have been sent to a peaceful town, or he could be sent south to the farm country where they're fighting for whatever scraps they can get, and they don't care who gets killed. But he held out against both of us, started training the day he turned eighteen, and never looked back.

I was sixteen and he was nineteen when he was first hired to run security out in the trading ports of Baypoint. We cried when he left home, promising to be home in the spring. But we rejoiced when he sent home his first paycheck, and we could afford new clothes and fresh fruit from the market. Leo sent every copper, outside of his expenses, home to us. He had always said he wanted to take care of us someday like Mom had for all these years on her own, and finally he had the chance.

Leo bounced around from job to job until six months ago when he was summoned to city hall with the other mercenaries in his company. We all thought maybe the government wanted to offer him a job, but no. It was the *higher* higher-ups.

The Fae.

The Fae have always had a hand here in the Middle Realm. They control the alliances, the trade, and the resource distribution. They all sit up there in the Upper Realm in their fancy castles and their bountiful homes with their magic and just watch us all run around down here like ants. This time, the Fae needed their worker ants, a group of mortal soldiers, to come run security for a top-secret operation of the House of the Sun. They offered more money than anyone in this realm had ever even heard of, and of course, Leo jumped at the chance. I have never seen him prouder to serve, and Leo could never resist an adventure.

A knock from the front door echoes faintly under my bedroom door, interrupting my thoughts. I pull the covers over my head in hopes I can stay in bed. "Will you see who that is, Grace?" My mom's faint voice calls from the kitchen.

Ugh. She knows I'm awake. I grab a robe and begrudgingly drag myself out of bed, stumbling to the door. I peer out of the hole in the top of the door and am faced with the back of a strange man's head. Behind him stand two other men. They stand rigidly at attention, mumbling quietly to one another. The leader's stance along with the navy-blue uniform marks him as a military man. Then I see the slightly pointed ears sticking out from under his rigid hat. My heart stops.

Fae.

No.

He turns slowly, and I see his face. His skin glows with an unseen light, and his purple eyes seem to bore into mine. It is as though he can see me through the heavy door. Perhaps he can. His features are too bright for this realm. His mouth is drawn tightly into a slight grimace, and I can't bear to think what it means.

"Mom!" I can't hide the panic in my tone. I hear a dish clank into the sink as my mom rounds the corner in a rush. I feel guilty for making her worry before she even saw what the trouble was, but my face says it all. She peeks through the hole herself before opening the door. She opens it so slowly, delaying the inevitable.

As the soldiers take a step forward into the doorway, I can now see that the leader is a Fae commander. The medals lining his breast and the swirling insignia mark him as such. His guards stand behind him. One of them holds a tightly wrapped scroll; the other holds the universal Upper Realm flag neatly folded in his hands. I stand behind my mother, staring blankly at the lot. I can't bring myself to move.

"I'm sorry," the commander says quietly.

My mother collapses to the ground, and I just let her fall. She sobs wildly into her hands as the panic rises up in my chest. I reach out and take the scroll and the flag, shaking my head over and over again. This can't be real. I tear open the scroll, ripping it violently in my attempts. *Leo Richardson—notice of death.*

I drop the flag, and it hits the ground with a soft *thunk*. The soldiers start when it hits the ground, but the commander stops them from moving into our home to retrieve it. *Thank the Lady for that at least. I would have charged them both if they had tried.*

Damn them. Damn all the Fae.

I kneel at my mother's side and pull her to my chest as she begins to wail. I haven't even begun to cry yet. I cling to her as tightly as I can, trying to shush her before the neighbors come to see what is going on. Our pain should be ours, not a spectacle for others to gawk at. I stare up at the Fae commander with what I hope is some sort of dismissive glance.

His even gaze looks down on me, and when we lock eyes, I am filled with a blinding hatred.

"Get out," I hiss. To my surprise, he only nods, and he and his men turn and leave immediately. I wonder how many death announcements he has had to carry out in his life. It may explain the flash of pity I thought I saw behind his glassy demeanor.

I despise his pity.

I see the flash of a maroon coat before my uncle Liam is kneeling by our sides. His door down the hall makes an audible click as it swings closed. "Grace, what happened?" He hugs my mother protectively before addressing her, "Anna, what happened?"

My mother is too incoherent to answer, and I can't find the words. I slide the scroll over to him slowly. Liam takes one look at it, and his breath rushes out in one go. "Ohhh, Grace." He hugs my mother tighter and holds out an arm to me. I lean my head into his hand for one small moment until it is too much.

"Take care of her," I say quickly as I flee to my room. I am being selfish. I know it, but I can't take the pounding in my head. I slam the door and begin to pace the room. The sunlight streaming in through the window is too bright, too perky for the moment. I try to yank the curtains closed, but the heavy fabric tumbles off the walls, causing more light to break. I have no patience for this. My hands tighten in my hair as I look for somewhere to hide. I catch a glimpse of the clothing shoved under my bed, and a rush of emotion hits me all at once.

I dive to the floor and reach far under my bed. Rummaging through my things, I search for the one box that has… *There!* I rip the lid off the jewelry box and throw it across the room. It hits the bookshelf and ricochets off the wall. I cringe and reach to get it, but I stop short when I see the tiny seashell bracelet lying in the case, curled up in the corner.

My hands shake as I pull it out of the box. I toy softly with the pure white shell on the end as I finger the smaller shells lining the string. It was the very last gift I received from Leo. He brought it home to me from the beach on his last mortal assignment in Baypoint. I can't even bring myself to put it on. I finally try to slide it onto my wrist, but it falls to the floor. I pick it up and try again, but my shaking fingers just can't hang on to it.

Finally, my tears come. I scream in my grief, crying out Leo's name to the heavens and praying the Lady would see him safely to the afterlife. I cradle the bracelet to my chest and rock back and forth as I sob and heave for breath. *Come home, Leo. Please come home. You can't be dead. You're coming home, Leo; I need you to come home, big brother, please... Please...*

I cried for a very long time. I don't remember much else of that day or that week, for that matter.

I can't stand the wintertime now. Too cold. Too dark. Too empty.

CHAPTER TWO

Two months later

My time of being compliant is up.

    I stand on the rooftop of the old abandoned hotel, overlooking Lisden below me. Being up here is the only way I can escape from the rest of the world. This place used to be a rooftop patio; you know, the kind where the upper class has their little soirees with drinks and music. Now it's just as sad and dead as the rest of the city. Plastic lounge chairs sit in tatters around the rooftop, minus two that may be usable if lying at the right angle. The lights have been broken for years, the glass still scattered on the concrete. There's no resemblance of those old lavish parties. The rubble and debris just show how far we've fallen.

    Now, this rooftop is just mine. Mine to keep. It's just above the smoke level, thick and grey from the factories. It's one of the few places I can breathe in clean air for a while. It's my safe space. Nothing centers me more than sitting up on this roof with nothing but the wind through my brown curls, even if it does blow the full length into my face if the breeze gets too strong.

And I need that today.

I buried my brother today.

Here lies Leo Donovan Richardson, a kind soldier and a loving brother. May the Lady guide his soul.

I never thought I would see those words as long as I lived.

I can still see my brother's coffin being lowered into the earth. The designs my mother and I took weeks to carve gave us one last glimpse of his life before it was covered over with dirt forever. My mother brought our childhood to life with her hands, chasing us through the park and following us over the hill into downtown. I tried to capture his confidence and his smile when he graduated from basic training as we gathered around him to celebrate. Each line, each cut was filled with a tear. I was so numb at the funeral, though; I couldn't bring myself to cry. I held onto my sobbing mother, trying to keep her upright as the pallbearers finished.

When the coffin was settled, my mother looked up at me with broken eyes. I knew what she needed me to do, what she wasn't going to be able to do herself. So, I passed her off to my uncle and reached for a shovel. I tossed the first layer of dirt onto the coffin.

Rest in peace, Leo.

After the death announcement, we never got a notice telling us when the body was meant to arrive. Weeks went by, and the Fae never brought him back to us. We were visited by only one other official in that time. He was a fool. He mentioned Leo was walking through the mine while on patrol and died during an unexpected cave-in. This foolish man harshly informed us that the body had been completely destroyed, leaving not even *a single piece* of Leo for them to bring to us. My mother broke down and didn't leave her room for a week. I hated him for being so explicit. My mother didn't need to know her son wasn't whole, let alone how broken he was.

That should have been the end of it. We should have been able to grieve and then find a way to move on. I could have gotten there eventually. But then I received a package from the Upper Realm—an unmarked box with nothing more than my name and the street address. Inside was Leo's dagger, perfectly intact with no blood or markings of strife. It looked exactly the same as when he had taken it with him.

That was when I first suspected the whole thing was a lie. Utter bullshit.

My brother never went anywhere without that knife. It was his first luxury purchase when he got his first paycheck as a soldier. He always knew where that knife was, and that blade was too flawless to have been pulled from a cave-in site. Before you think I haven't taken into account the whole magic aspect: if they had repaired the blade, they would have fixed the little nick I made down by the handle the one and only time Leo let me hold it.

The Fae pride themselves on being transparent. They like to say it gives them a better relationship with the mortals down in our realm, makes it easier for them to infiltrate our government, and leaves us less likely to rebel. That and the whole magic thing. When mortal mercenaries are asked to take part in a special operation in the Upper Realm, people pay attention. Mortals are never able to step foot into the Upper Realm unless called upon; it's too heavily guarded. A chance to see the Fae's world? No one wanted to pass that up, especially an adventurous soul like Leo.

Of course, being in the Upper Realm had its dangers. Being unequipped to fight against magic, a handful of mortals died within just the first day. But it became apparent the Fae wanted to take care of these families. Probably to diffuse tension. If a mortal soldier died while in service to the Upper Realm, they were celebrated. Parades were held in their honor in their hometown, and the Fae always covered a lavish funeral. Every man was treated like a hero.

But not my brother. They took my brother from me. My sweet innocent brother, who picked me up when he came through the door and spun me around no matter how much I had grown. My brother, who taught me how to read and how to spot the constellations when we could see them through the infinite grey and smoggy sky. Leo… my best friend. Leo…

But don't worry, Leo. I'm gonna make this right.

I can hear the faint noise of footsteps climbing up the back staircase. My shoulders tense, but I relax when I hear a characteristic knock and the creaking of the door opening. I turn my head back to look over the city. "What took you so long, David?"

The tall man in question moves to my side, rubbing the back of his neck and sighing in exasperation. "Some of us had business to take care of today." He runs a hand through the dark, shaggy mop on top of his head. He's always doing that, and it makes it worse. Sometimes I just want to reach out and fix it.

"Well, I told you I needed to see you right after the funeral. This is important," I say sternly. "I need your help."

David sighs and reaches out to ruffle my hair. I smile at the familiar gesture. "I told you I'd be here. And here I am. Lay it on me, Grace."

I take a deep breath. "I need you to sneak me into the Upper Realm."

The rooftop falls silent, and I cringe as I cast a glance over at him. David's staring at me like I've grown two more heads.

"I'm sorry," he finally says with a grating edge to his voice. "I thought you just said you wanted me to sneak you *into* the Upper Realm. I don't think I heard you right." When my expression doesn't change, he scoffs and starts to walk off. "You're insane. Not a chance in hell."

I grab his arm and hold on as tightly as I can. He tries to wrench it away from me as I plead, "David, no, come on. David!"

"Absolutely not," David protests. "Are you out of your mind?"

"Come on. Hear me out! Please!" I beg.

He manages to work his arm free. "Oh, I can't wait for this one."

"David, I have to find out what happened to him. You know he wouldn't have left his dagger if he was on patrol. You know he wasn't stupid. You know there's more to this just as much as I do. I have to know."

"So? What the hell do you think you're going to do? Just stroll on in unprepared and confront a bunch of Fae until you get what you need?"

"Of course not, David. I would—"

"You would be dead within a day, Grace. Mark my words. You have no idea what it's like up there. I don't even know what it's like there, and I'm a lot closer to the situation than you—"

"I'm not going to run in blind, David!" I shout. When he looks around nervously, I immediately lower my voice. "I'm taking combat lessons with Billy down at the ring. I'll do the research, figure out how to act like a real Fae. I'll be working more now to support our family. I'll put away some money and purchase what I need from the shop or from you."

"And you know you can't get everything you need from this realm," David counters.

"I know," I concede quietly. "I know. That's why… I'm gonna need…" I look around to double-check our privacy. There are ears everywhere when your overlords are magical. "I'm gonna need some things from your connections."

David sighs and looks at me with a hint of sympathy. "It's gonna cost you dearly, love. Black market product isn't cheap."

"I'll do whatever it takes."

David rubs his hands over his face with an exasperated sigh. "I don't approve of this."

"I know," I reply quietly. "But you know I'll do it with or without you." I move to hug him. "You were his best friend. You're mine too. He was my big brother." I rub my cheek against his shirt. "I know you'll make the right decision." A little cruel, I know, but it'll get the point across.

He chuckles dryly and finally hugs me back. "Fine. I'll help you."

"Thank you," I whisper back softly.

David sighs one last time before turning to leave. "I hope you know what you're doing, Grace. For your sake." As he slips out, I hear him mutter, "Let me know what you need. We'll be in touch."

By the Lady, I hope this works.

CHAPTER THREE

Ten months later

The city is always quiet at dawn.

Every time I pass through downtown Lisden on my morning run, I can't help but feel uneasy about the silence. The city sleeps only a few moments past sunrise before the smokestacks from the factories begin to puff out an unbreathable mess. The grocer flips around his sign on the ground floor of his apartment building and waits for hours hoping he'll make a sale. However, before the clanging of the factory bells, the city sleeps in dread of another monotonous day.

Not me. I have no time to sleep.

A strong gust of wind offers resistance as I purposefully change direction to run against it. I don't let it slow me; I fight back. I fight until I push enough to break past and into the rising sunlight. A brief surge of triumph washes over me as I come up over the hill and stop at the top, watching the sunlight graze the treetops of the park below me. My heart twinges as I glance over the swing set Leo used to push me on when I was younger, where we'd sit to have real heart to hearts.

People say you never really know what you've got until it's gone. I disagree. I think you know exactly what you have. You just never realize how much you should have given back until it's too late.

Shaking my head, I sprint in the other direction. No use in remembering. No point. Leo is still dead today, and he will still be dead tomorrow. Maybe tomorrow, though, I can start finding answers to why.

Once I reach the doors of the gym, I take out my keys and slip inside. I'm greeted instantly by the familiar smell of sweat and metal. I strip off my jacket and hang both it and my backpack up before turning toward the mats. Within minutes, my wrists are wrapped up, and I'm attacking a punching bag.

My life for the past year has been nothing but training. Every morning starts the same. I wake up at the crack of dawn to go for a morning run. It seems to help clear my head from another night of insomnia, and it maintains my fitness. Then I head to the gym for hand-to-hand combat training and weapons practice.

Billy has worked me hard over the last year. He owns the biggest gym in town, and he has always had a soft spot for me and my brother. We used to stop by and watch the combat tournaments that went on there. Thank the Lady he never told our mother. Leo would always bribe him with a few slices of my mom's pumpernickel bread, and I think that tipped us over the edge.

I told him I wanted to be a soldier like my brother, but it was incredibly slow going. I was nowhere near in shape. But with time and effort, I built up my body and my stamina, one bruise and callus at a time. Billy taught me how to conduct myself on the battlefield, how to take down a man twice my size in hand-to-hand combat, and how to keep up with the fastest of opponents in the ring. My weaponry knowledge expanded greatly, and I can now handle a broadsword and a bow with more finesse than the basics Leo taught me.

My brother always said I was the most stubborn person he knew. When I want something, I put my mind to it, and I always get it. Guess he was right after all.

I'm so deep inside my own head going over all the details for my departure that a low whistle startles me mid-punch, causing me to miss. My knuckles graze the fabric of the bag painfully.

"By the Lady, David, are you trying to kill me before I've even started?" I shake out my smarting fingers.

A soft chuckle comes from behind me. "Meet me outside when you finish your set." He departs as quickly as he came.

Once I unwrap my wrists, I leave the building and curve around to the alleyway. A pale hand darts out to meet mine, and I take it with a firm grip. The hand pulls me into the alley where I am greeted by a dark hooded figure with dark curly hair peeking out from beneath the cloak. I roll my eyes.

"Are the theatrics really necessary?"

David's hood falls. "You know it." His freckled face grins back at me. "Let me get a look at you." He strolls around me. "You've grown, Grace."

I roll my eyes. "Heh, sure. Let's keep this professional, David."

His grin falters for a moment when I smirk widely back at him. Suddenly, his arms are around my waist, and I'm being spun toward him. Laughing, I bury my head in his shoulder and hug him back tightly. "It really has been too long. How's work going?"

He waves off my question. "Not here, Grace," his voice drops to a whisper. "Too many ears and prying eyes." He looks up over our heads, studying the buildings for a moment as if they are the ones listening. "This way." A hand on my back ushers me down the alleyway, and I go quietly. I knew David had a safe house nearby, but I've never been there before. I've begged to be allowed in, but David was so paranoid about who may be watching. Not that I blame him. In this realm, it's never clear just how involved the Fae are in daily life. But there's palpable fear in the air of making the wrong move, especially when it comes to unlawful activities.

David drags me into the next alleyway and around the corner. "This way." He pushes me down a shadowy staircase that snakes around and under one of the canning warehouses. He conjures a key from his sleeve in a quick motion and unlocks the basement door. We slip inside to the open space, the graffitied walls greeting us. It's a wide-open space suited more for a party than a clandestine meeting place, but hey, I suppose you take what you can get in terms of hiding places in this town.

David leads me over to a dusty, sunken couch and sets me down on it. He sighs as he plops down next to me. "It's getting harder to get in and out," he finally answers, running both hands through his hair. "They recently increased patrols on the mortal side, and they're starting to bring in more guards."

I curse. "What about tomorrow?"

"We should still be fine," David reassures me. "They've only reinforced the main gate and the east side by the ports so far; they haven't reinforced the west side yet." He rubs his hands together. "My pipeline is still clear, for now. Some of the other guys are having a really hard time though. Pickings are slim on the black market these days."

I turn my attention to the bag he's wearing on his hip. "Do you have what I asked you for?"

David whistled and turned to open the bag. "Yes, my dear. I do."

"Please refrain from calling me dear."

He laughs and pulls a silver tie from the black velvet. I reach for it eagerly, but he pushes my hand away and wags a finger at me. "Oh no, I've got very pricey, very volatile items for other clients in here. I'm not risking you touching anything."

"Cause you're afraid I'll take it?"

"Pretty much."

I chuckle. "Fine..." I drag my reply out slowly.

David smiles at me and pulls a small purple vial out of the bag. "Item one!" he says with an announcer's flair. I groan and shake my head at his showmanship, but I can't help but hold my breath in anticipation. "This potion is capable of tricking the barrier long enough to get you across. I promise you it works. I've taken it myself many a time."

"What is it exactly?"

"This is an enhancement potion."

I nod in recognition.

"It has zero effect on the mortal body, but within the first five seconds of being taken, the barrier recognizes that the traveler possesses magical ability and allows them to cross. It's frequently used to get mortal mercenaries across the border. Without it... I mean, they'd disintegrate, you know," he says with a laugh.

I hold out my hand for the bottle expectantly. As David places it carefully in my hand, I run my hand along the smooth moonglass, hoping to soothe the growing fear in my stomach. "Be careful with that. That's a level-three spell. It wasn't cheap. I had to call in a lot of favors to get that for you." I nod. He didn't offer exactly how he came by the potion, and I really didn't feel the need to ask.

This is really happening.

"Item two," David interrupts my thoughts, pulling out a cloak that matched his. "Black cloak. Guaranteed to hide your face from unwanted attention by curious Fae." Taking the cloak, I start to stuff it into my backpack. "Woah!" he shouts. I freeze in alarm.

"Don't you want to try it on first?"

I hesitate. "Come on," he asks. "I want to see if I got the right size."

I pause and sigh, pulling the soft fabric out from my bag. "You know I hate trying on clothes." He doesn't reply but only waits for me in silence. The cloak slides easily over my shoulders, and I fasten the ties in a sturdy knot. I spin slowly and give David a little bow. "Is that better?"

His prideful smile gives me my answer. He takes a step toward me and gently pulls the hood over my head. He studies me for a minute and then abruptly turns to his bag again. To my surprise, he pulls out a small gold mirror and turns it toward me without warning. My heart pauses for a moment.

I'm taken aback by my reflection. The dark cloak shields my face enough to cast a shadow over me, giving me a very mysterious air. The silver lining makes my blue eyes seem more vibrant, more mystical, dare I say… even magical. I could certainly pass as one of the Fae now. *This is really happening.*

A cleared throat from David breaks my stare. "You did good," I say quickly. "I'll pass for Fae."

David laughs. "If I didn't know any better, I'd say you were one of my delivery girls, a true rogue."

"Shut up, David. Where's the other thing I asked for?"

He laughs at me again and reaches deep into the bag. "Alright, alright. Now, this was nearly impossible to find. You're very lucky. I paid an arm and a leg to get it out."

The second the shiny black handle peeks over the edge of the sack, I snatch it out of his hand. I can't help but squeal with excitement. In no time, David's hand is over my mouth. "Grace! What the hell? Are you trying to get us killed?"

I cringe and look at him apologetically. Yet I can't help but glance at the instrument in my hand—a small handgun with a cross-shaped barrel, easily concealed. He uncovers my mouth, and I whisper, "It's beautiful."

"Be careful with that thing," David replies. "It will go until it hits a target. Your aim has to be precise."

I only respond with a brief nod as I study the basement. "Will the grappling hook hold?"

"Yes. It's made of the strongest titanium in the Upper Realm."

I hum and tap the metal. "How high are the ceilings in this room?" I ask as I study a broken pipe near the top of the chamber.

"Fourteen feet. This used to be a pub." David looks at me with slightly narrowed eyes. "Whatever you're thinking about," he says warily, "don't do it."

I turn and face him with a big smile. "Too late." I spin about quickly, take aim, and fire the gun up at the broken pipe. To my delight, a tiny silver grappling hook with a nearly invisible titanium thread flies out, and I hear a soft clink as it connects and wraps itself around the pipe. I grin and tug on the gun to check how taut the thread is. It's secure. David reaches out to me, but I waste no time swinging toward the vandalized wall.

"Grace!" David whisper-shouts fervently.

I ignore his warning and laugh out loud as I hit the wall and begin to climb. Just like the rope at the gym, hand over hand, I practically glide up the side of the wall. I wrap my arm around the broken pipe and retract the grappling hook, laughing. "That's what I'm talking about!" I whoop.

"Grace, what the hell?" David looks perturbed, like he doesn't know whether to laugh or scold me.

"Just testing it out!" I fire again at a hook attached to the wall and take another swing. I'm bouncing from wall to wall, spinning in circles and soaring through the air with each new connection. The grappling hook works like a charm and doesn't let me down with any of my shots. Only when I miss the copper pipe running along the ceiling do I crash down onto the couch with a loud *oof*. When I regain my breath, I retract the hook, sit up with a wince, and smirk at him.

"It'll do." I nod satisfactorily. "Replicates flight magic fairly well. I might be able to pass for Fae."

David grabs me and pulls me into him, shaking me violently. "What the hell was that, Grace? Do you want to get yourself killed? What would Leo say?"

I freeze, and my eyes turn cold. All emotion has just left my body, and I lose that spark I just had, that little glimpse of thrill. I look up and say in a monotone voice, "He's not here."

We're both quiet for a moment as I look away. Nothing else needs to be said. David sighs and pulls me toward him for a hug. "I feel… I don't feel right… letting you go out alone to the Upper Realm. Leo would have killed me."

I hug him back lightly and repeat to myself quietly. "Leo isn't here."

"I wish I could go with you," he starts to speak.

"You know you can't," I interrupt. "You gotta get people what they need. Besides, your *connections* wouldn't be happy if you left town."

I feel him nod against my head. "I'll be outside early tomorrow morning. When you hear three stones hit your window, meet me in the alley outside your place."

I don't answer and just listen to his heartbeat for a minute. He holds me in silence, a quiet reflection on the lost life of his friend and my brother. I know it's killing him inside not to be able to do more. He served in our realm with my brother for two years. He was always in and out of our house whenever they came home on leave.

When Leo died, David lost his mind. Quit soldiering and got revenge on the Fae the only way he could think of—smuggling goods for the black market. He's the best damn runner they've got.

So, I have no choice but to go it alone.

This is really happening.

CHAPTER FOUR

My only regret about chasing my brother's ghost is leaving my mother behind.

She was never the same after Leo's death. It fucked her up in the head, you know? Losing your oldest child will do that to you. But it wasn't just the loss; it was the aftermath. The aftermath is always the worst. The fact that the Fae couldn't even give my mother a body, even just a piece to bury in his memory was just fucked up. It's affected her life in so many ways. Now she's just a shell of the woman who raised us.

My mom used to be this incredible artist. She'd been painting her entire life, and she had a way of capturing raw emotion through color. Blues and greens brought back the joy you felt when you touched the ocean for the first time and the bittersweet moment of the very last time because you couldn't afford to make it out to the coast another summer. Reds brought back the anger you felt against your father who had an affair with the shopkeeper down the street and destroyed your home. I'm making all of this up; I have no idea what people think when they look at my mom's paintings. But you get the idea. Those paintings could make you *feel*.

But when Leo died, she lost the will to create. Most days, she sits in the bay window in the living room and stares outside, searching for something that will never come. On her best days, I see her almost decide to pick up a paintbrush. I watch her fingers twitch as her hand skims over the top of the long-since-abandoned easel. But in the end, she can't bring herself to do it. Her inspiration is gone. I've tried to bring her things that would make her happy or play her songs that would lift her spirits. But nothing ever works. Not for long anyway. She has good days, and she has bad ones.

But the bad ones always outweigh the good in the end.

No matter what I do, I can never be enough for her.

"Grace?" she calls out to me from the kitchen.

"I'm here, Mom!" I call back.

"Out for another run?" She's asking about me. *Must be a good day.*

I hang up my coat and stash my bag in it before following her voice. "Yes, I went for a run over by the park." When I reach the kitchen, I find her at the stove, cooking breakfast for the first time in weeks. Pancakes… I can smell them, rich and buttery cooking away in the pan as a pot of blueberry jam bubbles on the stove. My mouth falls open briefly. I tread carefully. "Wow… Mom… I'm… glad you're up."

"I was craving some pancakes today; how do you feel about that, sweetheart?" Mom comes over to where I'm still standing, shellshocked, and kisses my forehead.

"I… I think that's a great idea," I finally utter.

"Why don't you set the table?" She turns back to the stove.

"Uh… sure!" I break out of my trance and rush to grab two place settings. Anything to please her. The longer I can keep her in this mood, the better it will be for both of us today.

I want to give her this one last perfect day.

She sets down two plates with a generous stack of pancakes on each. I'm pleasantly surprised by the sheer amount she made, and I dig in right away. She laughs at me. "Slow down, Grace."

I chuckle and begrudgingly slow down. "I can't help it, Mom. You make the best pancakes."

She smiles. "You're just like…" I watch her face fall slowly, like a breeze blowing over a feather. I know exactly what she was about to say.

I desperately want to see her smile again, so I try to change the subject. "The jam is great, Mom."

It works somewhat. Her smile is softer now, more of a hint of what I had seen earlier, but it's still there. "Thanks, sweetheart." We eat in apprehensive silence.

While I clear the table, I watch my mother move to her easel. *Is today the day?* She sits down on the stool and faces the canvas. Her hands brush across the paintbrushes and untouched paints. I hold my breath. She finally pops the top off a case of blue paint. I can't help but grin." You going to paint today, Mom?" I ask softly.

She turns to me abruptly, as if startled. I instantly regret asking the question. Her eyes furrow a bit in confusion, but then she smiles, and I just know this is going to be the day. A good day. "I read something yesterday that inspired me. I want to try and capture it."

"Go ahead, Mom," I urge lightly. "I'll come work with you." She nods at me absentmindedly, and I pray she finds what she's looking for.

As she turns to paint, I pull the map book down from the shelf. I bring it to the table and flip it to a well-worn page. Carefully, I unfold the pages and spread the four-panel map across the table. The entirety of the Upper Realm lays before me, marked with tiny, almost indistinguishable pencil markings of mine. Twelve Noble Houses to explore. Twelve lorddoms that could hold the answers I'm looking for.

I trace down to the border where the Middle Realm and the Upper Realm meet. I see the only clear opening in the energy field where one could possibly breach. It's feasible, but it's still next to impossible. About four hours north of the city is the only approved point of trade between the mortal and Fae worlds. Fae guard the mortal border to ensure everything is secure, and some heavy spellwork protects the Fae border on the other side. They want no interaction besides trade, and of course, they want to keep all political and military affairs at a distance. This is where David will be taking me in the morning. With the vial, it's the safest way of making it across.

I follow the border up to the first stop in my journey, Faraday: the biggest trading town in the House of the Day. There, I might be able to pick up something more to disguise myself and more of the specialty items that are harder to smuggle across realms. From there, the journey is pretty open-ended. The mining village Leo worked in was in the House of the Day, but the operation was carried out by a trading partner, the House of the Sun. They came to our city directly, searching for mercenaries who might be willing to make the trip to the foreign realm. When they offered to pay in gold, Leo jumped at the opportunity.

I can't blame him. A chance to get out of this place, a new adventure, and a hell of a payday. I would have done it too. But after that, the information stops. Unfortunately, that leaves me with twelve distinct lorddoms to work with. Twelve places I have to potentially make my way through.

No pressure...

"What are you looking at, Grace?"

I quickly shut the book on reflex. *Calm down, Grace. Way to not look suspicious.* "Just reading, Mom. Nothing important."

"Why don't you play your violin for us? I would love to work to some music."

"Sure, Mom."

I walk over to the bay window where my violin lies on the window seat. I brush my hand across its familiar body before swiftly bringing it to my shoulder and picking up my bow. Spinning to my mother at her easel, I ask, "Is there any song, in particular, you would like to hear?"

I can hear her smile. "Surprise me."

I take a deep breath, inhaling the heady smell of rosin that's been blown across my fingerboard and the wood for years. It's so familiar. I place my bow to the string and begin to pull. I start with a light-hearted melody, tapping my foot in time. Soon after, I see my mother start to tap hers too. My bow dances across the strings with practiced ease, and my fingers quickstep across them. They vibrate with longer notes and jump playfully on the quick sixteenth notes. I'm back in the parlor of some wealthy benefactor's home, moving my head and my entire body along with the music. The world rotates as I spin.

I change melodies and slide into something with a more irregular beat that's a little more danceable. My mother claps as I spin around the room, dodging furniture, books, and paint impeding my path. My feet create some indistinct yet perfectly coordinated pattern that adds to the musicality of the whole piece. I fall into the melody and get lost in the notes and the hypnotic movement of the bow.

I've always been a prodigy on the violin.

I heard the instrument for the first time when I was about three years old. I don't remember much about where we were, but if I think back hard enough, I can just make out the floating melody of a song. I begged my mom to let me try the pretty music. She and my brother had to physically drag me away from the performer. Mom let me take a few lessons when I was five, and then I began to learn on my own. I took to the violin like a bird to flight. I feel this energy flowing from my fingers into the strings and out into the world every time I play. It's special.

I entertain my mother for hours as she paints. I play until my fingers are numb and every slide of the bow feels heavy. I don't stop until dinnertime when my uncle comes over for the weekly roast. "You sure you don't want to bring your violin to the table, Grace? Do you think you can be parted from it for just a few minutes?" he jokes with me as he ruffles my hair. I chuckle and knock his shoulder as we fight over who gets to try Mom's roasted potatoes first.

We talk about idle things—his work, my music, and her art from today. We all avoid the elephant in the room, the empty chair on the other side of the table. Then, after dinner, I play some more—quieter, soulful tunes that bring peace. I want my mother to be at peace. I want my uncle not to hate me for what I must do.

I want them to remember me.

Finally, my mom can't keep her eyes open any longer, and with a soft "goodnight Grace," she leaves the room. My uncle leaves me too with a kiss on the head. The door clicks softly behind him, and I sigh in relief. I thought they would never go to sleep. I wait a few minutes to make sure my mother stays in her room before stashing my violin on its stand. I linger over it for one more minute and trace my fingers over the fine wood. It kills me to think this might be the last time I ever hold it. I allow myself one last trace over the swirl at the head before creeping back to my room. I grab my coat and bag on the way by.

Immediately, I drop to the floor and reach under the bed for my heavy leather trunk. I yank it out and swing it clumsily onto my bed. I detach my left earring and press it to the lock. It clicks, and the lid springs open. I pull items out in rapid succession.

I spared no expense with this. Any money I didn't give to my mother for us to live on went to preparation. Swords, check. Believable Fae imitation outfit to get me through the border, check. Satchel, check. Sixty copper pieces and twenty silver to get me started, check. Combined with the stuff I procured from David today, I should be set. I feel horrible essentially stealing from my mother, but to be honest, I've been the one making the money. I should be able to keep some of it for myself.

Maybe not half our savings, but at least some of it.

I strip down and change into the imitation Fae clothes. Not quite right, but the easiest to obtain. The cloak slides easily around my body and I tie the strings together, sliding both swords into the straps against my back. Holster to my left, satchel swung over to the right.

As I look in the mirror for the first time, I am transfixed by my reflection. The cloak's hood shrouds my face and my brown curls. When I brush one behind my ear, the mirror shows the softest point peeking out. Leo used to tease me about my slightly pointed ears, and I absolutely hated it. But how lucky they are now. I might be able to pass for Fae. I look dangerous, strapped to the teeth and my eyes glowing blue against the darkness surrounding me. My brother's dagger digs into my hip, but I welcome the sting. Better to know exactly where it is on my body than to be fumbling around for it when I need it.

My concentration breaks when I hear three distinctive thwacks on my window. *David*. I suppose I'm ready now. I close the trunk and put it away. I tell myself I'm ready as I close the door to my room and make my way to the front door. I pray I'll be ready as I stride down the hallway, the cloak flaring out behind me like some hero on a grand quest. I'm no hero. I'm not ready.

I take one last look behind me. The moonlight streaming in through the windows makes the apartment feel somber, almost showing me a semblance of what life will look like when I'm gone. Everything feels so empty. But I know my leaving doesn't truly make a difference. Our home was already broken. One crack is indistinguishable from another.

The door closes behind me with a soft *click*, and my fingers trail over the doorknob. Some part of me wants to turn around and go back inside, go back and climb into my mother's bed like when I was a little girl. Have her hold me for a while and protect me from the pain, keep me grounded, keep me home. Part of me desperately does not want to leave. I can wait another month, another year.

No.

It has to be tonight. Tonight… or never.

Leo is calling to me from somewhere beyond the grave. *Find me, sis. Bring me home.*

I let my hand slip from the door, and I walk silently down the hallway. It stretches out in front of me endlessly as I make my way to my uncle's apartment. Every step, I reaffirm my decision to leave. I fumble for the letter in my bag. I glance over it one last time and carefully slip it under his door.

I make my way to the staircase, and I tumble down four flights to the second floor and exit out into the alleyway. David's shadowy figure waits for me under the fire escape as a light shower rains down around us. I lift my face to greet it. There's something freeing about the rain and the way it soaks into your skin, leaving you breathless and full of emotion.

"Grace?" David asks softly. I can tell he wants to make sure I'm ready to go, but I really don't want him to ask. I hold up my hand to stop him, keeping my face up to the rain for a moment longer. I need a minute to breathe.

He waits for me patiently and then prods again gently. "Grace?" I let my head fall to meet his eyes. He's holding out his hand to me. I hesitate, and then take it and set off, pulling him along.

It's time.

> Dear Uncle Liam,
> By the time you read this, I will be long gone. So don't bother coming after me.
> You have always been an important figure in my life. Whenever I needed help with a math problem or even when I was learning to ride a horse, you always came to my aid. I have always admired you for your quiet strength, especially when my brother died.
> I'm going away for a while. I may never come back, but I have to know. I have to know if something happened to Leo down in that mine, if he was kidnapped or killed.
> Take care of Mom for me. Don't tell her where I've gone. Tell her I've gone to find work so I can keep her in comfort, or something like that.

Better I die in her memory as a good daughter rather than a woman on a fool's noble errand.

Please tell her I love her.

I love you.

Grace.

CHAPTER FIVE

We sneak out of the city under the cover of a smoky sky. As David guides me across town, I take one last look at the place that has been my home for my entire life. Everything I have brushed aside over the last year of training—all of the little shops and the alleys where Leo and I used to play in as kids and everything I have ignored—is now starting to make my heart twinge. In the darkness, the shadows of these buildings are like shades of memories I haven't been able to access until now. I have never known anywhere else but Lisden, and now I'm leaving it behind, probably for good.

After many, many twists and turns, David swings us around into a shady alleyway. I see a large covered wagon waiting for us and a short-bearded man leaning against the wall in front of it. David moves to confront him, and they exchange a moment of hushed words before David returns to my side. He gestures in the man's direction. "This is Layton. He's going to take us where we need to go."

I shake Layton's hand. David motions to me, and I climb into the back of the wagon. The wood scrapes my knees as I huddle behind the barrels designed to hide us. I smell some spices and something sweet coming from the containers.

It's a little foreign, yet a comforting smell. David joins me quickly after, and in very little time, we're riding off into the darkness westbound.

"We'll be riding for about an hour," David whispers to me. "Just enough time to get to the drop point."

"The border is more than an hour away," I whisper back.

"We can't get all the way by wagon," David explains. "Too suspicious. We're headed to the railroad tracks. There's an entry point that's isolated in the countryside. It's the best place to hop on a train without being spotted for the rest of the trip to the border."

"They don't check?"

"It's in the middle of nowhere; it's right before dawn by the time it reaches that section. Do you really think anyone cares?"

"Point taken," I concede.

David motions for me to inch closer. "Take a look, darling. Get a last glance of home." He pulls aside the canvas for me to peer out.

The hills roll by in soft peaks as we rumble over the gravel road toward the north. The countryside is so empty. Only a few farms lie scattered across the open land. The fields are completely torn up from the fall harvest, and the land is completely dead for the season. The farmers will come clear the fields once the weather clears up a bit more. I wave for David to close the tarp.

It's all the same for miles.

"Go to sleep, Grace," he says quietly. "Take a power nap. I'll let you know when we're there."

"I'm fine."

"It's gonna be a long night. Just take a nap. Trust me."

I sigh and close my eyes to satisfy him. I have no intention of sleeping, only thinking in silence for a while.

The next thing I know, David is shaking me awake.

"Come on, Grace!" David whisper-shouts to me. "Hurry up!"

I realize the wagon has stopped. I jerk up abruptly and stumble trying to exit the wagon. David grabs my waist and lifts me off. "Come on!" He pulls me along behind him. As we jog, I turn back to watch the wagon leave us.

"How close are we?" I ask.

"It's just up here," he calls back to me. Within minutes, he stops and drops to his knees behind a group of bushes. He tugs on my arm.

I kneel beside him. The smell of the rain-soaked ground is overwhelming. "When does the train come in?"

"About two minutes from now," he replies.

"And the chances of getting caught?"

"I told you, slim. Most officials don't check the early morning cargo train," he assures me. "The conductor's so sleepy, and the guys at the border just want to get everything unloaded and then off to the Fae realm so they can go home. We shouldn't have any issues." He looks down at his watch again. "Get ready. This is gonna be quick."

A few seconds pass, and I can feel the ground rattle underneath us. The wheels squeal against the rails of the track in front of us as the train rounds the corner. "Get ready!" David shouts over the noise. As soon as the locomotive passes us, David grabs my arm and yanks me to my feet. "*Run!*" He takes off down the side of the track alongside the train.

In shock, I hesitate a second too long before taking off after him. The back of the train passes me as I rush to catch up. I watch David suddenly take a flying leap and grab onto the door handle of one of the last cargo cars. Balancing precariously on a small ledge, barely two inches wide, he fumbles with the latch and rips the door open. He tumbles inside.

I sprint forward as fast as my legs will carry me, but I quickly realize I'm falling behind. That second of hesitation has put me that much farther behind. I pick up speed as best I can and manage to reach the edge of the cargo car.

David swings down, one hand firmly on a handle inside and the other outstretched to me. "Grace!"

With one last burst of energy, I reach out. My fingertips brush his, and it is just enough. David snatches my hand with an iron grip and swings me up, throwing me down to the metal floor of the car. We both collapse, breathing heavily.

As I catch my breath, I quickly roll over to look at David, checking to see if he's alright. He's looking back at me with a similar look of concern. I fall back over and burst out laughing. My laugh echoes against the sides of the car. I try to quiet my giggles, but they keep coming. David props himself up and moves over me, his brow furrowed.

"What are you laughing at?" he demands.

I can't answer him; I continue to giggle. I grin and breathe heavily, interspersed with remnant giggles. "That was fun." I gasp breathlessly.

He groans and rolls his eyes, shaking his head at me. "You're insane. You're actually insane." I barely hear him through my cackles. Suddenly, he pulls my hood down so the fabric is pinned against my eyes. "Go to sleep, crazy child. Our travel time's about four hours."

I roll over to face him. "Aren't you going to sleep?"

"I'm not the one headed into enemy territory. I get to go home and sleep for the next twenty-four hours. I can manage." David shakes his head at me.

I nod. Turning over to face the wall, I curl up with my knees to my chest. I draw my cloak around me like a blanket. It cradles me in its soft fabric. I rub my fingers over it lightly. He's not wrong. I could use all the rest I can get. I have a lot of sleepless nights ahead of me. I close my eyes and begin to drift off.

Just as I'm on the edge of sleep, David speaks again.

"It's not too late, you know. To turn back." My eyes flutter open. I don't think he realizes I'm still awake. I don't have the voice to tell him otherwise. We both just let the words sit there out in the open.

He doesn't understand. How could he? He can take his little pieces of revenge with every item he pulls off the black market. Leo was his best friend, but he had other people to turn to. He could throw himself into other pursuits. There was never any other choice for me. Leo was everything that I had. When my talent for the violin was discovered, I stayed home to study and perform. I never had any other friends, no one else to confide in. Leo was it.

And then he was gone.

Finding answers is the only option. *Revenge* is the only option.

I try, but I barely sleep.

Long before I'm ready, David lightly shakes my arm to rouse me. I open my mouth to speak, and he quickly covers it with a hand. "Shh…" he breathes. I keep silent. I hear the wheels underneath our car slowly grinding to a halt. Then there's a soft release of air as the train comes to a stop.

We have arrived.

David crouches low to whisper directly in my ear. "This next part is crucial. We will be caught and sent to prison if you do not do exactly as I say. Do you understand me?" I nod slowly, not trusting myself to speak. He nods sharply and uncovers my mouth as he moves to the center of the car. "Come here then."

I move to where he's kneeling. "The key to this… was getting through the gated checkpoint," David says. "We're through that. Now, as soon as the train stops…" He studies the floor intently. He extends a foot out and taps in three places, and an edge of a square section of the floor pops up. He picks it up and moves it to the side.

There's a perfectly square hole for a nimble person to slide out through.

He chuckles softly at my bewildered expression. "We've got people all over. This system is set up on the last car of most trains now."

The train slows to a stop. The moment it stops, David jumps through the hole, dropping to the dirt under the train silently. He beckons to me frantically. I slide down and drop to the ground beside him. He holds a finger to his lips and begins to belly crawl forward along the length of the underside of the train. I follow.

I see feet moving back and forth between cargo cars, undoubtedly moving boxes and crates down to the border. I am afraid to make any sound, so I hold my breath. When we reach as far as we can go, David turns to me and mouths, "*Wait for me.*" We wait in silence for a few minutes before he rolls out rapidly to the opposite side of the train. His hand reaches under for mine, and I take it.

As he pulls me up, his eyes dart with a controlled nervousness. I follow his gaze and see one of *them* guarding the stretch of the border tunnel. *Fae.* The soldier stands stoically, watching the mortals bringing crates to his feet. *Look how much pleasure he takes in watching the mortals scramble to him; he doesn't lift a finger to help them.*

David slips a vial out of his pocket, a brilliant purple liquid, and uncorks it. From his bag, he pulls out a dart gun. My eyes widen. "One thing to know about black market potions," he says to me. He dips a tiny dart in the liquid, loads it into the gun, and tucks the vial safely back in his pocket. "Surprisingly adaptable to mortal tech." He grins. "Watch and learn."

He trains the gun at the Fae's neck and fires a single silent shot. I could just make out the moment of impact against the Fae's neck as he swats at it like a mosquito. Then it's over. Nothing happens.

David nods definitively. "We're good."

I turn to him incredulously. "And what was that supposed to do?"

As soon as the mortals' backs are turned, David pulls me with him. I'm waiting for the fallout. Any minute, the Fae soldier will turn and see us. We're so out in the open. I shut my eyes tightly.

And then we're in the tunnel and running deeper inside.

"What the hell was that?" I exclaim.

David chuckles. "It renders a Fae's powers of perception useless for about fifteen minutes. Enough to get someone in and out. Very handy little thing."

"You could have told me that before I freaked out!"

"What's the fun in that?" He laughs softly as I slap his arm.

We reach the end of the tunnel, stopping just short of the edge. I freeze. The magical field shimmers with energy, and I can feel the sheer power behind it. Looking at this blank wall in front of me, I am terrified.

"You're gonna have to hurry on through, Grace," David apologizes with a glance over his shoulder. "I can't guarantee you more than a few minutes of protection."

I smile at him softly and lightly press a kiss against his cheek. "Thank you, David. For everything."

He leans his forehead to mine and ruffles my hair with a light touch. "Be safe."

I pull the cloak up over my head and smile one last time at him. "Don't worry," I reassure him as I turn and pull the vial of potion out of my bag. I throw it back in one fell swoop. "I have too much of my brother in me not to go out with a bang." I smile back at his skeptical face and salute him sincerely with a flick of my hand. As I step backward into the energy field, I keep my eyes on his as long as possible, saying a silent goodbye. Then I turn abruptly and face the Upper Realm for the first time.

CHAPTER SIX

Walking across the border between realms feels full and empty at the same time. Once I pass through the initial field, I am surrounded by a bright white light. It is blinding, so much so that I wonder if I'm truly seeing anything at all. I can't detect any edges to the space. I can only trust that I am moving forward by the steps I'm taking. With an air of trepidation, I just put one foot in front of the other slowly, hoping I make it out the other side. Something magical could annihilate me at any moment.

Still, I go on.

Suddenly, the white light recedes, and I'm standing on the edge of a mountain. The Upper Realm lies at my feet.

Whatever I was imagining before is nothing compared to this.

The wind whips past me, blowing my cloak out behind me. The ledge I'm standing on is mere steps away from the edge of the mountain, and as I peer over it, I can just make out the outline of the House of the Day through the dense forest. The sun shines down on me and reflects off the melting piles of snow.

Everything is bright and sharp and clear. I've never seen such bright colors in my life. The air is charged with the feeling of something vibrant, something *more*. A breeze teases its way through my hair, and I breathe it in deeply. *Oh, by the Lady, you can taste it... magic.* It's sharp and sweet, and I find my mouth watering. A smile creeps across my face as I stand, intoxicated. The fresh air is a welcome change from home.

Home. I remember why I'm here. The smile fades.

I've done so much to prepare for this trip, but I never actually sat down and considered what I would feel like once I was on the ground. Sure, I got every step of the logistics I could plan figured out by now. But I was not prepared for the rush of homesickness that flooded through me. *But for what? What home do I have to return to? A grief-stricken mother and a dusty smoke-filled life with no light like Leo to brighten it?* The homesickness is chased away by a rush of fear. *What am I doing here? I'm not ready for this.*

I shake my head violently as if to clear the bad thoughts away. *I've got to shake this.* I peer down the mountain again. Just down the side of this mountain is the House of the Day—supposedly a very light-hearted place with little likelihood of being questioned. Faraday lies at the base of the mountain, one of the largest trading towns in the entirety of the Upper Realm. I need to head there first for supplies. Then on to Shadowshore where my brother was stationed. *Logistics. Logistics, I can do.*

I'm so close. An hour down the mountain and then two hours' walk to the mining village. I just have to take the first step.

My inner monologue disappears as I finally traipse down the mountain. The scenery around me is too mysterious and too inviting for me to ignore. I have never seen trees this tall before. They tower around me, extending far past where I can see from the ground. While I try to keep moving quickly, I can't help but pause to kneel by the wildflowers gathering in little patches along the steep path. My fingers trail across them with care. It's been a long time since I walked through an environment this lush. Lisden is not exactly a prime spot for nature.

However, every once in a while, I find myself looking over my shoulder with a bit more caution. I have to remember where I am now. Danger could be around every corner. I'm without magic with a minor disguise and not enough physical training to get by. I have to be alert.

When I reach the town, however, it takes my breath away.

The dirt roads are open and spacious, even while bustling with wagons and carts. Painted buildings line the roads with delicately carved roofs and colorful shuttered windows. The sky above me feels limitless, and the sun shines down on the town like a spotlight illuminating scenery on a stage. That's what I feel like, as if I'm an actor in a play whose only part is a brief interlude in a scene that's surely going to collapse around me once it's over. I follow the road to the letter, trying not to let my head swivel and give away my curiosity. I'm on a mission here.

As I reach the market, my eyes widen. I've never seen so many different goods in one place. As far as I can see, the square is lined with carts, wagons, tables, and tents full of every item you can possibly think of. I see stalls with fresh fruit, and my mouth waters. How long has it been since I tasted a handful of fresh blueberries? Or an apple? I see tables with impressive weaponry, blades sharpened to the finest of edges and warring staffs with intricate carvings. An apothecary tent stands down a ways where the shopkeeper calls to all who will listen, pushing potions to cure all the world's ills onto any Fae who walks by.

And the people! The Fae! The only Fae I had ever seen were soldiers: stiff, stern, and stubborn. Men and women who always had an agenda in mind. But the ordinary people, the regular Fae, look nothing like that. They brush past me as I push into the crowd, swirling around me as they move toward their destinations. Each Fae is unique with beautiful shiny hair in purples and blues, reds and silvers. Their jaws are as sharp as their eyes, bold and powerful in just as many colors as their hair. You can practically see the magic swirling underneath them. The Fae carry themselves with such strength, so unafraid of the world around them. They have no reason to be afraid. Their magic will always keep them safe. They don't have to worry about immediate and sudden death the same way we mortals do.

Suddenly, a slow burning rage begins to trickle into my heart as I continue to see more and more carts of food. People are dying in the Middle Realm. Half the realm is facing famine while the other half is barely getting by. At least half of our production gets forcibly shipped off to the Upper Realm who produce enough on their own to feed their people! Clearly, they don't need what's ours to feed their people. They take it for their feasts and their excessive lifestyles, and no one gives a damn who they're taking it from.

It makes me hate them. I hate them for their happiness.

I find myself at the edge of the market square gazing with a careful eye before striding across the bustling marketplace with more confidence than what I feel. First priority is clothes. Certain nuances about Fae clothes make them instantly distinguishable from mortal clothes. They are more tailored, bolder. And of course, more colorful. The types of plants that grow in the Upper Realm, and I suspect some assistance from magic, create much more vibrantly colored dyes than down in the Middle Realm. While I have the one outfit, it would definitely raise some suspicion if I kept wearing it day after day. As much as I hate to spend money on something as frivolous as clothes when I have no idea what's ahead, I can't argue against the benefit.

I find a table laden with the finest silks I've ever seen. I can't imagine what they're doing in a trading market instead of taking their wares directly to the nobles. I can't imagine nobles do their own shopping around here. *Not quite what I need...* A few stalls down, I find a tent with peasant clothes: a little rough on the outside but sturdy and comfortable on the inside.

"Hello, young lady, how can I help you today?" A purple-haired older woman approaches me. Hands resting on her hips, she reminds me of my neighbor who would always invite me and Leo in for a plate of cookies. Her face looks kind, but I know better. I can feel the soft power radiating from her as she approaches me.

I keep my head down. "I'm looking for a couple of outfits. Nothing fancy. Something good for a journey."

"Oh! Where are you traveling to?"

I think for a moment and then reply, "I'm headed to Shadowshore."

"The mining village?" The Fae moves to pull some clothes for me. She glances over me calculatedly, presumably to check for size. "What business do you have there?"

Irritated by the continuation of the conversation, I snap a reply. "A friend invited me to visit."

She doesn't seem to pick up the stiffness in my voice. "Oh, how nice! Let's find you something nice to wear."

"Ma'am, I really only need basic travel clothes, please. I don't have much money to spend here."

She reacts to this almost immediately. "Oh, I'm sorry, dear. I didn't mean to presume. I get so excited when I see young people coming in. Would these do?" She holds out her cloth-draped arms out to me. "I've got two tunics that I think will suit you, blue and purple, and two sets of leather pants; I think you would look fantastic in these." She raises her right arm slightly. "This is a blue velvet dress with a patchwork skirt; I made it myself."

"And finally, this little number." She drops the pile of clothes in my arms and turns back to the table. She pulls up a dark brown half top and a black skirt that starts short and flares out long in the back. She holds it up for me to see, and I can't help but feel a little pang of desire. It looks fierce; it's perfect.

"All of these are wonderful, ma'am," I reply. In my head, I'm calculating. There's no way this is any less than three silver. "How much is this going to run me?"

The woman smiles at me. "For you, one silver."

I'm taken aback. "Excuse me, did you say *one* silver?"

"Yes, miss. You seem like a special young lady, and I can afford to take a little bit of a loss on this one."

I don't know what to say.

"Come on, I can see that hungry look in your eyes. Take them."

I look up at her and allow a small smile to creep onto my face. "Thank you very much, ma'am." I pull the coin from my bag and pay the woman.

As I leave the tent, she calls out after me. "Have a safe trip!" I turn back and wave slightly as she beams back at me. I can't help but smile back. *Such a kind lady.*

But she's Fae… don't forget that.

I stop behind a fruit stall to fold my clothes and put them in my pack. I look around me, taking a moment to just absorb it all. The Fae mill about between stand and stall and tent. I hear conversations all around me—loud and vibrant and friendly. There's haggling and good-natured ribbing. Children run around underfoot, their ears just starting to gain a small point.

I hate it.

It's too… normal. These children, no matter how old they are, are still Fae children. They still have immense untapped power building up inside their tiny veins. They will still grow up and study magic, perfecting their craft. They'll grow up to learn their superior position over the other Realms. In turn, it will change them to haughty, condescending creatures just like all the others I've ever encountered.

The Fae can never be fully innocent. Never.

With that thought in mind, I turn a calculated eye to the marketplace and move to pick up a couple more essentials for my pack. I buy some bread and fruit to tide me over until the next town. I find a leather canteen with a water purification charm for the times I can only gather water from a creek or stream. This would be useful because even though all the wells in the towns and cities on my planned route should have similar charms, I don't want to take any chances. I swipe it off the table and dart behind another stall to avoid being detected, a spark of conscience reminding me I'm stealing.

Yes, I stole it, I tell myself. Somehow, I got away with it. I guess whoever owned that stand didn't have any kind of detection magic. *I don't have enough money to spend, and I need the supplies,* I rationalize. I'm not a fan of stooping down to their level to accomplish my goals, but when necessary,

I'm willing to get my hands dirty. In addition to the canteen, I manage to swipe a healing cream for minor injuries and bruises and a stronger healing potion, should something more serious than cuts and bruises befall me. My satchel bulges with my haul. I've gotta get out of here before someone notices those are missing.

I breeze by the accessory carts as I wind my way out of the square. Hats, watches, scarves, silver, gold, copper; all of them fly by me as I make my way through the back of the market. The smell of roasted meat almost draws me off course, making my mouth water. I barely manage to get past that tent without stopping. I'm nearly out on the other side when something glints violet out of the corner of my eye. The glare off of it is so bright I have to turn my head away. But now I'm curious. I make my way over to the rickety cart, leaning in close to the model head on display.

A purple amethyst necklace sparkles up at me. Or at least, I believe it's amethyst. It's clear some magic has been infused into it as tiny flecks of silver glitter and occasionally swirl within the stone's surface. The delicate chain looks like pure silver, and it draws me to it like a moth to a flame. My fingers reach out and graze the surface; it feels smooth and comforting against my skin.

"She's beautiful. Isn't she?"

I startle. My hand flies to the dagger at my waist as I whip around. I relax a little when I see the elderly man leaning around the side of the cart, likely the proprietor. His wispy silvery hair spreads down his neck and meets at a prominent beard. His green eyes sparkle as he reaches out and takes the amulet from the case. "You know…" he starts, "That piece, in particular, bears a very precious stone mined in the mountains around the House of the Evening. The silver is from there as well."

I relax a little more, my suspicions confirmed. It's only the seller. "Yes," I reply softly. "It is beautiful."

"That necklace is infused with very powerful protective charms designed to protect the user from a wide assortment of magic and charms. I would say it's as strong as powerful deflection magic. If the user casts it at the time of the full moon, the moonlight will amplify the effects."

I resist the urge to roll my eyes. He's clearly trying to push this on me. "Thank you for your time, sir." I start to move away.

"Would you like to try it on, miss?"

I hesitate and turn back slowly. *It wouldn't hurt just to look again... would it...* "Alright..." I take the necklace from the old man carefully. Looking in the mirror hanging off the side of the cart, I fasten the clasp around my neck. The stone falls perfectly against my upper chest, cradling itself against my skin. I feel a surge of power against me and then feel it almost absorb into my skin and fade to a dull mist.

Incredible...

"Would you care to test it out?"

I shake my head in confusion. "What do you mean—test it out?" I turn to the seller to find a fireball flying at my face.

There's no time to duck; I have a split second to react. My head rushes and my lungs struggle to take in another breath. *Oh, by the Lady, this is how I die. I can't believe I was so stupid. One beautiful necklace and suddenly I forget everything about the Fae. This is how I die.* I raise my arms to shield some of the flames, knowing it will still burn through my skin. Maybe my body will be recognizable if my face only is partially burnt.

I'm so sorry, Leo.

But the heat never comes. My skin never burns. All I can feel is the rush of a soft breeze around me. I hesitantly open my eyes. A soft purple glowing mist surrounds me. The mist has deflected the fire, and it's burning on the ground in front of me. The shopkeeper stamps it out. I am in utter shock. My jaw won't shut. I'm a mortal... and yet the necklace protected me.

I have to have it.

"See? It works perfectly for you," the old proprietor interrupts my thoughts.

"Yes," I agree hesitantly, trying not to sound too eager. "Although I would have appreciated a warning before you chose to attack me." I smooth my fingers over the stone idly. "How much are you asking for it?"

"One gold."

There's the silver lining.

"I'll give you nineteen silver," I begin to haggle.

The gentleman wags his finger at me. "Oh no, no, no. No haggling, my dear. This is an incredibly rare piece. The strength of the magic itself is at least worth ten gold, not to mention the amethyst itself and the silver chain. It's a bargain."

I bite my lip. *There's no way in hell...* "Can you come down at all?" I ask politely. "I am... about to undertake a long journey, and I would like to save as much as possible for the road."

The Fae observes me pensively. "A quest, eh?" I open my mouth to correct him, but he interrupts me. "Oh, don't try to argue. You have such a determined look in your eyes; you're an open book, dear." He grins. "Tell you what, I'll give it to you for sixty silver and not a copper less. That's my final offer."

I curse internally. "What about a trade? Nineteen silver and… a healing potion. Moderate strength."

His eyes narrow ever so slightly, and I think for a moment I've pushed him too far. But then he smiles again and holds out his hand. "You drive a hard bargain. I accept." I clasp it firmly before pulling the potion out of my pack.

I count out the silver pieces into his hand, and he sweeps them away. "Pleasure doing business with you. Be careful on your journey, girl."

Nodding in acknowledgment, I turn my back to him and stride out of the market into the back alley. I look down at the necklace again. I can't get over how well it settles onto my neck. *And it fucking worked.* I can't even begin to imagine how much easier my journey has now become. I may be down a significant amount of money, but if this amulet can withstand most charms, I can get out of so many situations if I need to.

I grin widely. *I'm coming, Leo. I won't let you down.* And with that, I wander out of town, headed east toward Shadowshore.

CHAPTER SEVEN

My walk to the mining village is oddly peaceful despite the length. I follow the main road out of town, keeping an eye on the tree line as it curves around the corner and away from Faraday. Despite the cold, I see small white and purple snowdrops blooming among the taller trees interspersed with the bare ones. They are quite beautiful. I have never seen any flowers in the Middle Realm grow during the wintertime, not that there are many flowers in my home to begin with.

I walk for hours, only stopping for a midday meal of bread and fruit. Surprisingly, I only pass a handful of wagons moving in either direction. All of them are loaded with goods—fresh produce moving from Faraday and coal being exported from Shadowshore. Nearly all the carts headed the same direction as me stop to offer me a ride. I keep my hood down and reply politely that I rather enjoy the fresh air and would prefer to walk. My legs are actually aching like crazy, but I try to ignore it. Who knows what could happen if I hop on in? The Fae aren't offended by my dismissal; they only wish me well on my journey and go on their way. I almost regret swiping fruit out of their carts as they roll on. Almost.

It's so odd to me. In the Middle Realm, you would never find any merchants like that. None quite as kind; they tend to keep to themselves. I don't blame them. Moving goods down in my home realm is so much more dangerous. We're not starving in Lisden, but food is definitely not in great abundance. Other places are far worse off. Many merchants travel with armed guards just to ensure they get to the next town without being robbed or worse. Many members of my brother's old company were hired as guards for those trips. Several were killed.

These people make me crazy, these Fae. I mean, I would assume if they knew I was mortal, they would treat me entirely differently. *Yeah, chase me out of town with flames and stones, all right.* But, not knowing me, they have the ability to be kind and generous. *Is that normal?*

It takes a while for me to realize I have arrived in Shadowshore. The edge of the village actually begins out in the forest and in the fields along the road. I come across small pockets of domestic life and occasionally a one-floor house out where the land stretches out on either side for acres. Every once in a while, I see an older gentleman out on the front stoop, staring off into space, or young men in the fields sowing grain. I've never really thought about life being outside of the mine—a whole society in play. Although when you're focused on taking down the Fae, you don't really consider details like that.

I enter the center of village by mid-afternoon. Plenty of Fae are milling around the square in between shops and businesses and homes. A few men sit on the thatched roofs conversing with some people down below while they work on patching up the structure. Children play in the nearby fountain, splashing each other and some creating small orbs and animal shapes out of the water. I see a father teaching his son how to manipulate the earth in small peaks and hills with a flick of a hand. I try to ignore it, but I can't help but take just a little peek at the magic lesson.

I try stopping people on the streets and in the square to ask about the mine. But the friendliness I have been encountering all day appears to stop at this particular subject. "Excuse me, sir, I'm looking for some information about the mines around here," I say as I gently approach. "I'm in need of some assistance." But every man I stop either brushes me aside with a lack of information, or their eyes glint with the inklings of knowledge and then quickly knock me aside and disappear off to wherever they are headed. I try approaching the women carrying baskets from the grocer's, but they shy away from me as if I'm someone to be afraid of.

After a couple of hours with no luck, I finally spot the most crowded area in the entire village: a bar. Figuring it can't hurt, I stride over with purpose, my irritation from a lack of information fueling my steps. *Isn't the mine these people's livelihood? Why will no one speak to me?*

My irritation runs out when I slip through the doors to the bar. The place is bustling with people; every wooden table is packed. The noise level hovers between a low din and a dull roar. I've never been very good with a crowd of people in a tight space. From across the room, I watch the bartender mixing drinks with ease and slinging them down the bar to the waiting hands of the barmaids. Food is being shuffled around by these women in tight dresses with heavy brass trays who seem to fly around the chaos. Perhaps they are flying. As I make my way to the bar, I'm alert and scanning the crowd for someone who looks like they know something.

Someone in here has got to know something. I mean, this is a Lady-damned mining town. How can no one know what's going on with the mine?

As I stride toward the bar, I can feel eyes shifting onto me. I inwardly cringe. Maybe having the swords strapped to my back doesn't give off the "low profile" image I was going for. But it's too late to think about that now. Maybe if I walk with purpose and act confident, no one will question me or my odd appearance. *Here's hoping.* I sit down at the last open stool at the bar and signal the bartender with a hand.

"A beer, please, sir." I nod to the bartender.

He nods and shuffles off to get me a drink. Now, to be honest, I've never had a beer before; again, supply is limited down in the Middle Realm. But the drink should help me blend in while I take a look around.

The bartender sets the drink down beside me. As I take it, I confront him. "Sir, what can you tell me about the mine?

I'm taken aback when he looks at me with a piercing, almost menacing glare. "Who's asking?"

Thinking fast, I answer automatically, "I'm a mercenary looking for work in the area, just trying to get to the next House. I'm almost out of money, and this was the closest place. I heard the mine here is fairly profitable."

"It used to be," the bartender says shortly.

Feeling resistance yet again, I press on. "What can you tell me about the area? Who should I speak to about a job?"

Next thing I know, the man has a switchblade in his hand, the point pressed down on the bar's surface. My eyes widen, and I take a look around. This must be normal for the guy because almost no one looks over. The couple of people who do give me no sympathy. They shrug it off and turn back to their drinks. "Look, buddy," the bartender grimaces. "That's not the kind of question you want to ask around here. We stay away from it, and the soldiers stay away from us. They excavate, we take the materials and sell them. That's all you're going to get out of anyone here. And if the wrong people hear you, well, you're gonna have a lot of bigger problems than a lack of money."

I nod quickly, my eyes trained on his fingers curled around the handle of the knife. I only let myself relax once he slides it away. "The beer's on the house," he concludes roughly. "Do yourself a favor, finish your drink and get the hell out of here." He trots away to deal with other customers.

My heart pounds in my chest as I shakily sip my beer, cringing at the bitter taste. *Ugh. Why the hell did Leo like this stuff?* My thoughts are racing. *How did I manage to hit a dead end before I've even started? Why are these people so terrified of what is going on in that mine? What the hell was Leo mixed up in?* After another sip, I give up on the drink and begin to head for the door to try somewhere else. As I pass by a table against the wall, a hand darts out and grabs my arm to stop me.

"I can tell you what you want to know, sweetheart."

I jerk back in surprise, turning my head slightly toward the direction of the voice. A small man sits with his head low, clutching a beer in his right hand. His appearance is quite scraggly, but his face appears authoritative. I scan his face, and his smirk sends a chill through me. "You wanna know about the mines, little girl?" I bristle at the steel in his tone. But he's the best lead I have seen all afternoon, and I need information desperately. I nod slowly, and his smirk widens.

He lets go of my arm and motions for me to come over. Hesitantly, I make my way over and sit down in the empty seat across from him, the wooden seat creaking under me.

The man slowly looks up at me, his eyes glinting dangerously. "No information comes for free. Five copper," he says.

Ah, he wants to cut a deal.

I slip five coppers out of my bag and stack them in front of me. In a voice that sounds way more confident than I feel, I offer him a counter. "I'll give you five if your information is good. But I want the information first."

"Make it ten, and you've got a deal."

I cringe at the increase, but for information, I'll do anything. I nod once as he chuckles and holds out a sweaty hand to me.

"The name's Finn. I used to be the owner of the mine. My information will be worth it." I shake his hand once firmly, resisting the urge to wipe off my hand as I pull away.

I take five more coins out and lay them on the table. "Go ahead."

"What do you want to know?" He takes another swig of beer.

"Tell me why the House of the Sun is mining in the House of the Day."

He chuckles. "You already know a few things. Don't you? Smart girl." He grins. "It's true; the House of the Sun took over for the House of the Day about two years ago."

"Took over?"

"Well, of course, we were mining here first," he continued. "I was the owner of that mine for fifteen years. It was the main economic provider in this area. The farming's alright, but the mine was the far more lucrative option. We had men of all ages in and out of that mine every day."

This was news to me. "So… what changed?"

Finn drums his fingers on the table before throwing his hand out carelessly. "One day, a particularly powerful mage came to visit Shadowshore. No one had ever seen him in town before. The power radiated off him in droves. Turns out this man was from one of the more powerful Houses of the Realm, and he was interested in the contents of our mine."

My eyebrows furrow. I try to take note of every word. "What was he interested in?"

"A particularly..." he hesitates and then grins, looking around shiftily, "rare substance that he believed our mine was the last to possess. He bought the mine on the spot. In gold."

I raise an eyebrow. *In gold?*

To my knowledge, very few Fae possessed enough gold to purchase an entire mine, and very few carried it around on their person. Then an errant thought crossed my head, something I hadn't considered in my excitement for information. He said he was the owner of the mine? Shouldn't he be swimming in gold? He certainly shouldn't need to ask me for money in exchange for information.

I continue anyway, hesitantly, but keep my guard up, now even more unsure of whether I could trust him. "So, this mage... did he hire the soldiers?" I am trying to keep all of this information straight in my mind, and I just have so many more questions. *It must have been a decent amount of gold to buy an entire mine; he would also have the money to pay the soldiers, right?* "Finn, you said he was from one of the more powerful Houses? Did he come from the House of the Sun?"

Finn shakes his head. "The House of the Sun came two weeks later with a group of mercenaries from both the Upper Realm and the Middle Realm. They took over, bought out everyone's contracts with the mine, and set them straight to work digging."

I feign interest. "Soldiers from the Middle Realm? Why would they need mortals?"

"Hell if I know." He takes another drink and signals to the bartender for a refill. "I never understood why they would bring those bastards in. Can't do anything to save themselves."

My fists tighten under the table. "Yeah… strange…" I manage to reply.

Finn looks at me curiously. "Oh, don't tell me you're one of those mortal sympathizers."

I quickly reply, "Oh no, sir. They're horrible. They do everything the hard way. No magic." I cringe at my faltering response.

With narrowed eyes, Finn continues. "They've been searching for something important for the last two years. No progress yet, as far as I can tell."

"Do you know what they're looking for?" I ask.

Finn leans across the table close enough for me to feel his hot breath against my cheek. "I would tell you, sweetheart, but uh…" His eyes flick to the doorway of the bar. I look up quickly and gasp. Four Fae soldiers are staring in our direction intently as if they know if I was asking questions. My worst suspicions are confirmed when they start moving purposefully toward our table. "I think you have a date with a higher power."

I whip around to look at Finn, who is grinning wickedly. He turns his head to shout out the soldiers, "She's the one, boys!"

Oh fuck.

CHAPTER EIGHT

The bastard sold me out. I swear loudly. Finn laughs.

"A word of advice, sweetheart, although I doubt you'll need it when they're done with you. Be wary of telepathic magic." He smirks broadly. "Didn't even have to leave my chair to tell the soldiers that someone is snooping around the mine. I wish you a painless death."

"You bastard," I spit out, backing up toward the bar.

"That's the way the world works, darling. Sorry I had to be the one to teach you."

I have to think fast. The soldiers close in on me. The tallest of them speaks to me. "Miss… we're going to need you to come with us."

I shake my head. "On what grounds?" Maybe I can talk my way out of this.

"Miss, do not resist; it will only make things worse," his voice steamrolls right over me.

I groan and whip around, searching for a way out. The small window behind me catches my eye. *The glass looks thin enough. If I can get close enough…*

"Miss! Now!" the Fae soldier shouts. The three men behind him keep their hands poised over their swords, ready to fight if necessary.

I sigh. *Lady... protect me.*

I turn my back to them slowly. "Alright," I answer. I hear them stop behind me. "I'll come with you." My hands wrap around a mug of beer the bartender has just set down.

"I'll meet you in hell."

Whipping around, the cup flies out of my hand straight up to the chandelier hanging from the ceiling. As the glass shatters, the liquid coats the glowing candles and ignites. Fueled by both the oil and the alcohol, the blaze coats the flimsy chain and sends the fixture crashing down. Patrons scream as it hits the table in front of the soldiers, sending up a burst of flame that causes them to cover their faces with their arms.

Wrapping the bar cloth over my hand to protect it, I punch through the glass of the window and leap out headfirst. I hit the ground hard, rolling to a stop and cringe slightly as smoke begins to pour out of the window.

Not ideal. Already bringing attention to myself, and it's only my first day!

With no time to berate myself, I scramble to my feet and sprint away from the bar. My legs burn as I try to push through after hours of walking from Faraday to here. A small crowd of Fae begins to gather, moving toward the bar, and I push my way through them as best I can.

"Stop her!" I hear the shout from behind me.

I take off running, pushing over the last few people in front of me. Throwing a glance over my shoulder, I see the four soldiers bust out of the crumbling bar. Their arms show minor burns. It was a pretty big explosion, so they must have some sort of shield magic. Within seconds, they're gaining on me, their legs are almost a blur. *Speed magic. Damn!* I fumble for my bag, trying to unlatch it while I run. They're too close. Thirty steps behind, twenty steps behind, ten steps behind.

My fingers finally close around the grappling gun, and I yank it out to fire up. The lead soldier's fingers grasp the edge of my cloak as the hook winds around a chimney behind me. As I feel the thread pull taut, I close my eyes and jump. The retraction pulls me upward rapidly. The soldier's grip threatens to hold me back on the ground, but with enough effort, I'm able to wrench away. I soar backward over the Fae's heads while they look up in anger. I smirk and laugh.

I collide with the chimney with a hard *oof*. My feet slip and slide on the angle of the roof. After I catch my balance, I look around quickly at my surroundings. The rooftops rise and fall all the way back to the edge of town where I came from. *How am I gonna do this?* I muse.

With one hand gripping the top of the chimney, I disengage the grappling hook and refire it at the chimney two houses down. I let go and run across the roofs over to the next section, disengaging and refiring as I move along. My feet tumble down the wood and straw, pushing pieces off the roofs as I run.

Below me, I can hear the soldiers pacing me on foot. *Fuck, this isn't working at all.* As we move toward the edge of town, the soldiers double and then triple. When we reach the edge of town, I slide down to the ground and take off into the woods, assuming naively I can lose them in the dense trees.

That plan immediately fails as they catch on to my location on sight.

Now I've got to find a place to make a stand. I can't outrun them. At least I have a shot at fighting a few of them off.

May as well go down swinging. My legs move as fast as they possibly can, tearing through the woods and dodging trees left and right. I change direction abruptly, buying myself a couple of extra seconds.

The shouting moves closer. I can hear it from all directions. *They're surrounding me.* I curse their tactics. My heart pounds deep in my chest. The shouting gives way to a heavy buzzing in my ears.

Suddenly, an arm reaches down from somewhere in the foliage and yanks me upward by the straps holding the weapons on my back. I scream, but a rough, callused hand stops it by covering my mouth. A deep, woody smell fills my nose. My body is roughly pulled onto a branch several feet up, covered by a curtain of green leaves.

"Shhhh…" a harsh voice hisses in my ear. I'm too frightened to move or make a sound. My heart's leaping out of my chest. "There's a good girl…" The male voice slides over me like molasses, making me shiver. "Now, don't make a sound."

In my peripheral, I see the soldiers under the trees searching frantically for me.

"By the Lady, where the hell did she go?"

"I saw her turn this way, I swear."

"Split up, men. She can't have gotten far."

I watch in relief as they disappear in all directions into the woods. My shoulders relax a fraction. *Thank the Lady they don't have sensing magic.*

Then I become hyperaware of the hand at my mouth and the solid broad chest at my back. "Now what do we have here?" A warm breath blows at my ear.

Fuck.

The arms slide away from my body, allowing me a little space to breathe. I feel the man shift behind me and slip down the tree trunk. "Come on down," he calls up to me. "It's safe for now."

I hesitantly climb down. As I hit the ground, I take a minute to get a good look at my rescuer. He's dressed like an off-duty soldier, his regulation shirt stretching against a muscular frame. He's nearly as strapped as I am, jeweled sword at his hip held on by a tight leather belt. He makes no move toward his weapon, though. I have no idea why not. Instead, he takes the time to stare at me, hands tucked behind his tousled blond head in such a nonchalant manner.

"Interesting outfit," he says lightheartedly with a smirk stretching across his lips. "What exactly are you supposed to be?"

My eyebrows furrow. "Excuse me?"

"I mean the costume. What are you trying to be? Female assassin? I can't quite tell."

A costume? My jaw tightens as I grind my teeth. "This is not a costume," I enunciate angrily. "I'm traveling, and I prefer to be armed." I tighten my weapon straps. "It's dangerous."

"Where's your family? Do you need help finding your way back to them?"

What the hell is going on?

"How old do you think I am?"

He shrugs. "Fifteen? Maybe Sixteen?"

I throw my hands up before sliding my dagger out from my belt. I hold it up threateningly. "Seriously? I'm nineteen. And I suggest you keep your mouth shut, or you're going to find this blade in some less-than-desirable places."

"Woah... really?" He seems genuinely surprised! "But... you're so tiny!"

The next thing I know, I've got the man pinned up against a tree with my dagger at his throat. "Don't you say… another word, you smug Fae bastard."

To my increasing fury, he chuckles at me. "You don't really think you can hold me here, do you?" In one swift motion, my arms are held tightly in his hands as he physically lifts me up and off of him. He keeps me suspended between his two hands, kicking freely in the air. I attempt to swing the knife at him, but my motions are limited by how firm he is keeping my arms at my sides. My wrist movements are wild and erratic, and eventually my blade falls to the earth. My stomach drops as I swing weightless. This Fae can crush me at any second, and I can't stop him at all.

Somehow, he doesn't seem to notice this. He laughs instead. "Easy, woman." He sets me down. I straighten up and pick up my dagger, attempting to ignore the burning in my cheeks. "A thank you would suffice."

"Thank you," I snort.

The man smirks again. "I am Aiden Çaelic, at your service, darlin'." He sweeps into a low, cocky bow. His bold blue eyes glint up at me teasingly. In another world, in another time, perhaps I could find him attractive. Now, I just find him utterly irritating.

I roll my eyes at his antics and turn back toward town. "Nice to meet you," I drawl. "Now, if you'll excuse me…"

"Oh no you don't," he cuts me off, bodily blocking my path. "You're not getting away that easily. I saved your ass. Now you owe me."

"Oh, I owe you. Is that how this works?" I retort.

Aiden smirks. "You owe me at least two answers. First, what's your name?"

"Karen."

He laughs. "Oh honey, you are a terrible liar. Besides, Karen doesn't suit you. Tell me the truth this time."

I scoff and try to move around him. He moves to block my path. I change direction. He follows. I glare. He smirks and raises an eyebrow expectantly. I sigh. "Grace."

"Grace," he draws out my name. "That's much better."

I try to step around him another time; he slides to block my path. "Do you get some enjoyment out of this?" I ask irritated.

"Yes, as a matter of fact, I do. Besides, you haven't answered my second question, sweetheart."

"Don't call me sweetheart."

"Alright, angel."

"Angel is worse," I groan.

"But I like angel. Grace, angel. It's perfect," he insists.

I roll my eyes. "What's the second question?"

"Why were my buddies chasing you?"

I take a deep breath. "There was a disagreement."

Aiden laughs. "What kind of disagreement?" I shrug. He leans against another tree. "Oh, come on. Spit it out."

"Yeah, I tell you, and you immediately turn me in."

"Okay, look, I pulled you out of the way. Didn't I?" His voice takes on a slight hint of irritation. "If I was going to turn you in, I would have left you to those guys. Right?"

I sigh softly. "Fine. I was asking questions about the mine."

"The mine?" Aiden asks, confused. "What business would you have with the mine?"

"That's my business."

"Tell me," he says with a playfully smug smile. "Or I won't let you pass."

"Get out of my way, Aiden!" I am fed up with his antics.

Aiden just chuckles. "I like the way you say my name, angel."

"I'm trying to find out about what happened to my brother, you irritating—"

"Your brother? Interesting." *Fuck.* I mentally panic as I realize he's pondering the new information. "Are you from the House of the Sun? Do you have family up there?"

"No...," I say slowly. "My brother... was a mercenary," I say plainly, praying I can talk my way out of this one, "from the House of Earth. He died somewhere around here, and I know it has something to do with that mine. And now I'm looking for answers."

There, good, mix a little truth in. Make it seem believable.

Aiden looks pensive for a while. My palms start to sweat a little. I don't like how long it is taking for him to answer nor how long he is scanning me over with those blue eyes. "A mercenary, you say?" he finally says.

"Yes."

"See... the only mercenaries traveling with the army... were from the Middle Realm. They were mortals. So, the only way for you to have any relation to them... would be..."

No...

"If you were mortal yourself."

...

"That's ridiculous." I try to play it off. "Why would I be mortal? How could I have gotten up here?"

"I'm not sure how." Aiden begins to circle me slowly. "But there's no question about it. You are mortal. Aren't you?"

"No," I protest.

"Yes, you are. I can see it now. That's why you look so out of place."

"I don't look out of place!"

"Oh, darling, you can play dress-up all you want, but without the magic, it's just a costume."

Oh, this is bad.

Without warning, Aiden grabs my arm and drags me forward. "I'm escorting you back to the border now."

"*No!*" I shout and struggle violently. He keeps a tight grip on my arm. "Please, no, I can't go back now."

"Oh, you can, and you will. This isn't up for debate. You're lucky those guys didn't catch you and kill you. Hell, you're lucky I don't kill you."

I wrench my arm from his and tumble to the ground. Aiden reaches down to grab me, but I scramble back quickly. "Please!" I beg. "Will you just listen? You don't understand!"

I must sound incredibly desperate because he finally stops and stands above me, arms crossed. "You have two minutes."

"Look," I stand slowly and shakily, and in seconds I realize I'm spilling everything I've tried so desperately to keep secret. "My brother's name was Leo Richardson. He died in this town a year ago. He was a mercenary hired to come here to guard the mine for some sort of special project carried out by the House of the Sun." I am pleading with him, begging him to hear me out with my voice and my eyes. I just need him to listen; I don't know why.

"When they came to our door and told us he was dead, it broke my mother and me. My mother barely gets out of bed anymore. He was everything I had…" I pause to catch my breath before continuing. "They didn't give us his body; they didn't pay for a funeral. We ran ourselves into a serious financial slump just to pay to bury an empty coffin. They couldn't tell us *anything* about how he died, couldn't produce even…" I choke softly. "Even a finger."

Aiden's eyes don't give anything away.

"I'm here..." I take a deep breath. "I am here to find out what happened to him. I'm here to take my revenge... and then I will leave this Lady-forsaken place. That's all I'm here for." My eyes close involuntarily. "Please, please don't take me back yet."

When I open my eyes again, I see Aiden's face change. The stern face melts into a pained grimace, which eventually shifts into a neutral expression. He sighs. "Alright."

"Alright?" I dare to get my hopes up. "You won't take me back?"

He shakes his head. "No, I won't take you back."

I grin widely through the remnants of the tears on my face. "Thank you, Aiden. Thank you. I will never forget your kindness." I turn to leave quickly.

"Of course you won't—because I'm coming with you."

I whip around. "Wait, what?"

Aiden strides up beside me. "I'm coming with you. You don't think I'm just gonna let you traipse around the Upper Realm by yourself now, do you? No, I'm gonna follow you, keep tabs on you."

I shake my head rapidly. "Oh no, you're not coming with me."

"Take it or leave it, sweetheart. It's me or the border. Take your pick."

I cringe. I don't want to take this Fae man with me; there's absolutely no way I can trust him. But I don't have a choice.

"Fine."

Aiden grins at me. "There we go. Where to, angel?"

I hiss softly at the pet name. "Just walk." And with that, I storm off, Aiden chuckling behind me as he follows.

CHAPTER NINE

Aiden is… a very strange character.

He walks beside me without saying anything, but he keeps an amused smirk stretched across his lips as if he has a million things he wants to say but is purposefully making it a point to keep them to himself. The boyish look lets you know the more time you spend with him, the more he's investigating you. Despite the whole soldier thing, he seems so lighthearted. I've never seen a single Fae soldier look anything but stern. Not this one. Aiden is too… happy?

It's unnerving.

As I lead us through the forest, I'm re-evaluating my plan. I don't know whether to head back to town or to try and find out where the mine is. *Maybe Aiden knows how to get there.* And exactly how much can I feasibly do with this Fae man beside me? Or really, how much can I get away with? Am I going to be able to carry out my plans without interference from the peanut gallery?

My gut says absolutely not.

I just have to make sure he knows who's in charge.

Though I suppose I do need to let him in on some of my plan if I want to get started. "I want to see the mine." I turn to Aiden. "Can you make that happen?"

He nods. "I can make it happen. But we can't get too close. No offense, but you don't exactly look inconspicuous."

I roll my eyes. "As you keep telling me."

"Is that the only outfit you've got?"

"Not the only one," I answer indignantly without thinking. *Why do I keep taking the bait?* I forcibly bite my lip to keep from replying to anything else he says. Aiden seems to notice because he just chuckles at my pursed lips. He leads us the rest of the way to the mine in silence.

When we finally reach the edge of the forest, Aiden stops me short from stepping out into the light. "Stay behind me, but stay close." I follow him carefully out into the sun, trying to move within the shadow of his tall, broad frame. A few moments later, we stop at an outcropping of rock, which he ushers me behind. "Down there. Take a look."

I peer around the corner and down at the mine below us. The actual entrance is just below our feet. More people move about the mine than I saw in the entire village. Dusty workers bring ore out of the tunnels by the cartful, dumping it into a massive pile off to the side. A group of men sort the ore by hand, tossing it into one of two sets of wagons. I watch as one wagon moves into a soldiers' camp and another heads back toward the town. The place is just crawling with soldiers. Tents and temporary wooden structures cover the field. The flags of the House of the Day and the House of the Sun are both flying.

"The House of the Sun is still here then…" I say aloud to myself.

"Yes, that's where my unit is from," Aiden says in my ear.

"You're from the House of the Sun?" My eyebrows furrow. "Why the hell are you here? This is House of the Day territory."

"We got called in by somebody. Said they needed more protection around here. My commander wasn't really forthcoming on why. But we go where we're needed, even outside of our own land."

I nod slowly as I try to take this all in. I turn away from the mine and lean back against the rock. "Same reason the mortals were brought in. More protection. And we didn't ask as many questions as we should have," I say quietly to myself. I peer around at the mine again. "We need to figure out what they're mining down there and why it's so important that the mine needs extra protection from whoever they can get to."

"How do you want to do that?"

I turn back to Aiden. "There was a man at the bar," I start firmly. Aiden's head tilts slightly my direction to hear me. "He seemed to be the most willing to talk, and he clearly knew more than he was letting on. He sold me out to the soldiers. His name was… Finn?" I question, hoping my memory serves correctly.

Aiden groans. "That guy…"

I turn to him. "Do you know him?"

He sighs. "Yeah, he's an informant."

"Figures," I chuckle dryly. "The one guy I actually get an answer from turns out to be the guy who sells people out for a living."

Aiden chuckles. "You're pretty funny for a mortal girl."

I give him a look of absolute loathing. "Seriously?"

"Oh, don't act all high and mighty, angel. I can tell since I picked you up, you're judging me for being what I am." I fall silent. He's not wrong; I can't stand the Fae.

"I bet none of the information he gave me is even real."

"Oh, it's real," Aiden assures me. "Finn gets a kick out of telling people real information and then sending them off to their deaths because he knows they'll never be able to use it. Sick enjoyment, if you ask me."

"Do you know where he lives?"

"Yeah, he's got a place back this way. I can take you to him."

"That would be appreciated. Thank you." I nod definitively and follow him in silence.

After a while, Aiden turns to me with a wry smile. "I like you, Grace." I ignore his comments. "You're very focused and such a curious girl. I like that." When I don't reply, he chuckles. "Not gonna talk to me? You know you're stuck with me, doll. Might as well speak to me. Maybe we even can get to know each other." He wiggles his eyebrows suggestively.

"I don't need to know you," I snap. "I don't need to speak to you unless absolutely necessary. You signed on to come with me. I'm in charge; I'm calling the shots here. Not you. Now shut up and leave me alone while I work out a plan." All I hear is the same wry chuckle before there's finally blissful silence.

When we reach the rickety-looking cabin, Aiden pounds on the cabin door hard three times with one fist. Finn opens the door a crack before swinging it wide open. "Heyyyy, how you doing, soldier?" he drawls drunkenly. "What can I do for you today?"

Aiden glances over his shoulder at me with dancing eyes. *Watch this,* he mouths. "I need answers," his voice booms out.

"I have lots of answers. If you're willing to shell out a little," Finn smirks, "I'll give you whatever you need." That's the moment I choose to step out from behind Aiden. Finn's eyes widen exponentially, and he moves quickly to slam the door. Aiden stops the door easily with his hand.

"Let's talk inside, shall we?" Aiden suggests. I can tell he's getting a kick out of this. All I care about is finding out the rest of what Finn knows. I storm into the man's house, and he immediately begins to back up. My eyes darken, and I slowly begin to back him into a corner.

"Heyyyy, you're alive?" Finn looks around nervously. "Good for you?"

I chuckle darkly and move to draw my sword off my back. "Now, now," Aiden interrupts, stopping my hand. "Let's give the man a minute to explain, angel." He gives me an imperceptible wink. I glare at him and then turn calculatedly to the man trembling in the corner. *I swear by the Lady if you interfere, Aiden, I will rip your head off myself.*

"You have exactly two minutes to tell me everything you know about the mine before you find yourself without something valuable of yours." My eyes slide suggestively down his body.

Finn gulps. "I told you everything I know, miss..."

This time Aiden doesn't stop the swing of my sword as it collides with the wall just above the man's head, causing him to cower under it. "No, you haven't. What are the Fae mining?"

"Miss, please... please have mercy," he begs.

"Like the mercy you showed me? You're not in a place to be asking favors, Finn. Answer the question," I snarl.

Aiden pushes me back with a hand at my waist. "Let me handle this," Aiden interrupts.

"I think I'm doing just fine, thank you very much." Instead, I find myself brushed aside as Aiden takes a stance in front of the man. "I'm completely capable of getting the information on my own," I huff.

CHAPTER NINE · 89

"Oh, I'm sure you are. But I would say we need it a little faster." At his words, his palms begin to glow softly with energy. Two tiny flames appear against his hands that slowly grow the more they are exposed to the air. I watch in fascination as he combines them into one large ball of fire and holds it directly in front of Finn's face.

Before long, Finn is screaming in fear. "*Alright*! I'll tell you, I'll tell you anything you want. Just don't hurt me!"

I scoff as Aiden extinguishes the flames. "You have no problem selling other people out, but you'll do anything to save your own skin. Won't you?" I mock, reaching out and yanking him close to me by the collar. "What are they mining?"

"Black obsidian!"

My brows furrow. "Black obsidian?" I hear Aiden hiss sharply behind me. "What's that?" I swivel my head and look back at Aiden.

"I don't know!" Finn begs. "I don't know anything else. I swear. I just know the name, black obsidian." His eyes glance around wildly.

"We need to leave," Aiden interrupts. "Now." He kneels down, overshadowing Finn. "If you tell anyone we were here, I will kill you myself." Finn nods quickly in fear. Aiden grabs my arm roughly and pulls me out of the cabin, rushing down the path as I struggle against him.

"Hey!" I shout. "Let go of me! I wasn't finished with him!"

Aiden stops abruptly once we're away from the cabin and out of sight amidst the trees and then lets go of my arm. "What the hell was that?" I ask, rubbing my arm ruefully.

"Black obsidian, Grace. It's..." he hesitates. "It's a legend. It hasn't been seen in literal centuries. He has to be wrong.

It wasn't worth staying any longer." He rubs the back of his neck, a hint of nervousness creeping across his features.

My eyes narrow. "If it was only a legend, it wouldn't have mattered if we stayed or not. What do you know?"

He doesn't answer.

"Aiden, what do you know? What is black obsidian?" I ask again.

He sighs and looks down at me. "Look, I'm really not supposed to tell you anything. Mortals aren't supposed to know about these things."

"The more I know now, the faster I can get out of this realm and back to my own. Which we both want," I argue. "So tell me."

He pauses in thought. "Alright," he concedes before taking a deep breath. "It's a type of stone that is said to harness the power of the Lower Realm."

It takes a moment for me to recognize the gravity of his statement, but when I realize what he's saying, it causes me to rock back on my heels in surprise. The Lower Realm is the place you only hear stories about—an uncontrollable territory beyond the southern mountains of the Middle Realm, heavily fortified by magic, controlled by the founders of the Fae. It's a dark place where demons run wild with no check on their powers, a complete wasteland filled with uncontrollable magic. No Fae would ever dare to venture down there, let alone any mortal. The only writings about the third realm were ancient texts written in an old, indecipherable language.

"What kind of power does it harness?" I ask curiously.

"I haven't read about it in a long time…" Aiden's eyes look far away. "But from what I remember, its primary function is to harness enough power to reveal prophecies."

The hell? "Prophecies?" I chuckle. "You're worried about a little prophecy? I thought we needed to be worried about a demon apocalypse."

He runs his hands nervously through his hair. "It very well could be. Prophecies are few and far between. There's only been a handful throughout the last few thousand years, but every time one arises, it always comes from the Lower Realm. And it always marks a new era in the history of the Upper Realm… even potentially the last age." He groans. "But black obsidian… there's no way they could even find it in a mine in the House of the Day. Those mines have been scoured, and nothing new has ever been found."

My head reels. "Then why would they be digging there with armed guards? Why would they hire mortal mercenaries to assist them? Why else would they be so secretive?"

"I don't know!" Aiden shouts, pacing back and forth. "I don't know… it doesn't add up; it just doesn't make sense. I don't know anything else." We stare at each other, both breathing heavily as we wait for the other to say something.

I finally break the silence. "We need to get back to town. I need to figure this out."

"Fine by me," Aiden groans. "I could use a drink."

CHAPTER TEN

―

While Aiden grabs a drink at another tavern in town, I pace back and forth in the alleyway behind it trying to come up with a plan. I don't like this. I don't like this at all. Working in close quarters with a Fae is not on my to-do list for this mission. Certainly not a soldier, of all Fae. Who knows how this is going to work.

Can I ditch him? I look to the end of the alleyway, but there are too few Fae milling around to make a clean getaway. Besides, if Aiden did catch me again, he would drag me back to the border without a second thought. Before I can make a final decision about darting, the back door to the tavern swings open and Aiden joins me.

Suppressing a groan, I grit my teeth and confront him. "I'm telling you, you need to get me down into the mine," I argue. "I need to get inside."

"You've lost your mind," Aiden chuckles with a hint of irritation. "Full-time surveillance by at least twenty soldiers at all times, all of which have infinitely more magic than you currently possess. Plus the entire camp as backup? You'd be killed instantly."

"There's got to be a way you can get me past them. You've got magic."

"That doesn't mean I can get you past everyone! We need a better plan than that."

"I don't like your attitude."

"Well, darling, I don't like your—"

"Excuse me?" an unfamiliar and shaky voice interrupts us.

I whip around with my hand to my dagger hilt. An elderly woman with soft curly white hair stands behind us with a delicate wooden cane in one hand and a bag of food in the other. She peers at me and Aiden. "Don't be afraid of a little old woman, dear," she speaks directly to me. I take a step back, and Aiden automatically moves forward to meet me. I don't have time to analyze how quickly he moved to that protective stance.

"What do you want?" I cringe out how harsh my words sound.

"I only wanted to say that you should both probably keep your voices down," she said, not unkindly. "The walls here have ears." She gestures to the sides of the buildings around us. "And the army really doesn't like it when people discuss the mine." She frowns. "You should know this, soldier." I see Aiden blush sheepishly. "I've seen people who mention it in passing remarks taken into custody for questioning. They often come back with no memory of the conversation."

I sigh softly. "Thank you, ma'am." I move my hand away from my weapon. She seems to be fairly harmless. I feel Aiden relax a bit behind me. "We will be quieter."

"If you would like a safe place to talk, I would be glad to open my home to you."

Aiden interjects, "Thank you, ma'am, but I think we're fine."

"You have nothing to fear from me, children. My husband worked down in that mine for many years. Gave the army the layout of the place when they moved in."

"We have no way of confirming your story, ma'am," Aiden argues. "We'll be fine."

The elderly woman peers at me carefully. "How strange," she says.

I feel uneasy. "Is something wrong, ma'am?" I reply cautiously.

"You look very familiar, dear," she says gently. She studies my face with an odd fascination. Her eyes bore into me. A fogginess descends over my brain, and I can't seem to tear myself away from her gaze.

"Hey!" Aiden shouts in my ear before physically pulling me behind him. I break out of my trance abruptly, and I begin to shiver in the cold air.

"I meant no harm—" the woman tries to speak.

"Sure, you meant no harm," Aiden snaps. He turns and puts his hands on my shoulders, peering into my eyes. "Are you alright?" he asks.

"I… I'm fine." I shake my head to try to shake the fuzzy feeling. "What was that?"

"She was scanning you. Empathetic magic. She was trying to read your emotions." Aiden glares harshly at the old woman. I feel the ground begin to shift and hum lightly, and to my surprise, I see the Fae man begin to glow with a soft, yet dark golden glow. "I suggest you be on your way, ma'am."

"Please listen. I had to know if she was who I thought she was." The woman leans around Aiden's shoulder to speak to me. "Are you a soldier, child?"

My palms begin to sweat. I can't believe she tried to invade my head. "Why do you ask?" I stutter.

"Well, you're with another soldier, I only assumed… Are you his girlfriend?"

"No!" Aiden and I say in unison.

"Then are you a soldier?" she pushes again.

"Yes," I snap. I just want her to stop questioning us and walk away so I can breathe again and get my head on straight.

"Do you know… a Leo… Leo Richardson?"

My jaw drops. Aiden tenses and the glow grows stronger. I stutter, "L… a Leo?"

"You look very familiar… almost like him. Did you join the ranks recently?"

I stumble over my words. "I… yes, recently."

"You're his little sister. Aren't you?" My fingers slide back and tighten around my blade handle. "Grace, is it? Your brother talked so much about you; I knew if you ever came, I could recognize you on sight," she continues. "That's why I wanted to look. I am sorry to pry. If it makes you feel better, I couldn't see much of anything. Only a few flashes of emotion, no memories."

"Did you really know my brother?" The words slip out in shock. I can't believe what I'm hearing. *Who the hell is this woman…*

The old woman smiles. She beckons for us to follow her. "Come to my house, child. It's only a little ways down the road. I can tell you all about him and his time here. Anything you want to know…" She pushes by us softly as she makes her way down the alleyway. We let her go.

I stand there dumbfounded. I don't know whether to follow or to turn tail and run in the opposite direction. But once she reaches the other end of the alleyway, she turns over her shoulder and motions for us again. This time, I feel a little gust of wind, a purposeful one, press up against my back and knock me slightly forward. *She's not taking no for an answer.* I glance over at Aiden in hopes of an answer. His jaw is drawn tight, but his eyes stare at me. They betray nothing.

I know I should be cautious. Every bone in my body is screaming at me to let Aiden have at her. But to hear Leo's name from a Fae woman's lips stirs something in me. I have no choice but to find some strength and accompany her home.

***

The old woman leads us to a small cottage just past the market square. She unlocks her door with a flick of a finger. "Come in," she calls out as she makes her way inside. "I'll only be a moment."

Aiden follows her first, and I trail behind. I wasn't expecting to find quite a simple home. My vision of the Fae world had always been of these grand homes full of magical artifacts and curiosities. But here, I see wood tables and wooden chairs with small cushions to soften their backs. The only luxuries I can see are small oil paintings and what appear to be tiny glass bottles. Potions, maybe? If it hadn't been for those, I might have thought it was one of the Middle Realm homes.

Aiden and I sit down at the small table in the woman's kitchen, looking at each other pointedly. His gaze warns me, and I nod shortly in solidarity. Our hostess makes herself busy, summoning three teacups from a cabinet and setting them at each place. The soft whistle of a tea kettle echoes through the tiny home.

"Pardon me for approaching you so bluntly," she apologizes while she pulls the kettle off the stove and places a tea bag into it. "But I swear you have your brother's eyes."

I can't help but smile. "My mother always said that," I say politely. I hesitate. "Ma'am... how do you know my brother?"

"Please, call me Elaine," she offers. "Your brother used to come visit me when he wasn't on duty. I met him in town one day when I made my weekly run to the grocer. My family was coming into town, so I really needed to pick up supplies. As I was leaving the grocer trying to balance multiple baskets and satchels at once, your brother spotted me from across the square and came to offer to carry food home for me. From then on, he became a good friend."

I smile brightly. It's so nice to hear a good story about Leo again. It's been so long. "That's…" I pause, holding back a moment of sadness. "That was my brother, Elaine. Always willing to help." I'm acutely aware of Aiden's eyes on me. I hope I don't look too emotional.

"I heard a lot about you."

"You did?" I ask quietly.

"Oh, lots." She pours Aiden and me a cup of tea. "Leo wouldn't stop talking about the little sister he had back home waiting for him." I nearly lose my composure at that point; I feel the tears well up in my eyes and shake my head quickly to get rid of them.

"Thank you," I whisper softly.

"Did you happen to see Leo?" Aiden chimes in unexpectedly. "Before he passed?" I nod in solidarity.

Elaine looks very pensive. She sinks into her chair and shakily brings the teacup to her lips. She sips it carefully before looking directly at me. "Yes."

My heart breaks at her pitiful expression. "Yes," she repeats. "I saw him the day before."

"The day before?" I choke out the words, much to my dismay. Aiden stares at me.

"Yes, child." Her eyes look toward the door for a man who isn't there. I do the same. "He was very quiet that day. He seemed... agitated. But there was such a determined look in his eyes. It was almost like he knew he was going to die."

She lays her hand on mine comfortingly. "He gave me that dagger for you. He told me to get it through to you somehow. I'm glad it arrived."

"He sent it to me?" I choke.

"Yes, child. He loved you very much."

I sink back into the chair. This is all too much for me. To know he actually set it aside for me, it's almost like he knew I was going to come here. He knew I was going to need a way to protect myself.

Even from the grave, Leo, you're still trying to protect me.

Aiden stands slowly from the table and beckons to me to follow. "Thank you for your time, Elaine." He gives a slight bow. My chest tightens, and I want to ask so many more questions. I can't just leave now.

But Aiden flicks his head pointedly toward the door. Overwhelmed by the conflicting feelings in the pit of my stomach, I just obey and stand. "Thank you."

Elaine nods. "Take care, the both of you." She looks at me pointedly; I shiver slightly at the frankness of her gaze. "Be careful."

Unsure of what else to say, I silently follow Aiden out of the house.

***

Aiden and I begin strolling down the country road in silence, the afternoon sun just starting to make its slow descent above us. My head is reeling. Did Leo know he was going to die?

Did he think I would come up here to avenge him? Did he plan on it? In sending me the dagger, was he giving me his approval? Or did he never want me to venture up here in the first place? Was I supposed to stay and protect my mother? Was that the message?

"Grace," Aiden interrupts my thoughts. "Are you alright?"

I shake my head. "Don't go there."

He holds his hands up. "Alright. Alright… What do you want to do now then?"

I stop in the middle of the road and stare down at the dirt. "I'm… I'm not sure. Give me a minute to think." I walk off a little bit.

He stops beside me and pulls out his sword from his back. "Alright. Hope you don't mind if I do this." Pulling out a cloth from his bag, he sits down right in the middle of the road and begins to clean the sword. I watch him in my peripheral. The cloth swipes methodically over the blade in careful, even strokes.

I remember when my brother would come home from training. He would sit in the living room with me at his feet cleaning his blade with the same care. *I guess it's a military thing.* The familiarity of it relaxes my shoulders a fraction of an inch, and my brain finally starts working clearly again.

"We need information on black obsidian," I state abruptly.

"I've told you everything I remember," Aiden replies without looking up from his blade.

"No, we need more information." I pace away from him. "There's gotta be a way…" I turn around suddenly. "There's a library… in the House of Peace. It's the biggest library in the Upper Realm. It's supposed to have copies of all of the ancient texts and magical tomes over the last three centuries, right?"

Aiden nods thoughtfully. "Yes, that could work. But how are you planning to get in? That library is reserved for scholars and those with proper clearance."

I shrug. "I'm gonna sneak in. Obviously."

Aiden chuckles as he sheathes his blade. "I can get us in, no problem. But it's a few days' walk from here." I furrow my brow. *No problem? What kind of clearance does this guy have?*

Well, if he can do it, who cares where it comes from? "Then we better get moving. Shall we?"

CHAPTER ELEVEN

Aiden and I make our way back to town to stock up on supplies for the journey, and of course, he just has to continue to make things difficult.

"Aiden, I do not need anything else!" I insist. "I have barely enough space for what I've got."

The man will not budge. "You do not look good enough to pass as Fae in the places we're traveling to," he presses. "We've got to get you done up."

"What's wrong with how I look?" I ask indignantly. "I have other clothes."

"First of all, you look like you're wearing a costume. Second of all, even if you did get past the fake image, you look like a peasant woman. Peasant women don't often travel. You have some decent clothes, but they won't hold up for a long journey. You need sturdier clothes, and you need to look like a scholar or a rogue or something to sell that you're a Fae traveler." To my chagrin, Aiden actually is making some sense. *How disappointing.*

"What would you suggest then?" I'm going to regret asking this.

Aiden grins. "I know just the place."

We ditch the back alleys in favor of the open square. I keep my hood up to cover my face, and Aiden leads me forward with a hand on my back. To the outsider, we may look like a couple out on a nice walk. As much as I hate the idea, I can't deny it works well as a cover. Every time a soldier waves to Aiden, I try hard not to flinch. "Relax," Aiden murmurs. "You're too tense. You look like you have something to hide." He pulls me a little closer. "Follow my lead." I let him wrap his arm around my shoulders, and I pray to the Lady for this ruse to end soon.

When we reach the shop, I practically dart through the door and away from his arm. "Don't do that again," I hiss under my breath.

Aiden chuckles. "Oh, don't pretend like you wouldn't be my girl in a different life." My horrified expression makes him break out into a full belly laugh. I blush furiously and turn my focus onto the clothes. He stops me before I can pull a shirt off of the table. "Oh, no. Not a chance, doll. You had a chance to pick out your own clothes. Now it's my turn."

No. No. Absolutely not. I am not taking fashion advice from a Fae soldier. I have got to be dead, and this is hell.

Aiden pulls outfit after outfit for me and shoves them into my arms. He and the shopkeeper usher me into a dressing room, and Aiden refuses to let me out until I try everything on and show him. I try to put a shirt on and take it off without interruption, but Aiden's arm reaches through the curtain and pulls me out before I can get it all the way off.

"*Hey!*" I grip his arm and shove him backward as I spin in a circle to get away. I pull the sides of the shirt together to cover my body. "What the hell?"

"I want to see everything," he protests. "I have to see what's going to work best."

"Uh, uh, no way! I'm not—"

Aiden gives me a look. "I'm buying."

...

I storm back into the dressing room with a very loud huff. Begrudgingly, I show off combo after combo: shirts, pants, dresses, and for some reason, countless pairs of boots. "Adventurers need a good sturdy pair of boots," Aiden assures me as he passes me two more pairs.

By the end of it, I'm dressed in a white blouse with black leather pants that blend into black leather boots. Aiden carries two more outfits besides. "Aiden," I whisper softly as the shopkeeper begins to add up the total. "I can't... I don't have..."

He cuts me off quietly. "I've got this. I told you, don't worry about it." He pays the bill in silver, and I load up the clothes in my satchel. We make our way to the market then and fill our bags with food and medicine. He again refuses to let me pay for my own.

I don't know what he's playing at, but I don't plan on giving him any credit just because he's gifted me some supplies. No, I'm still in charge. No buts. No mercy.

***

We set off the next morning after a night of rest at a local inn. Several hours of walking, and I'm already getting exhausted. *One thing I will never understand about the Upper Realm is why they don't have trains.* I tell Aiden as much as we trudge forward on the dirt road.

He chuckles and turns to me slightly. "We prefer tradition around here."

"Ugh," I groan. "But tradition is so inconvenient."

Laughing, he pokes my arm in a strange gesture of friendliness. "It's how things are done. The only place that's really moderned up would be the House of Darkness. They began adapting mortal tech to magic several noble families ago." I roll my eyes at him as he pokes me again. "I'm impressed with you, Grace."

"Why?"

"You actually managed to get here. Look at you, you're a mortal in the Upper Realm. It's been almost two thousand years since a mortal set foot here until the hiring of the mercenaries."

"So?" I reply. "Do you have a point?"

"Where did you get all the information you needed to navigate your way through all of this?"

I shrug. "Books, primarily. Sometimes my brother would come back from training and tell me the latest story he heard about the mysterious Upper Realm."

"There's no way you learned all of this through books available in the Middle Realm," Aiden presses on.

"Well, not entirely," I chuckle softly. "You know how prevalent the black market is in the border areas. The rest of my information and stuff came from there."

Suddenly, I forcibly collide with his arm as it flies across my chest, stopping me in my tracks. "Hey! What the hell…" I turn to look at Aiden and immediately freeze. His eyes glint dangerously.

"What was the last thing you said?" His voice rumbles.

I bite my lip. "The black market…?" I'm very confused. The Fae don't condone the black market, but they mostly leave it alone. Or the Fae running it are just too elusive for the others, and they just can't keep a handle on it. Either way, I'm concerned the mere mention seems to shake Aiden.

"By the Lady, dammit Grace, is that how you got into this realm?" He spins and grips both my arms tightly, nearly lifting me off the ground. I thrash violently. "Do you have contacts on the black market? Who helped you?" His voice steadily grows louder, shaking me a little.

"Aiden, stop, you're hurting me," I struggle in his grasp.

"*Tell me!*" Aiden shouts and shakes me hard. Without thinking, I react instinctively, and my boot comes flying up to his crotch. He drops me, and I scramble backward, my hand clenching the handle of my dagger.

Something in his eyes shifts and he looks down at me almost horrified. "Grace…"

He takes a step toward me, and I hop to my feet, dagger out and poised to strike. "Don't come any closer," I growl. I whip around and sprint as fast as I can away from him. *Who the hell is this guy? He's a maniac!* "Grace, wait!" I hear him shout after me; I ignore him and keep running. His long strides echo behind me, and unfortunately for me, it's only a matter of time until he catches up.

Aiden reaches out to grab me. I make a split-second decision and lash out, slashing at his forearm. He yanks back just before the blade grazes his skin. "Grace! Calm down!" He manages to catch the back of my shirt to slow me down.

I flip around and scramble backward. "Absolutely not! You tried to kill me!"

"Please… I'm sorry!" he shouts. "I lost my head."

"Yeah, you got that right!" My hand tightens around the hilt. He takes another step toward me, and I scream at him. "Stay *back*!"

"Look, I'm sorry! I'm not trying to hurt you!" he begs. "Please… just listen. I'll explain." He holds his hands out as if trying to soothe a wild animal. "My best friend was killed in a skirmish with black market movers three years ago. We caught a group of guys headed for the border with nearly eight hundred gold worth of stolen magical ware. They turned violent."

I nod slowly, my hand loosening ever so slightly from the blade handle. "Mortal or Fae?"

"Fae," he sighs. "You do know no one really cares about what the mortals do on their end, right? It's all a bunch of fanfare. The guards at the border barely need to lift a finger's worth of magic to catch anyone stupid enough to try to make it to the edge to make the swap. Most of 'em just don't care enough to enforce it."

"Did you get them?" I ask quietly.

"Oh yeah…" he replies with a more determined air. "We got 'em alright." His voice deflates again as he shakes his head. "Look, I shouldn't have grabbed you. I'm sorry. The black market just… it's one of the worst things to come out of our realm. I've seen it tear apart the lives of many here who run afoul of the Fae runners."

I nod. "I won't give up my contact to you," I say firmly.

"I don't expect you to. Just… use it sparingly, alright? It can be dangerous." Aiden shakes his head. "I really don't understand why you all feel the need to use it at all."

I sheath my dagger and chuckle dryly, continuing off toward our destination. "You don't understand? Have you ever been to the Middle Realm, Aiden?"

"Well," he starts, jogging a little to catch up with me, "no. Most Fae haven't. It's against universal realm law."

Scoffing, I turn to him and walk back to talk. "Have you ever paid attention to what's going out? Has anyone even tried to keep track?" Aiden shakes his head. I laugh dryly and sigh. "Figures." I absentmindedly kick a rock along the road.

"Tell me then," Aiden said. "Why do mortals need all these magical items?"

I scoff loudly at that. "Are you kidding me? Wow, you Fae really don't know anything." I shake my head in utter disbelief. "We're not just importing magical material."

"You're not?" Aiden stops short.

"Aiden... the mortal black market is mainly importing food."

"Food? What do you mean food? You all grow your own."

I groan. "Oh, by the Lady, help me. It's not enough, Aiden. Our population is nearly four times the Fae population, and we only have the resources to grow about twice the food that you do. Then on top of that, the Fae take almost half of what food we do have. So, whereas you have a small surplus, we are stretched thin just to make ends meet. And in a lot of towns, they don't."

Aiden watches me with furrowed eyebrows. "I... had no idea." He seems puzzled by the idea.

I shrug. "Well, now you do." We continue walking in silence for a little while. I glance sideways at him and notice his downtrodden expression. *How strange.* I feel the need to continue. "Look, I'm sorry about your friend. I know how dangerous it can be chasing after runners, especially on the Fae side. I really am sorry." I cautiously reach out and touch his arm lightly before quickly pulling back at the awkwardness of such an emotional movement. "But you have to understand, we're all desperate to survive. That's all." With that, I turn and continue to walk.

We move along in silence for a while before Aiden stops me again. "Did I hurt you?" he asks. I shrug and try to move on. He moves in front of me to block my path. "Did I hurt you, Grace?" he repeats.

With a sigh, I pull up my sleeves. Two handprint-shaped bruises mark my upper arms. Aiden takes a sharp breath, and I bring my sleeves down quickly. "Don't worry about it; they don't hurt," I reassure him. He scoffs. I roll my eyes. "I'm serious. Don't worry about it."

"Let me fix it," Aiden pleads.

"No, Aiden, look, it'll fade in a little while, and I don't have enough healing potion to use it on something so minor. Besides… I can handle it."

"I have some."

"We don't have time for that."

"I'm not moving from this spot until you let me do this."

"Fine, I'll keep walking."

"Grace." Something in his voice makes me stop just as I pass him. "Please."

By the Lady, he's stubborn. "Fine." I turn back around and move over to the edge of the woods on the side of the road. I plop myself down in a pile of leaves. "Go ahead."

Aiden nods in thanks and kneels beside me. He pulls a small vial of a green elixir out of his bag and reaches for my arms. As I shift to meet him, his fingers carefully pull the fabric of my sleeves up and over my shoulders. I fail to hide my slight wince as he brushes one of the bruises, eliciting a soft sigh from him. He uncorks the bottle with his teeth expertly, spitting the cork into his lap. I wonder how many times he's done that before.

Slowly, he pours a single drop onto each of the bruises. As the liquid sits, I feel my skin tingle pleasantly. I watch in fascination as the purplish handprints begin to recede, retreating inward until they disappear altogether. All that is left is a slight prickling and a sickly-sweet smell of magic.

"Thank you." I stare in fascination.

Aiden shakes his head. "Don't thank me for that. Please." The guilt still shines from his eyes. I'm not sure why he still feels so guilty. No one has ever looked at me that way since Leo. Like... I was important enough for them to worry whether I would forgive them or not.

Something prods me to try to cheer him up. "So, you're not a healing mage, I would assume?"

My joke has the desired effect; Aiden lets out a small laugh. "Nah, not a healer."

"What kind of magic do you have?" I ask curiously, leaning back against a tree.

Although a little taken aback, Aiden replies, "Well, I have two types of elemental magic, fire and earth. Elemental magic is..."

"The ability to control the elements of nature. Water, fire, wind, earth," I interrupt him. "I know a lot more than you think."

He chuckles. "I'm starting to see that." He glances at me before continuing, "I'm particularly adept at energy magic. Energy conversion... Uh.... force fields, detection, drawing on power from other sources. Then there are a couple other things." I look at him pointedly. When he doesn't get the hint, I exaggeratedly beckon for more. Laughing, he begrudgingly finishes. "Alright, alright... flight magic and shapeshifting."

My eyes widen. *That's a lot more than I remember reading about.* "I thought most Fae were born with like... two, three, maybe four gifts?"

Aiden shrugs. "I'm gifted, what can I say?" He laughs when I roll my eyes and sits down beside me, offering me his arm to lean on. I ignore it, so he just rests it at his side awkwardly. We sit together and collectively catch our breath.

My head bumps against the bark behind me. "Do we have to walk all the way to the House of Peace?"

Aiden chuckles as his head falls sideways to bonk mine lightly. "Well," he says. "There is one other option... if you like it fast."

***

I whoop loudly as we take off down the road. The horses' hooves pound against the road, sending a cloud of dust flying up around and behind us. My hair billows in the breeze as I bounce with every gallop. *Best idea ever.*

Apparently, the area we were in is horse-trading country. They travel back and forth between the House of Peace and the House of the Sun frequently, and the best market for horses is in the heart of Cara where the library is. A few words and some silver from Aiden, and a horse seller in the next village was willing to let us bring the horses to his buyer in the city who would pay Aiden back.

A chance to make a few coins and not have to walk the several days to Cara? Aiden is a genius.

We're flying down the road at top speed, racing each other. Aiden rides with such ease it's clear he's been doing this for a while. I don't know why I'm so interested in this Fae man. Something feels too off about trusting him. I gotta bring my guard back up. But as I watch him steer his horse through a turn, I can't help but let a small smile cross my face. Maybe having a partner in this expedition isn't the worst idea in the world. *Let's just hope I don't regret this.*

CHAPTER TWELVE

I thought Faraday was beautiful. But there aren't enough words in any language to describe the ethereal atmosphere of Cara.

Aiden and I arrive in town just before sunset when the bustle of daily life is just beginning to quiet down. The fading light from the open sky shines down on the city like a glittering chandelier in a wealthy man's parlor. I'm used to cities being modern and dull, but this one... this one screams ancient with a touch of brightness. Instead of skyscrapers, white marble temples rise around us on all sides. Neat, delicately carved wood and stone houses stand in clusters, forming small communities. Businesses and shops lay interspersed in between, the streets below lined with neatly trimmed patches of green and wildflowers.

And everywhere I look, I find some of the happiest people I've seen since I started this journey. With loose-fitting clothes that swish and flow wherever they walked, the Fae practically flit from place to place. That's the best word to describe it: *flitting*. Like... pixies, I suppose, from a fairy tale. I can't get over how happy everyone is. Does no one in this world frown? Is there really that much happiness to go around, or is it magic-induced somehow?

As I stroll down the main street, I can't find a single thing wrong. It's so peaceful. I can almost hear music playing in the background. It only takes me a few minutes to find out there really is music, strings coming from the temple. Perhaps a lyre. My violinist's fingers itch to play along. I glance over my shoulder at Aiden, who appears to be busy speaking with the horse buyer who's just approached him. I bite my lip as I face the temple again. *One peek can't hurt.*

I cross over the threshold of the open-air temple and feel a wave of calm wash over my body as the music grows slightly louder. I still can't see the musicians, but the temple itself captivates me just as much as the notes floating past my ears. The columns stand sturdy against the backdrop of blue sky all around it fading into purple and pink. When I inspect the structure a little more, I see tiny intricate carvings along the stone, carvings of Fae and birds and flowers intertwined into the grooves. Small candles float above the temple in a nonsense pattern, glowing strong in the fading sunlight.

It fascinates me, this House, and how artistic the whole city feels. Every detail seems purposeful and reverent to the sanctity of magic itself. How odd that feels to me. I have always seen magic as something to be feared, something so powerful that it can take away everything you know in a heartbeat. That's always been the mortal way of seeing this; pissing off the Fae was never a good idea. But looking up at the floating lights, all I can think of is the few times I've seen good, honest magic since I started.

Which Fae world is the real one? The one that takes, or the one that creates?

"Grace!" I turn around quickly. Aiden's voice brings me out of my reverie as he motions me over to him from the stairs. I reluctantly leave the temple and bound over. "It's getting late," he says. "The library closes at sunset. I suggest we wait until morning. Gives us a little more time to look if we need it." I nod in agreement. As he ushers me down the street, I turn around and glance back at the temple. I never did find where that music was coming from.

We find an inn just past the temple with lodgings open. I insist on paying for a simple room for myself, but Aiden insists on paying for a suite for both of us in silver. I follow him reluctantly up the stairs, and I feel instantly more comfortable to find that it is two separate rooms with a bathroom joining them. I plop myself down on the bed and flop back onto the pillows.

Aiden chuckles. "Happy?"

I smile back lightly. "Mhmm." I want to just stay here for a minute and sleep.

As he slips into the bathroom and over to his side of the suite, he calls back. "Hey, you should go ahead and get some sleep. There's something I want to show you tonight."

I sit up and call back, "What do you mean?"

"I figure your introduction to the Upper Realm wasn't that great." He peeks his head through the bathroom doorway one last time. "I'd like to give you a better one." His eyes dance with mirth as he disappears. I roll my eyes at his antics, but I feel an odd sense of warmth fill my chest.

I chalk it up to being exhausted and immediately collapse into bed. *A short nap sounds wonderful…*

***

A light knock from the bathroom door stirs me from my sleep. To my surprise, the sun's long since gone down, judging from the look of the sky. *How long was I asleep?* "You okay in there, Grace?" I hear Aiden's muffled voice through the door.

"I'm fine," I call back.

"You were asleep for a while. You sure you're feeling okay?"

I rub my eyes as I reach for my satchel. "Yeah, I'm alright. Was just tired. I'm sorry I overslept."

The bathroom door flies open, and I struggle to rapidly fix my hair so I don't look like I've just rolled out of bed. Which of course, I have. Aiden stands in the doorway in his soldier's uniform. His left side is decorated with unfamiliar medals and insignias, but my heart aches with how much it reminds me of Leo. He sees my face fall, and his eyes narrow with concern. "Oh… I… didn't really think… I'm sorry."

"Don't be," I interrupt and grant him a rough smile. "You look like an upstanding soldier."

He laughs at that. "And I'll have an upstanding Fae woman beside me once she gets dressed." He winks playfully. I roll my eyes and shoo him away so I can change into something clean. I pull out one of the new outfits I picked up from the market, a flowing white tunic and brown pants. Aiden then escorts me downstairs, out the door, and into the street.

Cara glows gently from tiny string lights that flicker softly and hover over the streets. Everywhere I look, the city is bathed in the silver glow of moonlight. The hustle and bustle have long since died down, but the light and enticing music still call to me as I'm led down the street. The best sign of life comes from inside the taverns we pass along the way, filled with dancing people and tambourine and fiddle music. But Aiden leads me past the excitement and further into town.

"Where are we going?" I ask.

He glances over his shoulder and presses a finger to his lips to silence my questions. "You'll see," he says cryptically as he pulls me down a dark alley. I'm immediately on my guard; nice things don't usually occur in dark alleyways. But once we're on the other side, I can see why he wanted it to be a surprise.

We're standing on the outskirts of town on top of a giant grassy hill that tumbles down toward a calm river at the base. The river is lit up along its banks, creating a snake of light in both directions as far as the eye can see. I can just make out tiny fireflies darting in and out of the tall grass. It takes my breath away. I see Aiden smile at me out of the corner of my eye.

"This used to be my favorite place to go when I was stationed here," he says softly. "Come on," he beckons me with his hand and pulls me down the hill to the bottom.

When we reach the river, he pulls me down beside him and motions for me to look up. My heart skips a beat as I see Cara in all its lit glory towering above us. It makes me feel so small, so insignificant as a human being, but I can't tear myself away from staring at it.

"It's beautiful. Isn't it?" Aiden breathes in my ear. "Makes everything else feel pointless." I nod absentmindedly.

"Not everything…" slips from my lips. I shake my head and look down sharply, cringing at myself for ruining the moment.

Yet Aiden doesn't seem to mind. He leans back on his hands and turns his head to me. "So… where do you come from, Grace?"

I chuckle dryly. "This isn't a date."

"I can't try to understand my partner in crime?"

"Look, if anything, you're *my* partner in crime." I turn to him. "I'm in charge here. Don't forget that."

Aiden laughs. "I got that, alright? I just want to figure out why you're here."

"I told you why I'm here—to find out what happened to my brother and get revenge on the people who took him from me."

"Woah, woah, woah, revenge? You didn't mention any revenge."

"I absolutely did. What did you think was gonna happen once I figured it out?" I shake my head incredulously. "Did you think I was just going to go home?" I shake my head again. "No..." I lay back in the grass, letting it rise up around me. "Would you pass up an opportunity to kill the ones who took your friend from you?"

I see Aiden's lip tighten, but he doesn't respond. *That's answer enough.*

We stay there in silence for a long time, listening to the lapping of the river and the wind whistling lightly through the grass. I let out a small sigh as Aiden lies down away from me, facing the water. I feel a little guilty for shutting him down so quickly. *He did give me a chance to stay here... I suppose it couldn't hurt.*

With a long internal groan, I roll over to face him. "I'm from Lisden." The single sentence echoes against the silence. Aiden turns over to look at me. Seeing as that's probably not going to cut it, I continue. "It's a factory city a little way south of the border. Not much happens there. A lot of factories, a lot of smoke." I shrug. "Where are you from?"

"Brighton in the House of the Sun."

"Did you grow up there?"

"Ah, ah, ah. A question for a question, doll." Aiden wags a finger at me teasingly. "That's the only way this is gonna work."

I roll my eyes and begrudgingly accept. Aiden nods and raises his head up on his arm as he faces me. "What's your story?" he asks.

"That could mean any number of things. What are you looking for?"

"What do you do? Do you work, do you study, what do you do?"

"Ah," I breathe. "I'm a performer. A violinist."

"Violin?" Aiden grins. "That's fantastic. Are you any good?"

"Any good?" I raise an eyebrow. "I'm the best there is in Lisden. I'm always requested for rich people's parties and gigs at the bar. I've been playing since I was five years old." I chuckle. "Am I any good…"

Aiden laughs. "I'm sorry for asking then. And I did grow up in Brighton. Brighton born and raised."

"What's your story then?"

He looks pensive for a long time, just looking at me. I can't read what he's thinking. A small smile dances across his lips. "I've been nowhere and everywhere in my life," he finally speaks. "I've been at the very peak of high society, and I've been deep in the mud fighting for my life. I joined the military to escape from the conventional boundaries that had always surrounded me. I want adventure in my life. You know? Something different. Something worth fighting for."

I watch him carefully as he tells his story. It's a curious thing to be coming from a Fae who appears on the outside to have everything he could possibly want. But more than anything, all he wants is something to chase after. I wonder what it would be like to have dreams like that.

"What do you want out of life, Grace?"

The question hits me and presses like a stone against my chest. I don't know how to respond. *Have I never really thought about what I want to do with the rest of my life? At my age?* I feel shocked, but of course I know the answer. Don't I? When Leo died, there was no reason to prepare for any sort of future. I'm going to die here, eventually, carrying out my revenge against whoever killed my brother. I don't think I ever prepared for a Plan B, a plan for if I survived.

Aiden's waiting for me to answer, but I just don't have one. I can't even come up with a good excuse to give him because I can't even remember what I wanted to do before Leo died. I shrug. "I… don't really know."

He studies me curiously but eventually turns over onto his back. The unanswered question lingers in the air around us. He doesn't press for more answers, and I appreciate that. Perhaps he's noticed I'm finished talking. We lie there on the riverbank together, looking up at the stars.

And I just try not to think anymore.

CHAPTER THIRTEEN

We arrive at the library at first light. I was too nervous to wait any later than that. I couldn't sleep most of the night, my head a whirlwind of thoughts. I hope, by the Lady, today goes well.

The library lies just outside of the city center, yet it feels so isolated from everything else. Surrounded by tall trees, it towers over even the largest temples in Cara. Its marble columns rise to the sky and meet underneath a big beautiful black dome. The stained-glass windows stretch nearly up the full length of the walls. Each of the images represents an old Fae scholar, Aiden tells me, and each is lined with real gems and gold. My palms begin to sweat as I stand there in its shadow.

Aiden nudges me softly. "You good?"

I nod silently as I stare up at a front door that must be four times my height. I'm stuck to the spot. Aiden sighs impatiently and steps in front of me, pushing the door in. It creaks with a squeak that's both chilling and oddly satisfying. I stare into the darkness that is revealed, lit only by soft candlelight. Looking back at me, Aiden grants me a soft smile. "Come on, Grace," he says in a sing-song voice. I roll my eyes and push past him.

As I creep softly into the lobby, I gasp. My lungs feel too full. Almost immediately as I step through the door, I can see the floor-to-ceiling shelves covering whole walls in their entirety. Books upon books span the cases, and the deep, heady smell of old parchment wafts into my nose. Along hallways that must lead to more rooms of wisdom, marble statues of the Fae's greatest scholars are lined in reverence. I recognize some of them from my old history books. I inhale deeply again and shudder.

It's incredible.

I wander further in, transfixed by the sheer size of it. Aiden slips in behind me and closes the door. I pause where the highly polished wood floors transition to plush rugs. Slowly, reverently, I take a step across the line where the entry ends and the library begins. I feel at home immediately when my foot hits the rug. Spinning around, I try to take it all in at once. When I turn back to look at Aiden, he's got another peculiar small smile on his lips. I try not to dwell on it too much.

"Excuse me," a voice chimes out from a desk beside us. "Can I help you?" A small elderly gentleman stands up and moves to greet us.

Aiden steps in to speak to him before I can open my mouth. "Yes, we're here to do a little research." I watch him pull a chain out from under his shirt and show it to the clerk. "You should find my credentials in order. And she's with me," he says firmly.

The clerk's eyes seem to widen. Mine narrow curiously. "L…"

Aiden interrupts him. "No need for titles here, sir. I'm trying to keep a low profile." I see his hands twitch. My curiosity only grows. *What is he so nervous about? And what the hell is around his neck? Some sort of identification?*

"Yes… of course. The two of you may enter," the clerk responds nervously. "Please let us know if there is anything we can do to help you… Sir."

Aiden nods before glancing back at me and motioning me forward with a jerk of his head. I shake off my questions temporarily and step forward. Within seconds, I turn back around. "I… have no idea where to start," I admit.

He laughs softly and pushes me forward a little. "Just pick up a book."

"… any book?" I hate how silly I sound.

"Any book," he whispers teasingly with a smirk. "They're all open to you."

That's all I need to hear. I leave Aiden behind without a second thought, striding purposefully over to the first shelf. I pass directly through the center of the room, blowing past a handful of older mages who sit reading at various tables. They give me odd looks, but I couldn't care less. When I reach the bookcase, I carefully brush my fingers along the spines of the books at eye level. The leather binding feels fantastic under my hand.

I finally draw a book from the shelf: *An Encyclopedia of Upper Realm Lore*. I turn to Aiden, still standing back at the entry staring at me with an amused smile. I give him a playful smile. I barely manage not to laugh at the shocked look on his face.

Alright… let's get to work.

***

I wish I could say Aiden and I found what we needed quickly and were on our way to the next destination within the hour. But nothing is ever that simple.

We search through the morning, through lunch, and through most of the afternoon with absolutely no luck. I lost count of how many books we flipped through. I ran up and down the stairs to the second and third floors, carrying larger and larger stacks of books each time. By the end of the day, our table looked like we had bought out an entire Middle Realm bookshop (not that that's an astounding number of books, but it's definitely enough to spread from a table onto the chairs and across the floor).

We looked through practical books on rocks and stones and magical texts on prophecies. Hell, I even looked through a collection of fairy tales and legends hoping I would find a helpful word on black obsidian. But luck was not on our side. We could not find anything more than Aiden had already told me about black obsidian.

As the sun's dying rays filter through the window, I collapse back into my chair, my head resting against the back. Closing my eyes, I let the cool air gently streaming in from the upper windows wash over my face like mist. I breathe heavily, like I have been running through the city for literal hours. Researching takes so much out of you mentally; it's exhausting. Wiping the sweat off my forehead, I glance over to find Aiden in a similar disheveled state.

"Do you want to try again tomorrow?" he asks me softly.

I shrug, unsure how to respond. On one hand, I can't just give up on this. On another, we have torn apart nearly every book that could possibly have some information on that Lady-damned stone. "We'll see," I finally answer.

He nods knowingly. I hate that he pretends to know what I'm thinking.

We both slowly get up to leave, stretching. Just as we're about to leave the room, a voice calls down from the staircase. "Aiden?"

He turns, and his face lights up. "Master Xavier!" He breaks away from me and bounds up the stairs to meet an old mage at the top of the stairs. I think he's going to hug the man, but instead, Aiden drops down to his knees on the stair below him. I watch in fascination as the mage lays his hand against his forehead, and a soft orange glow encircles Aiden's head.

"How are you doing, son? What has brought you to the Mages' Library? I thought you were stationed in the House of the Day." The mage pulls Aiden to his feet and wraps an arm around his shoulders familiarly.

"I'm actually here with a friend, sir," he replies politely, more formally than I've ever heard him. "Maybe you can help us." Aiden escorts the mage down to me. His long white hair bounces on his broad shoulders as the two men make their way down the stairs. The old man's face appears frail, but his body seems strong. His tall frame looks like it has seen military training and battle, and a flash of the calluses on his hands suggest the same. My hands clasp behind my back to show respect. "This is my friend, Grace."

I ignore the warm feeling in my chest at his admission of friendship. Instead, I focus on the slight panic rising as I have no idea what to do. I panic and drop to my knees with an embarrassingly loud thud. I bow my head to hide my flushed cheeks as my heart pounds.

"You don't have to kneel for me, miss," Xavier replies. I scramble to my feet. "Aiden here was a student of mine way back when." He smiles at him warmly. "One of the best I've ever taught. The kneeling is a sign of respect between student and teacher. I imagine your teacher did not use this?"

I shake my head quickly. "No, I apologize, sir."

Xavier shakes his head and smiles at me. "No matter, child." He turns to Aiden. "What kind of assistance are you looking for?"

Aiden glances at me before answering. "We're looking for more detailed information on black obsidian."

Xavier lets out a soft slow breath. He looks back and forth between the two of us. "What do you need the information for?"

Aiden hesitates. "It's for… a research project of sorts."

Xavier gives a wry smile. "You and your research projects always got you into trouble, young man." I want to laugh as Aiden turns sheepish. *That's a story I would love to hear.* With a sigh, the mage turns back toward the stairs. "You two, come with me."

Aiden and I turn to look at each other before following him up the stairs. The staircase winds in steady spirals as we make our way up to the third floor. To my surprise, we find ourselves moving past both the second and third floors. Suddenly, a section of the staircase that had not existed before opens up to us. We continue up to what appears to be an entire secret fourth floor I had not seen before.

"We're going up to Master Xavier's private study," Aiden leans over and whispers to me.

My eyes widen. *The study of a mage… Leo would have loved this.* I mouth back to him, "Wow."

Xavier stops about three quarters of the way up the suspended flight of stairs and waves his hand, revealing a simple wooden door with a gold engraved nameplate. He swings the door open and ushers us inside. The study feels practically like an extension of the library itself, another room overflowing with books and a fireplace at the end. But upon entering, unlike the library downstairs, it is evident these books hold specific meaning to Xavier. Each is arranged so carefully and pristinely on the shelf. There's something so calming about a room like this.

"Take a seat," Xavier beckons toward the wingback chairs over by the fireplace. I gladly take my place closest to the fire, resisting the urge to curl up there. Aiden settles to my left. The old mage takes his seat in front of us. "Now, why are you searching for black obsidian?"

Aiden and I look at each other nervously. "We would prefer to keep the reasons to ourselves, sir, with all due respect," Aiden finally answers.

Xavier smiles grimly. "I had a feeling you would say that." He stares absentmindedly into the fire. "You're after a prophecy. Aren't you?"

Aiden begins to protest, but I cut him off quickly. "Yes." Aiden looks at me in confusion, but I shake my head imperceptibly. *Not now.*

"Chasing after prophecies is very dangerous, children. Rarely does anything good ever come of it."

"With all due respect, sir," I reply, "I need answers."

He sighs. "Black obsidian," he begins, "is a substance that is rare and beautiful to behold. It glistens and thrums with power, but is black and cold like the night itself. It is said... that the Lady herself wore a bracelet of it to increase her strength and perception." I look on, enraptured by his words, wishing I had a quill to take notes.

"The stone has the ability to harness demon energies from the Lower Realm, transmit it to the Upper Realm, and concentrate it to emit a tremendous amount of power. That kind of power, though, is risky, you know. Many have died trying. That's why its primary use is for the revealing of prophecies. It's the least risky magic to use it for," he finished. We looked from each other back to him, nodding silently in understanding.

Xavier sighs and looks to me. "It has been lost to the Upper Realm for hundreds of years now. The only known place where it may exist is in the Lower Realm, and no one will dare venture down there."

"Why?" I ask.

The master looks pensive for a moment before standing abruptly. He wanders over to a shelf behind his desk and thumbs over the volumes. He selects a large thin black book and passes it to me, taking his seat again. When I open the text, I pour over a speculative map inside the front cover.

"The Lower Realm," Xavier finally says, "is the most dangerous place in the entirety of the Three Realms. That map you're looking at is over fifteen hundred years old.

"What makes it so dangerous?" I ask carefully.

"The demons, child. What else? I have studied demonology for centuries, and I have barely scratched the surface. Many… many more demons exist in the Lower Realm than there is magic in the Upper Realm, each with their own unique magic and disposition. A trip down there is suicide."

"Yet… that is the only place black obsidian can be found in the current age?" Aiden chimes in.

"Yes." The room is silent save for the crack and snap of the fireplace.

"Is there no safe place in the entire Realm?" I frown.

"I have heard tales… legends of a traveling oasis that runs on the magic of the Half-Fae Coven…"

"The Half-Fae Coven?" I interrupt.

"It's just an old fairy tale," Aiden shakes his head. "A group of eight mages born of both mortal and Fae during the ancient times was exiled to the Lower Realm when the Fae couldn't abide their mortal blood. Legend says that they have survived all this time through the creation of a magical traveling oasis that protects them from all demonic magic. But there's absolutely no basis in fact."

"I would be careful believing in your convictions so strongly, Aiden," Xavier interjects. "All legends often have their basis in fact. And no one has been down there to explore the possibility of its truth. Not since my time, at least."

"Your time?" Aiden's jaw drops. "There were Lower Realm explorers in your time?"

"I was one of them."

"What?" Aiden and I both exclaim loudly.

"You went down to the Lower Realm?" My jaw falls.

"Once. It was my first and my only expedition down there. I barely made it out alive."

"By the Lady..." Aiden sinks back into his chair.

"Yes," Xavier says quietly. "But it was a very long time ago. All sorts of adventurers were looking to try their hand at exploring the Lower Realm. Every man wanted to be the first one to document the realm. We ventured by the drove, sometimes alone and sometimes in packs. Most did not return."

"How did you survive?" I whisper in awe.

"I don't know, Grace. I truly don't know. I catalogued as much of the eastern half of the realm as I could. I fought countless demons. Most of my memories of it are a blur. All I know is one moment, I was being blasted into the air by a demon, and the next moment, I wake up in front of the exit. If there's one thing I know, it's that I was not saved by a demon. Something... or someone must have saved me."

He stands suddenly and begins to pace, circling the room. "This is not a good time for you two to be investigating prophecies. If the wrong people discover your interests... I cannot guarantee your safety."

Aiden's eyes widen. "What do you mean, sir?"

Xavier turns sharply to us. "What I tell you now does not leave this room." We nod quickly. "There is legend of a prophecy... a prophecy as old as the Lady herself. It is foretold that this prophecy contains information about what it will take to unite the Houses as they once were in the ancient times. It also contains information about what will ultimately be this realm's destruction. The prophecy is said to only be known and held by the Coven of the Half-Fae."

"Why would we be killed for going after the prophecy?" I ask quietly.

Xavier studies me with contemplating eyes. "I have said too much already," he finally speaks. "Do not go chasing after prophecies, children. The fates will reveal everything in their own time." He reaches out his hand to Aiden to help him up and then me. "It is time for you both to leave now. Remember what I said." Aiden kneels to him again as I cross to the door to let them finish their reverence rituals.

I trail my hand across the doorway as I leave, nimbly tucking a tiny folded piece of parchment into my sleeve. *That map will come in handy for what I need next. I'm sorry Aiden, Master Xavier... But I won't be deterred by an old wives' tale. Prophecies, ha. I'm not afraid.*

CHAPTER FOURTEEN

Aiden and I leave the library in a dazed state. What Master Xavier said has me very uneasy. A Fae realm desperately in search of some prophecy that signifies dawn or destruction? Okay, maybe I can get behind that. But where does Leo fit in all of this? Black obsidian appears to be the key to the whole puzzle.

"What are you thinking?" Aiden asks carefully.

And if it takes a little perilous escapade to find out the truth, so be it.

"I think I need to head back home," I reply suddenly. I try to ignore the hint of surprise I see in his eyes.

"Really?" he answers in disbelief.

I nod. "Yes," I lie. "I need to re-evaluate what my next move should be. I need to train more, get more supplies. Maybe I'll come back in a year or so and find a new way to get what I want. Right now, I just need to see my home and my family again." I turn away so he can't see the deceit, which shows too easily in my eyes. "Leo would understand."

I watch Aiden out of the corner of my eye. His surprise has faded to stoicism, resigned to ending the journey where it is. I don't have to ask him; I can see it in his eyes. He's ready to take me back to the border and usher me back to the Middle Realm without a second glance. I'll be damned if I let that happen. I'll placate him into thinking I'm just gonna walk away from all of this. Then when the moment is right, I'll slip away.

My heart pangs a little bit at the thought. *Traitor.*

"The question is how to get back to the border," I muse aloud. "It's a decent distance from here."

"Well," Aiden starts. "There is… another connection between the Upper and Middle Realms."

I stop short. "What?" My mind races. *Another connection?*

"Yes," Aiden continues. "It's a bit of a well-kept secret," he chuckles sheepishly. "But the House of War has a port on the river that trades with the Middle Realm. They're the only house that has a direct connection."

"Why? How?"

"They have the means to build ships that can withstand the sheer power that's infused into the border, allowing them to sail by ocean straight through the barrier. They trade with towns on the mortal coast. We can hop a ship tonight and get you back home by dinner time."

Another portal. Just wait until I tell David. My heart skips a beat at the thought of seeing my friend again. He would be happy to know I made it out alive. Then with a small inward sigh, I remind myself that it's not quite over yet. David will just have to wait.

"What are we waiting for then? How soon to the House of War?"

"Just a short ride over the river. But… we're going to need to get some paperwork in order."

"Paperwork?"

Aiden rubs the back of his neck. "We need a travel visa in order to get into the House of War. They like to stay as closed off as possible from the outside world."

My eyes widen. "Aiden, how am I supposed to get paperwork? I'm not Fae. I have no… identification or anything, I'll be found out in a heartbeat!"

Aiden sighs. "I know a guy."

I raise my eyebrows. "A guy?"

"Yeah…"

"That guy wouldn't have to be a black-market contact. Would he?"

"…. Is that actually a question you have to ask? Do you really think I would use someone like that?"

I wait.

"Look, he's a guy we use for some of our informants so they can be cleared to get into certain places—certain restricted areas we need surveillance on. We grant them transportation in return for valuable intel. He's shady… But not black-market shady." He groans when I look at him skeptically. "Just come on."

***

Aiden's contact was able to give both of us valid visas to the House of War by identifying me as a traveling student. Turns out he's fantastic at drawing up official-looking papers specifically to get people into the House of War. He usually helps merchants get their goods through, but occasionally he extends his assistance to others, particularly soldiers. These papers are some damn good forgeries.

As I hold the papers in my hand, I can't believe how official they look. I feel almost like I am betraying my roots. I kept my head down so much in the beginning, but as I have traveled, I find myself hiding less and less. I must look so much like a Fae that no one is giving me a second glance. *Is it the clothes? My ears? What is it?* The longer I stay in the Upper Realm, the more I am adjusting to acting Fae. Now that I have this supposed proof of Fae heritage in my hand, I hate myself for even faintly enjoying the experience.

I've got to get my head together.

When Aiden leads me onto the ferry at nightfall, my stomach is in knots. Every time I get one step closer to finding out what happened to my brother, the trail twists in an unexpected direction that I am just out of reach from. And I have no choice but to follow where it leads. For Leo. But that begs the question too. Is this what Leo would have wanted from me? Is this what he would have expected of me, chasing after vengeance? Would he have stopped me from going?

These questions haunt me as we glide across the river.

As we approach the House of War border, I can feel a shift in mood. Gone is the serenity of the House of Peace. As we approach the dock, we notice the officials on board begin to double-check people's visas to make sure they are valid. They stoically evaluate everyone and seem to remain suspicious of various people long after they've been approved.

I don't know a lot about the House of War, only what Leo told me from the research he did when training to be a mercenary. He told me how the House prefers to keep to itself. It's nearly entirely self-sufficient; they grow ninety percent of their own crops and import very little product. They can afford to be stingy with trade. With the river to their south and the mountains to their west, they have enough natural protection to make it difficult for others to reach them without them knowing.

Leo also told me that it's the House with the largest army, keeping their people trained and ready to mobilize on a moment's notice. He admired their preparation and meticulous care in military and diplomatic strategy.

Only when we reach the riverbank do I truly appreciate their strength. We dock under the shadow of a large stone fortress lined with armed guards, positioned at the ready to strike down a traveler if they make a wrong move. Once we pass through the arches in the fortress, the town widens into open market squares filled with traders, forges, and weapons dealers. In the distance, a stone castle just as impressive as the opening walls stands tall and proud over the surrounding countryside.

Despite the gruffness of the soldiers we pass on our way off the ferry and the solemn expressions of the people as we pass by, I feel more secure here than I have at any part of the journey. I mean, of course, there's always the risk that I'll be caught here by one of these people. But since the outside world can't get in here without extensive processing, there's statistically less of a chance of me being found out. That gives me a moment of reprieve to just enjoy where I am.

Enjoy where I am? A literal war zone in the most dangerous place in the Three Realms? What the hell are you thinking, Grace? Get your head out of your ass before you either a) forget your mission or b) let your guard down just enough that you seal your own death sentence.

Dawn is creeping up the horizon by the time Aiden and I arrive at the ship heading for the coast of the Middle Realm. As we approach the gangway, I stare up at the deck in awe. Leo always told me about how wonderful it was to be riding on the sea, feeling the salty air on your skin and the wind at your back. He used to travel about once a year by sea as a temporary subject of the navy, and he always brought back the most wonderful stories.

The ship is massive, almost as tall as some of the tallest buildings in my city. The cloud-like sails raise even higher, billowing majestically in the wind. As we climb up onto the deck, I'm fascinated by the swirling activity around me as the sailors prepare for departure. Even the deck is packed with barrels and crates full of produce and raw materials strapped down in hopes of keeping them secure during the journey.

"We've got a cabin on the third deck down," Aiden steers me toward a trapdoor.

Panic strikes me. "Wait, below deck? Why can't we stay up here?" I ask hurriedly.

"We'd be in the way of the sailors. They want passengers to stay below deck as much as possible," he replies.

I nod slowly. But inside, I'm a mess. As we descend into the depths of the ship, I can't help but feel a sharp shiver go through my body. I wrap my arms tightly around my body to stop it. I see Aiden purse his lips out of the corner of my eye, but he says nothing.

Three flights of narrow stairs later, Aiden leads me down a long, narrow hallway. At the end, he pulls a key from his pocket and unlocks the nearby door. When he pushes the door into the room, I peer in. To my horror, the inside is small and cramped. My heart pounds in my chest.

Aiden beckons me forward, and I slowly follow. The room is really only big enough for the bed and a small armoire in front of us, presumably to store whatever we carried along with us. To distract myself, I begin to strip out of my gear and store it away. But when I open the drawers that practically take up the rest of the remaining space in the room, my panic only grows.

"Um," I stutter out softly. "How soon do we dock?"

"It's a ride," Aiden replies. "About twelve hours. We'll be there just before dusk. You can watch the sunset on the beach," he teases. "Isn't that what all girls love to do?"

I force out a small chuckle. "Yeah…" I trail off.

Suddenly, we feel the ship jerk, and I tumble to the ground. Aiden laughs. "You've never been on a ship before. Have you?" I shake my head. He offers a hand to me. "Come on up top! I think they can make an exception for a woman's first ocean voyage!" I take it eagerly and practically sprint up the stairs behind him. *Anything to get out of that cabin.*

When we reach the top deck again, I gasp and run to the edge, flying into the rail. A grin spreads across my face. The sailors shout to each other around me, shifting sails and readjusting ropes. The helmsman stands on top of an upper deck, steering the ship out of port. The ship slowly turns away from the dock, inching along the edge of the harbor.

Then…we're out on the open sea. All I can see is ocean stretching in front of us to the horizon. As the wind shifts, the ship picks up speed, and we sail off into the vast unfamiliar. I close my eyes as the wind begins to hit me, smiling as it tickles my face and neck and ruffles my hair lightly. The salt air feels amazing.

All too soon, however, Aiden places a light hand on my upper back and ushers me back down to the cabin. As we descend, I feel my anxiety creep back in again. When the cabin door shuts for the last time, I jump.

"Hey," Aiden interrupts my thoughts. "I'm gonna catch a few more hours of sleep if that's alright with you."

Thank the Lady. "Sure, that's fine," I reply. *With him asleep, he shouldn't notice any... complications with me.*

"Good." He reaches into his bag and pulls out a leather-covered book. "In the meantime, I thought you might want to get a good look at this." He hands it to me. I trail my fingers over the cover. The title reads *Magic: A History*. Aiden smiles down at me. "I figured you might want something to add to your library at home."

I struggle not to show him how impressed I am by the gift. Who would have guessed he would have gotten me a present to remember all of this by? I bite my lip before granting him a small smile. "It's beautiful. Thank you."

"No problem." With that, Aiden plops down onto the bed and rolls onto his side. "Good night, Grace."

"Good night."

As Aiden drifts off, I open the book carefully and begin to read. The words distract me from the impending sense of doom looming over my head, and I'm sucked in immediately. I don't start to panic again until several hours later when the ship takes a sudden, violent swing to the right.

The book flies out of my hand, and I tumble to the floor as the ship takes another pitch to the left. I clutch the sides of the walls and fumble my way to my feet. I barely manage not to crash again as the ship swings yet another time. Over the course of a few minutes, the ship lurches back and forth, left and right, never ending. The second I think it will stop, another jerk happens. *What is happening?*

Aiden groggily comes to his senses, rolling over to look at me. "Hey."

"Hey? That's all you have to say?" I shriek as I hear something in the hallway crash.

He chuckles. "It's alright, Grace. There's always a bit of stormy weather going across the border. It's a magical field. Tries to deter the sailors from sailing on. Don't worry, the ship is built to withstand it."

I scream as I tumble into the wall with the next wave. Aiden chuckles at me. "Grace, calm down, it's just…" He trails off when he gets a good look at me. Huddled up in the corner, I press my face to my knees and rock back and forth. The walls are closing in around me; the cabin feels restrictive and growing tighter.

I crawl forward rapidly, flinching hard every time the ship rises and falls. "Grace?" Aiden sits up in bed.

"I need to get out of here!" My hand reaches the doorknob and pulls it open hard. "I need to get out of here!"

Aiden is out of bed in two bounds, grabbing me around the waist and pulling me back in. As he slams the door shut, I tumble down to the opposite wall with another wave. To my horror, the rational part of my mind has shut down, and I can't do a single thing besides whimper and cower.

"Grace." Suddenly, Aiden is down on his knees in front of me. "Grace, what's wrong?" I can't answer him. He reaches out to touch me, and I flinch. "Grace, talk to me."

Trembling, I choke out. "I'm… claustrophobic."

The room is silent except for the sounds of the violently crashing waves and the wailing wind. I curl up into a tighter ball. Then I feel a soft hand on top of my head. It rests there gently, giving me something new to focus on. He rubs very lightly. "Hey… Hey, shh… Come here." He cautiously reaches over and grabs my arms, lifting me up and pulling me to his side. "Breathe with me, Grace," he says quietly. "Take a deep breath in…" I shakily follow his lead as he exaggeratedly takes a breath. "And out…" I breathe out slowly. "In… out…

that's it, just keep doing that." His arm pulls me a little tighter. "I promise it's going to be okay. This will pass soon."

As the ship tilts again at his words, I instinctively bury my head in Aiden's chest, my hands tightening around his arm. I realize too late what I've done. But at that point, my fear and anxiety and desire to be comforted are too great to overcome. I breathe in slowly, hoping not to be rejected.

Aiden's arms tighten around me, his other hand moving to rub my back lightly. I relax slowly and take solace in his embrace. His arms aren't unlike Leo's, strong and steady. But his scent is uniquely different, like a warm crackling fire. He sits with me, sustaining my flinches and slightly uneven breaths.

"Come on," he says as he grips my arms, pulling me onto the bed. He throws the blanket over us and tucks it around my back. "Cover your eyes." I hide my face in his chest. He lays his arm over my head, blocking out most of the storm's noise.

"Try to sleep, doll," he says quietly. "It'll be alright. I'll keep you safe."

I take a few deep breaths and shut my eyes tightly. Before I realize it, the dull roar of the storm behind Aiden's arm fades away as I descend into sleep.

CHAPTER FIFTEEN

I am startled awake by a loud whistle from the ship's upper deck. I nearly leap from the bed, but Aiden's arms steady me. "Hey, hey, hey, breathe," he hushes. "It's alright, Grace. We've made it."

"We're on land?" I blink dumbly as I adjust to the room again. It takes me a few moments to regain my bearings, and at that point I realize Aiden's and my arms and legs are intertwined. I immediately jerk my legs away. I hope my face isn't turning colors.

"Yes, we're safe. You'll be home soon." Slowly, Aiden slides his arms away from me. I uncurl from my position and keep my eyes to the ground, unable to look at him head-on. "Get your stuff together," he says as he picks up a few of my things that were disrupted in the storm and lays them at the end of the bed. "I'll be up top when you're ready." He pats my head once, and I see him smile out of the corner of my eye. He then leaves the cabin to check up top. I sit alone as I try to catch my breath.

I have to admit, I'm entirely surprised by Aiden's actions. Frankly, I'm surprised at myself too. I hate letting other people see me with such weakness. Only my family ever knew about my fears, but I didn't really have a choice with them. But Aiden stepped in and comforted me, kept me from hyperventilating. He didn't have to do that. And I... I trusted him to help me and didn't push him away. I didn't have to do that either. And yet, it felt natural to do so.

All I can think is that this is only going to make it more difficult to say goodbye.

Those thoughts escape me as I make my way to the upper deck. When I reach the top of the stairs, I am greeted by the vibrant pink sky of the mortal realm. The sun is slowly setting, and a soft breeze teases my hair. A grin crosses my face at being back home. *Where I belong,* I remind myself. *Where I belong.* Forgetting I'm supposed to rejoin Aiden, I take off down the gangway, away from the docks and into the street.

I sprint through the streets of Baypoint, flying past the last few stragglers returning home for dinner who look at me with puzzled looks. I rush past thatched roofs and lanterns in doorways all the way down to the edge of town. I can hear Aiden's shouts behind me. I turn over my shoulder and wave at him in the distance to follow me. I continue on my path headed straight for the fabled beach. I reach the coastline within minutes, careening down the beach toward the ocean.

I crash down to my knees in the sand, overcome with emotion. I breathe in the salty air deeply, feeling it creep into my very soul. My eyes close softly as the cool wind ruffles through my hair. They fly open as the high tide sweeps up to soak my legs in seawater. I grin widely.

By the Lady, the ocean feels fantastic. I burst out into a deep belly laugh, bubbling up from the smallest shreds of happiness left inside of me since my brother died. I tumble forward onto my stomach, flipping onto my back to stare at the wide-open and brilliantly blue sky. The water creeps up with another wave to slide over my hair and under my back. I relish the cold, tipping my head back into it.

Needing to feel more, I scramble to my feet and rush into the ocean. I wade in up to my thighs and let the waves slide and crash around me and onto me. My hands glide through the water reverently. I scoop it into my hands, let it go again, and in a surprise fit of passion, toss it into the air. It rains down around me in tiny crystal-like droplets. I breathe in slow, deep breaths, trying to take it all in.

Aiden calls out to me from the shore. *Good, he finally caught up.* "By the Lady, Grace," he cries. "Why were you running? Haven't you ever seen a beach before?"

I chuckle lightly and close my eyes. "No…" I whisper to myself before shouting back at him, "No!" With that, I hold my arms out and let myself fall back into the sea.

I hear Aiden shout just before I hit the water. The water rushes around me in a swirl of foam. I force my eyes open, and before the salt overwhelms them and forces them back closed, I catch a glimpse of a long stretch of sand scattered with seashells. I blindly reach for a handful before bouncing back up on my feet, narrowly avoiding another wave.

"What the hell are you doing, Grace?" Aiden yells. "Do you even know how to swim?"

I laugh again. "No! Not a clue!" Aiden's loud groan echoes to me.

"Get out of the water now!"

Erupting in another fit of giggles, I dismiss him with my hand and hold my arms open to the sky once more. "In a minute!" I catch Aiden throwing his hands up in defeat as I turn back to the sea. The waves crash over me again and again. I don't move an inch.

It's another full half-hour before Aiden is able to coax me out of the water. Shivering in the slowly cooling air, I collapse down in the sand beside him, spreading out to air dry a bit. Aiden drops his military jacket on my chest. "Try not to catch your death of cold." I smile and take it gratefully, draping it over my legs and pressing it to my pants in an attempt to absorb some of the water. When that fails, I bring it up to my hair and ruffle it violently, wringing the water out of it.

"You are absolutely insane," Aiden shakes his head.

I chuckle. "You don't get it," I reply. "I was so jealous of Leo always getting to travel places with his work. At least once a season, he would end up here on the coast. He would always bring me back a handful of seashells he collected while patrolling." I smile and glance off back at the ocean. "He always picked the small ones for me, or the ones with little holes in them." I trail off softly. "I liked to make bracelets with them…"

A hand lightly ruffles my salt-tinged hair. "You've got a lot of good memories with Leo," Aiden says quietly, sliding in to lie beside me. I nod absentmindedly as I stare off into the sky deep in thought. We lie together for a while, lost in our own heads. As Aiden's hand lightly brushes mine, I dare to slip my pinky over his. His own pinky slides under mine and locks there in a comforting gesture.

I try not to think about how much I like the feeling. "Yeah," I finally answer. "I really do." We lie together in silence for a while, taking in the night sky.

"Are you ready to go back home?" The question jars me from my peace. I cringe slightly, and it doesn't go unnoticed by the man beside me. He turns on his side to look at me. "Are you nervous about heading back?"

I sigh and shift on my side with a slight grimace. I feel the need to warn him, to at least let him know. It's not like he can stop me anymore; he's headed back home. "Actually... I'm not headed home quite yet."

Aiden's facial expression intensifies into a glare. "What do you mean you're not headed home yet?" He sits up fully and stares down at me.

I try not to shiver under his harsh gaze. "You might as well know. I'm traveling to the Lower Realm. I'm getting on the next train to the southern border."

Aiden flies to his feet, kicking sand over my chest. "You're doing what?" he screams at me.

This is what I was afraid of. I scramble to a sitting position. "Look, I really appreciate you escorting me back home, but I need to get on with the next phase of this operation. I'm out of the Upper Realm now, so you're no longer obligated to keep an eye on me."

"You had me..." Aiden's voice trails off, and I begin to detect something similar to betrayal in his voice. *Betrayal? No... that can't be right.* "You had me bring you, escort you back *home* to the mortal realm just so that you could go traipsing off into the Lower Realm and get yourself killed?"

"I'm not going to..."

"Oh yes, you are!" Aiden shouts. "It's the fucking *demon realm*. Would your brother really want you to get yourself killed over this?"

I freeze. "Don't you dare bring Leo into this."

"That's what this whole thing is about. Isn't it?" As Aiden rants, I slowly rise to my feet. He ignores the impending storm brewing in my eyes. "Let's be honest, Grace. Your brother had no intention of you ever traveling to the Upper

Realm. Come on, Grace, do you think he wanted his little sister put in danger?"

"Leo would have understood why," I argue. "Leo understood me. Leo knew that... he sent me the dagger!"

Aiden explodes. "You are not strong enough to do this."

I growl, "You have no idea what I have the strength for, Aiden."

"I know you can't do this on your own."

"Yes, I can."

"By the Lady, you are so stubborn."

"Why do you care?" I fire back.

Aiden suddenly grows very quiet. "You're right."

My eyebrows furrow in shock by the sudden change of pace. "What?"

"You are right, Grace. Why do I care about you?" I suddenly can't breathe. "I have no attachment to you. You're just some mortal girl who got lucky. *You got lucky.* And I will make it my mission to find the flaws in the border and seal them up so you or any other mortal who gets some fanatical dream about finding their way to our world will never be able to get there again."

Picking up his bags, Aiden turns back toward the town. "You want to get yourself killed? Go right ahead. I won't stop you."

I am frozen as he storms off. *What just happened?* The echo of his words hit me deeply. How dare he bring Leo into this. While I know it's not ideal, I know Leo would have understood my need to understand and avenge his death. I know that. I hate the doubt creeping into my head.

And to my horror, there's a soft pang for the loss of my companion. Sure, he might have been Fae, but he made the journey a little more bearable. His conversations made me feel less alone, and even his cocky, smirking attitude brought just the tiniest bit of light to my often overly concentrated moods. And he just… walks away without a second thought.

And he wished me dead.

He actually sent me off without as much of a goodbye.

Obviously, my judgment has slipped. I need to rebuild those defenses, block out those words, and remind myself that Fae must always be untrustworthy.

Hopefully, before my traitorous heart decides to grieve for the loss of a pointless, pointless encounter with a cruel and heartless man.

CHAPTER SIXTEEN

―

When I get too cold to remain on the beach, I wander slowly back into town. At every turn, I find myself looking around the corner, hoping to catch a glimpse of Aiden leaving. When I stop at an inn to ask directions toward the railway, I half wish to see him sipping a beer at the bar with that soft smirk and a glint in his eye, asking me why it took so long. Everywhere I look, I am further reminded of the fact that I am now on my own.

After being with Aiden on my journey for so long, I forgot what it was like to feel so alone. I am right back where I started. And… I tell myself that's for the best. I have let myself get distracted from my goal. I shake my head, straighten my shoulders, and stride toward the station. *Never again.*

I board the train headed south to Lorraine, the southernmost town in the Middle Realm. From there, I'll walk to the border. There's so much magic surrounding the border to keep the Fae out and demons in that I would imagine there's no such protections for mortals. Unlike the Upper Realm border, the Lower Realm doesn't require guards. No one in their right mind would ever suspect a mortal would want to go into the demon realm.

Which is why there shouldn't be any problem walking right up to the edge.

I manage to find a window seat in the far back of a crowded third-class car. People file in behind me, pressing me close to the wall. No doubt this entire car is headed home for the night after a long, hard day of work. Some sit quietly with a newspaper while others converse with weary eyes but full hearts.

I envy them. Baypoint doesn't have the same kind of interaction with the Upper Realm as Lisden does. Lisden deals with the bureaucratic side as well as the trade. Baypoint moves cargo off the ships, and then the Fae disappear back to their realm. I envy their hope, their families to return home to at the end of the day, their innocence as a people.

What do you mean as a people, Grace? These are my people. I'm one of them. Even as I repeat the sentiments to myself, I am strangely unable to believe it.

In the Upper Realm… I just felt… okay. Okay to be the way I am. Not strange, not right, just… okay. Something about it made me feel like *more*. More than what I am.

The train starts. I stare at the window as the little coastal town fades away. We rumble across the countryside, stopping every so often to let people off. The crowd trickles away until about halfway to my destination where the last couple finally disembarks. And then I am alone. I keep my head pressed to the window frame, staring at the hills as they roll by. Towns and cities blur together as my eyes start to slowly shut.

I wake up a long while later with a jerk as the train stops. The conductor suddenly opens the door connecting the other cars, peeking his head in. He smiles softly at me. "I was hoping you would awake soon, miss; I was sure I was going to have to wake you myself. This is our last stop, Lorraine

Station. You're going to need to get off now unless you're headed all the way back."

I nod groggily and stumble to my feet. "Thank you, sir."

"Safe journey home, miss," he replies before turning around and walking away.

Home. My heart pangs.

As I step off the train, I close my eyes and breathe in the night air. The smokiness, although somewhat bitter, calms me just enough to keep me moving. Instead of walking toward the town, I turn and disappear into the forest instead. Although I could cut through civilized society, I only want to take the memory of Baypoint as my final memory of the mortal world. In case I die before this is all over, I want to remember the world Leo once knew.

However, I regret my decision to not wait until morning almost immediately. The black night casts shadows over the trees that make the forest seem darker and more dangerous than it would in the daylight. I feel like I'm walking through a living nightmare. *Although, I suppose there's nothing more fitting than walking through a dark forest before reaching a land of literal demonic chaos.* For the first time since I left home, I feel genuinely vulnerable. Without any phobias to blame, I can only conclude that I, myself, am afraid of walking into this alone.

Aiden...

If Aiden were here, I imagine he would have done something to reassure me. Maybe with a joke or two and that stupid smirk of his. Or he'd lay a comforting hand on my shoulder. It's ridiculous to me that instead of worrying about what happens after I reach the Lower Realm, I'm choosing to think about Aiden, a man whose very existence I should be focusing all my efforts on forgetting.

Why am I thinking about him so much anyway? It's not like he gives a single thought about me; hell, he sent me off to my grave without so much as a second glance. It becomes increasingly more alarming that I'm already seeing this as the place I am going to die. Even with the amulet around my neck, I am painfully aware that I am a mortal woman who has no real way to defend herself against demonic magic.

What scares me more is that I don't have any qualms about my death. I must be a horrible daughter; I don't have a second thought about leaving my mother behind. Although, I wonder if she already thinks I'm dead. I don't know what my uncle told her, if anything. No, I'm willing to die for this.

Maybe it will erase the guilt I feel.

Then I finally reach the border between the Middle Realm and the Lower Realm. My eyes widen. A jagged rock face with protrusions up and down its length juts out from the ground and soars high above me, disappearing into the sky. I swear it may go all the way up to infinity. It's solid, with no visible opening in sight. There appears to be some sort of black fog surrounding it, a further sign of foreboding. *By the Lady...*

My heart pounds like it wants to leap out of my chest. I am frozen.

After what feels like ages of standing still, I approach the wall cautiously, my hands held out in front of me as if to ward off whatever is beyond it. I lean forward and reach out to graze the rock wall with the tips of my fingers. When the wall doesn't explode before me, I allow my shoulders to relax the slightest bit. Then I begin to walk the length of the wall slowly, searching for an opening.

Finally, I find a small, two-foot-wide crack in the rock. It appears to form some sort of tunnel. I sink down to my knees and pull out a little handheld light from my bag. I shine it into the crack. As the light sails through, I can see a short tunnel to the other side, where there's a swirling gray vortex of sky. The tunnel is tiny, and I can feel my claustrophobia starting to kick in. Before I can think too much about it, I take off my bag, push it in front of me, and crawl forward into the small space.

Now I know I have a fear of tight spaces, but these walls might actually cave in on me.

I try to move as quickly as I can through the tunnel to get out of the tight space. But unfortunately, it is slow going. The narrow channel only allows me to inch forward one limb at a time. My back is pressed up against the ceiling; my sword handles clang against the rock every few movements. I can barely lift my knees to crawl forward. When my hand grazes the dirt on the other side of the tunnel, I press down hard and pull myself out as rapidly as possible. I get to my feet, stretching… and finally get my first glimpse of the fabled Lower Realm.

I was expecting nothing. I mean… literally nothing. Wide open spaces, no cover, no ground, no sky, actual nothing. Dark space, maybe. Or a space that is so cramped with demons, there is only room for raw magic and pain and destruction.

Instead, the world in here doesn't look too different from the world out there. It's at least a solid ground and a sky. I only see one endless dark forest stretching out in all directions. Yet the atmosphere feels different. The sky swirls black and grey and red, so intertwined that I can't tell which color is more prominent. The shadows hold more fear than the mortal realm. Every odd shape or reflection could be an enemy.

I hesitate just before making my way into the forest. I can't imagine what waits for me in this realm. *And how the hell am I going to get back to the border?* There's no clear distinctions or landmarks around besides this rock wall. Getting back to this point may very well be impossible. But I really don't have a choice. Maybe the Coven can help me once I find them. *If I find them.*

Without feeling very reassured, I step forward slowly. My foot cracks the twigs on the forest floor, and the crack echoes out into the darkness. I freeze, waiting for something to happen. When nothing arises, my grimace straightens into a determined line. I stride forward as confidently as I can muster.

My confidence may have been a little premature.

Because only moments later, three entities land in front of me, emerging directly from the shadows.

By the Lady… Demons.

Each of the demons is distinct in its own way, unassuming and yet terrifying. The first appears almost human, but with a marred face scraped up with oozing cuts and bloodshot eyes covering the entire surface of the skin. The second reminds me of an imp from a fairy tale—short and green with a glaringly devilish look in his eyes. And the third… the third is something straight out of a nightmare. A minotaur-like figure towers over me, at least triple my height with a massive staff and golden-tipped blade ends. His upper lip curls dangerously, almost as twisted as his horns. I am frozen in their presence.

A fight breaks out in a violent surge of wind as the three demons fly toward me. I barely have time to draw my swords before the ram's blade collides with mine. The humanoid and the imp knock me onto my back as they collide with me. I don't hesitate, surging to my feet and swinging one sword at the humanoid's head before connecting back with the minotaur's blade with the other. The humanoid suddenly throws a fireball at me. It catches me off guard, and I don't have time to react. I hope my amulet will protect me.

Instead of deflecting the threat, however, the amulet's magic only shields me from most of the fireball. The rest of it hits the skin just below my neck, searing into me. I cry out in pain as it continues to burn. I slap at it furiously until it finally goes out. Fighting off the discomfort, I scream in rage and whirl my swords with increasing speed.

Round and round we spin, swords clanging, my legs lashing out whenever possible to catch one of them off guard. All the while, the demons attack. None of the magic is coordinated. I'm dodging flames and lances of ice that come wildly from all angles. Sometimes it almost appears they're fighting both me and each other. I manage to damage the imp, wounding it enough to slow it down. But instead, it only throws ice at me from its place on the ground. I have to do some impressive acrobatics to avoid it and continue to stay on my feet.

I feel like the combat goes on for ages, but in reality, I know it's only been a few moments. The intensity is eventually too much to handle, and I collide hard with the ground, losing one of my swords in the process. The demons close in on me. The ram-like demon swings his massive blade high over his head while the imp and humanoid demons swarm me with teeth bared.

It's the closest I've come to death in my life, and there's a real chance I'm not getting out of this.

I hear some sort of a shout from behind me, and an arrow protrudes from the imp's chest. In a startling turn of events, the demon falls beside me. I cringe as it lands, and a blackish tar-like substance pours from its wounds. The other demons back up slowly, weary of the new addition on my side. I spring to my feet, and I find him standing there in furious glory just before he charges into the fight.

Aiden.

CHAPTER SEVENTEEN

In battle, Aiden is an absolute whirlwind. Eyes blazing, he wastes no time in his attacks. He fights fire with fire, casting intricate and intense swirls of flame. He slams down a fist to the earth, and tendrils of roots rise up from the dirt to intertwine around the minotaur. The demon struggles against the binds, and although he's held tightly, he's very close to breaking loose. I stand frozen, staring at the mage as his hands begin to glow a soft yellow. He pulls something flickering and strand-like from his hands and winds it into a sphere. I realize it's one of his forcefields.

He throws the forcefield at the two remaining demons, surrounding them in a dome. It lands strongly, and as the humanoid pushes against it, I'm relieved to find he can't break through it. But as the minotaur struggles and the humanoid pushes, I can see the beginnings of tiny cracks. *"Run!"* Aiden shouts at me, sprinting toward me. I don't think; I follow his instructions and take off. He follows right behind me.

We run as fast as we can and as far away from the demons as we can get. The trees blur together, and my vision practically leaves me. The only thought on my mind is getting as far away as possible from the demons before they break loose. Even so, I am increasingly aware of the man running behind me. *He came back for me. He saved me.*

Where the hell does he get off doing that?

When the demons and the border wall is but a distant memory, Aiden calls out to me. "Grace! Stop!" I skid to a stop, breathing heavily. He slows behind me and leans over with his hands on his knees. I imagine I look as exhausted as he does. Avoiding his eyes, I turn my back and walk off a little way, plopping down in the dirt and leaning against a tree. When I find the courage to look up, Aiden is looking at me with a strange expression. Perhaps a cross between stoicism and relief. We stare at each other for a while.

Then Aiden's eyes snap to my neck. "Your neck!" he says in alarm.

I shake my head quickly. "It's alright. Just a minor burn."

"That looks painful."

I hesitate. "It is," I concede quietly.

Aiden kneels next to me. "Let me…"

"No!" I shout and jerk back.

"Grace, just let me…"

"No! It's fine, Aiden."

"It's not fine, Grace!" Aiden lashes out. "If I hadn't come after you, you would be dead right now and food for the demons!"

"I was handling it just fine!" I shout back.

"Like hell you were. Now, will you just shut your mouth for once and let me heal you, you Lady-damned, stubborn woman?"

I freeze where I am. I hate how my shoulders shake. After a moment of silence, I nod slowly once and whisper, "Okay." I turn my head away from him, giving Aiden a better look at the burn. He sighs quietly in a slight breeze of air that tickles my hair. When he lays a soft hand against my skin, I flinch hard. His hand stalls before moving forward and lightly touching the burn. I barely stifle a gasp as my hands curl into fists.

He pulls the healing vial out of his bag and gently brushes a little of the healing potion on my skin. I can feel the burn shrinking, but it does not fade entirely. Aiden furrows his eyebrows and tries a little more. The burn then shrinks to the size of a large freckle, but it still does not vanish. With that, he moves back and slides the vial back into the bag. "I'm sorry, Grace. That's the best I can do. It won't fade completely; it's demonic magic. It's likely to scar."

"I understand," I reply softly. He sits next to me. I can feel how hesitant he is. I sigh and turn to him. "Thank you. For saving my life."

He nods. "You're welcome." He dares to put his hand on my head. I welcome it, going so far as to lean into his shoulder. I can hear the slight smile in his voice. "It was my pleasure."

He leans his head against mine. "Hey…" he sighs. "All those things I said back on that beach… I didn't mean any of them. I… I don't want you dead, Grace."

I nod, mostly because I don't know what else to do. "It's okay."

Aiden grips my shoulders lightly and turns me to him. "No, Grace. It's not alright. I shouldn't have abandoned you, especially knowing what you were heading into. It goes against everything I believe in. Please forgive me."

I look into his pained eyes and sigh. I don't know what to do. My gut is telling me he really does feel sorry and he needs this, and dammit if his eyes didn't look so sad, I might be able to turn away. *By the Lady, help me, let me turn away.* But no answer arrives; I'm just stuck staring into those beautiful sad eyes that beg me to give him what he needs. And I find myself giving in with little to no resistance from my head.

I finally smile at him. "I forgive you." I stand slowly. "Besides, I think I owe you a life debt."

His eyes grow happy again as he chuckles and stands with me. "No, angel. You don't owe me a thing. Only let me continue with you on your trek."

"Even at your own peril?"

He shrugs. "Well, I've been searching for adventure for forever, so… might as well go down in flames, you know?" He smirks widely at me, and I can't help but smile back. "What now, angel?" I notice he's taken to calling me angel again. I decide I don't mind.

"We're searching for the Coven," I answer. "Happen to know where we're supposed to find them in here?"

Aiden shakes his head. "I suppose we just start searching?"

I nod in agreement, and the two of us set out from that very spot.

***

Days blur together in the Lower Realm. If one can even define days in this realm. There is no sun or moon to detect the passage of time. The sky never wavers from its swirl of menacing colors. We walk until we are weary, and then one of us settles down for a few hours of sleep while the other keeps watch. We run into demons constantly. But with each encounter, we get a little closer to each other.

Aiden has all of the magic and I've got none, but that doesn't mean I can't help out. Aiden fights with his magic, and I attack with my sword as much as I can. He says he doesn't expect me to be able to keep up with him, but I'll be damned if I let him protect us both alone. We battle in tandem, taking hits for each other and fighting off each other's enemies. During the confrontations, I get to see more of his power. Fireballs, growing mountains from the ground, converting some of the demons' magic into explosions that ricochet off the trees in the forest. If I wasn't fighting for my life at every turn, I might have been able to appreciate his skill more. The last few sleep cycles, we have come off worse for the wear. We fight on, though. Our lives depend on it.

From my best estimate, it has been about four days since we had arrived in the Lower Realm and I am beginning to give up hope. Fighting battle after battle against a variety of horrifying and all-powerful demons eventually becomes devastating on the body and the mind. We have been beaten up over and over again, and I just can't take it anymore. I collapse to my knees behind one of the thousands of trees we've been hiking through.

"Woah!" Aiden shouts as he manages to catch me around the waist before I hit the ground. "Grace?"

"I can't do this anymore, Aiden," I breathe out.

"Yes, you can, Grace; we gotta keep going. For Leo, Grace, you can do this."

I shake my head violently. "I can't walk another step, Aiden." I hate the way my voice wavers.

"Then let's sit down." Aiden drops to my level beside me, grimacing the whole way down. "We can stop here for a while." He takes his bag off his shoulder and pulls out the little healing potion bottle that's almost empty by now.

I can't find the strength to pull off my own bag and swords.

"Come on, love," Aiden murmurs before leaning over and beginning to pull my satchel off my shoulder. "Let go."

I snap out of my stupor long enough to shrug off the bag and pull the swords off my back.

We face each other quietly, Aiden with vial in hand. I'm taking stock of our injuries. Aiden's got a busted ankle; he's been limping since the last fight. His arms are covered in multiple bruises and scrapes. My right arm is almost too burned to be able to pick up a sword properly. Even after several applications of the potion, the burn has barely faded. He opens his mouth to speak, but I quickly shake my head. "No."

"Grace, don't fight with me on this."

"No, we're not doing this again. You can't keep giving me the potion and not yourself. It's your turn."

"Your arm—"

"Aiden, you need patching up."

"We'll split it then, what's left," he offers.

I sigh softly. "Alright," I agree. "But I'm doing you first."

"Absolutely not, darlin'." He pops the top off the vial. "I don't trust you not to use the whole thing on me. I promise I'll split it fairly if you let me do you first."

"Fine." I offer him my arm. He pours half of the liquid onto my arm before very carefully rubbing it in with his fingertips. I try hard not to wince. He pats my shoulder apologetically when he pulls away and passes me the vial. I lightly dot the potion on my fingers and then slide it over his ankle a few times. The cosmetic injuries fade a little more than mine did, but when Aiden moves his ankle, it is clear nothing deeper has healed. I let my hands trail over his other injuries a couple more times before letting go.

"That's it," Aiden says. "That's all we got."

"We're not gonna find it, Aiden." The panic has really begun to creep up on me. "The oasis, the Coven, I don't know why I came here."

"Grace, we have to keep going," Aiden replies quietly. "I don't even know where we are. That map you took, it's only given us basics. I don't know where the border is. We can't get back without the Coven's help, whether they're real or not."

My head just falls into my lap at that. I feel helpless. I can't even remember why I thought this was going to be a good idea. Even Leo would have understood there was a limit to what I could do in my search for him. *How could I have been so stupid? I didn't want to die this way. I wanted to go out on revenge for my brother, not on the journey because of my own stupid pride.*

"I'm sorry, Aiden." I look up at him. He watches me carefully. "I never should have dragged you into this. You don't deserve to be here right now."

"Hey," he reaches over and ruffles my hair lightly. "Look, I coerced you into bringing me along. I chose to be here."

"Not here. Not in this realm."

"You're right." He sighs. "Not originally. But then I *did* make the choice to be here. That's my choice. That's not on you."

I wrinkle my eyebrows. "Why did you come back?"

"What do you mean?"

"Why did you come back for me? You could have gone back home. You could have lived your life. Why did you come back for me?"

Aiden's quiet for a while. I can't quite tell whether he has an answer and doesn't want to share it or whether he's trying to work it out in his head. "You're fighting for something real," he finally says. "You're following something that means so much to you that you're willing to put your life on the line to find what you were looking for. I've never seen someone with as much passion and drive as you. And… you're mortal, but you've got the spirit of a Fae." He shrugs slightly and offers me a small smile. "I wanted to see what else you had in you."

I don't know what to say.

He seems to know that because he brushes my questioning look off with a chuckle. "Get some rest, Grace. I'll take first watch."

CHAPTER EIGHTEEN

―

The next thing I remember is being shaken from my sleep what felt like shortly after I had closed my eyes. "Grace!" Aiden whisper-shouts excitedly. "Look!" I look up to where he's pointing, and my breath catches in my throat.

The oasis has appeared. Not five hundred yards away from us, it has emerged from whatever magic it's been enshrouded in. *It's beautiful.* My heart pounds in my chest as I scramble to my feet. "Aiden, is it…"

"I don't know what else it could be!"

"That wasn't there before. Was it?" My voice catches in my throat.

"No," Aiden breathes in awe as a grin brightens his face. "Come on!" We grab our stuff and take off toward the horizon. Aiden grabs my hand, and I'm so happy I don't think twice about letting him. We reach the oasis, and by the Lady, it's real. We can feel the power radiating off the area, and when we pass through the entrance to it, we have clearly passed through some sort of magical barrier. The Lower Realm and its dangers literally vanish behind us. I really think there's magic here that's able to keep the demons out. *Where it came from, I have no idea.*

When we emerge from the mist, we were not prepared for what awaits us on the other side. Trees tower around us as we approach a small courtyard with a lake in the center. The water is crystal clear, beckoning us, and Aiden and I both kneel in the sand to drink. I collapse on my back in sheer bliss and look up at a brilliantly blue sky. "We made it," I whisper to no one in particular.

Aiden hears me, looking over with a soft smile. I turn to him and smile back.

His eyes suddenly widen as he looks at me. I flinch a little bit in surprise. "Aiden?"

Aiden hovers over me and reaches out to lightly touch my skin. To my surprise, I feel no pain when he brushes my burned arm. "Grace, look," he whispers insistently, forcing me to sit up and look at my reflection in the lake. As I gaze into the water, I notice the burn mark is missing. Gone. *By the Lady...*

"Aiden..." I breathe his name. "It's gone..." I look over Aiden. All his injuries are gone as well. We stare at each other dumbfounded. *The water.... How powerful is the Coven? How the hell...* He glances over my shoulder, and his eyes change to an expression of surprise and then horror, before settling on shaken. "Aiden, are you okay?" I spin around, and the breath is snatched from my lungs.

There must be a hundred people behind us, staring back at us with the same surprise and curiosity. *By the Lady... men... women... and children. There are children here.* I leap to my feet, causing the crowd to take a few steps back. I see a few create orbs of magic, ready to strike if I make a wrong move. I keep a hand on my dagger. Aiden slowly stands up beside me. We face off with the strangers with no intention of moving a muscle before figuring out what we're dealing with.

The strangers are Fae for sure; they have similarly pointed ears to the race I've met. But they don't have the same natural glow to the skin I've seen throughout my travels through the Upper Realm. Men and women are dressed simply in white shirts and brown leather pants, and nearly all of them have mortal-style weapons hanging off of belts or inside shoes. I can see the tell-tale outlines.

I don't think they mean us any harm, but one can never be sure when playing with magic.

"My name is Grace," I say quietly. I feel Aiden startle behind me at the use of my real name. "I'm here to see the Half-Fae Coven. Do you know where I might find them?"

A man with steely blue eyes steps forward from the crowd. "We are the Half-Fae Society. The Coven are our elders. How have you found this place?"

Suddenly, it all makes sense. The combination of features would certainly mark them as half-Fae. The weapons, the clothes, it's all a combination of both cultures. *By the Lady, there are so many of them. How have they survived all of this time down here? Why are they all down here?*

"How have you found this place?" the man shouts louder, interrupting my thoughts. I see more weapons drawn.

"We came upon it by coincidence," Aiden interjected quickly. "We don't mean anyone any harm."

"Nothing happens by coincidence," a new, more powerful voice speaks over the crowd. The Half-Fae part instinctively as if it were a routine part of everyday life. My hand tightens around the handle of my weapon. A whisper of magic freezes Aiden and me in place. "Do not be alarmed, children," the voice continues as a woman steps out of the shadows.

I can feel the magic rippling off her, this beautiful tall woman shrouded in flowing white robes. Her purple eyes and deep red lips stand out starkly against her ghostly pale face. She glows with a soft white light. "I am the Enchantress, leader of the Half-Fae Coven. I wish to welcome you to the Guarded Oasis, our home and sanctuary. We know you have traveled far, but answers are near now."

She holds out her hands to us. "Come." As we move to meet her, a cave materializes behind her. Aiden and I glance at each other cautiously before falling in line behind the Enchantress and following her into the cave. The people watch us as we pass by, ushering children behind legs and cloaks as they peer curiously from the ground.

We move carefully toward the center of the large cave. Seven shrouded figures stand in a daunting circle around the edges. They make no motion and make no sound; they stand perfectly still. I almost question whether they are people or statues. The Enchantress joins them at the head of the circle. She looks at me, beckoning me with a nod of her head to speak.

I am compelled to kneel before her. "Fabled Enchantress, I ask for your assistance. I am searching for answers about my brother, Leo Richardson." As I look up, I see the Enchantress nod in recognition. Emboldened, I push on. "I need you to tell me why my brother was searching for black obsidian."

She nods. "Answers are not easy, Grace Richardson." Her voice echoes with force against the cave walls. "You must earn them."

"I will do whatever it takes."

"Stand, Grace."

I stand quickly and move to her.

The Enchantress looks to me and Aiden. "Do you know where you are?"

"No, my lady," Aiden answers slowly. "What is this place?"

"You are one of the few to have found the Guarded Oasis, a sanctuary for children born of Fae and mortal blood."

"I've never heard of a Half-Fae Society," I breathe softly in awe. "I didn't know how so many of you could have existed. The Fae have always hated us… I mean…" I stumble over my words as I realize it may not have been wise to reveal my mortal status.

"Relax, Grace Richardson. We know you are mortal, and no harm shall come to you while you are within these walls. Many do not know or do not remember that the Half-Fae used to be a part of regular society. We were deemed too different, too dangerous, too *other* to remain with the rest of the Fae thousands and thousands of years ago. We were banished down here to die out, but we survived. We have survived everything this realm has thrown out us, and we will continue to fight for our lives and our existence until the end of time. We refuse to surrender to the Fae's will made all those years ago."

Aiden looks like he's about to faint. I don't know that I feel much better. This is all too much to take in. *Another race?* It's almost too much to bear. The Enchantress beckons us forward, and we comply. "You will listen, children. Your mission is the same as ours. You will heed these words accordingly."

The Enchantress raises her hands. My eyes widen as thin, white smoke spirals from her fingers. The strands intertwine to form indistinct shapes that eventually solidified into demonic figures with gaping mouths and abstract bodies. "This world," her voice booms as if amplified to address an entire crowd, "was born of demons who have existed for over one hundred thousand years." The shapes change to show Fae figures whose magic swirl around in blues, reds, and purples.

"The Fae people were originally born of these demons, a people with less power, but more finessed."

She casts a new strand of smoke that rotates to show a sphere before searing it with a red flame into thirds. "After thousands of years, the Fae grew tired of the persecution and the endless death that surrounded the ever-shrinking community. One of the elders of the community, Master Annacht, devised a spell that would shatter the world into two: one for the Fae and one for the demons. Draining his own magic and lifeforce, he managed to generate enough power to shatter the realm into what is now the Upper Realm and the Lower Realm."

"And mortals?" I ask hesitantly.

The Enchantress shakes her head irritably. "Child, that is irrelevant to the point." She waves me off with her hand before suddenly throwing her arms wide open. The white smoke explodes into colors in mid-air, forming nearly an exact replica of the Upper Realm map that I had combed over for years. The map grows from a few towns to a few cities to the entirety of the Upper Realm of what I had now come to see. The landscape moves with people and goods and the bustle of everyday life I had slowly come to expect from a world such as this.

"Listen carefully," the woman hisses. *I haven't stopped listening, Enchantress. But I can't see how this relates to anything that has to do with Leo.* "The Fae began to prosper. They began to grow in population; they began to live lives that weren't solely fraught with peril. They chose a leader, the brother of Master Annacht, who was extremely powerful in his own right. He was a benevolent ruler, although perhaps a bit naive. When he was blessed by his wife with twin children—one man and one woman—he could not decide whom to leave the kingdom to. In the spirit of fairness, he split the land into two, giving each of them a half to lead." The smoky map suddenly split in two.

Slow, black tendrils begin to encircle the two halves of the map. "The brother and the sister grew to resent each other for the land they believed should have been theirs," the Enchantress speaks quickly, her voice growing louder. "War broke out, killing thousands and thousands of innocent men and women caught up in the nobles' power struggle. The queen watched her children destroying themselves and the world they had worked so hard to build. She couldn't bear the destruction. She stopped the war in its tracks with the power from her own lifeforce. She consumed her own children in a flash of brilliant light, and with the last of her power, split her children's souls into five pieces each. Then she split herself into two and let the pieces scatter to the hills."

All the while, the smoke is swirling with magic and color and light until it explodes into nothingness. "The souls inhabited the bodies of the people who would be the first patriarchs of the Twelve Houses," the Enchantress concludes her story with folded hands.

Aiden and I stand in silence. My thoughts are swirling. Aiden looks just as confused as I do. What does this have to do with the black obsidian? With my dead brother? With anything at all? "I... I don't understand," I finally say. "What does this have to do with my brother?"

"It has everything to do with your brother," the Enchantress says firmly. "It has to do with everything your brother has done to protect you."

"How?" I barely manage not to snap at her.

"*You will listen!*" the Coven suddenly speaks in unison. I stumble backward, caught and held in place by Aiden. The air around us becomes much more ominous.

Low and booming, the Enchantress's voice echoes against the cave walls. "The Lady has foretold to us the Coven of Eight; That shall overturn impending war; To shift the balance of an impossible fate; Even an uneven score."

By the Lady… is this a prophecy?

The first dark hood falls to reveal a glowing man with one eye who steps forward to the Enchantress's right. "The Bringer of Light burns the longest and the brightest," his high voice titters. "For his sacrifice for the greater good shall not be the lightest."

Another hood falls as a blind woman with smoky eyes steps into the light. "The Soothsayer shall bring clarity to that which is blurry; But a sharp word of warning, as her words cannot be hurried."

"The Potioner will craft her potions like her spells," a black-caped man speaks firmly. "Intensely pure, combating those who rebel."

A loud, booming voice echoes from the giant. "The Deliverer shall bring more than sheer strength and power; he will bring in the last known ally to usher in the final hour."

A violet woman joins the circle. "The lost child shall be the Spinner, the strongest of the women's breed." Her lighthearted voice almost made me more uneasy than the others. "Spinner of tales and spinner of winds, only she can commence the final deed."

The final two cloaked twins step into the circle, surrounding us now entirely. They speak in unison, "The Witch and the Conjurer, knights of the red; upon darkness and shadow will they always tread. But in the light, what the others won't expect: The Witch is to serve, the Conjurer to protect."

The Enchantress shoots out her hands and hits both of us directly in the chest, pressing her fingers over our hearts. We are both frozen. "The Enchantress shall unite the mages..." Her eyes bore deeply into mine. "And rewrite every inch of the realm's history pages. With untapped power that spans both mortal and Fae, she is the only one who will call night to an endless day."

In a creepy, yet immensely powerful chant, the eight mages speak together. "The Coven of Eight must protect the many, from mortal and magic, both and any. With a bond that's stronger than the fabric of magic, to override the destined to be powerful and tragic."

The words of consequence echo purposefully. I can't move. Aiden is frozen beside me, his heavy breathing, the only sign he's still alive. I clear my throat nervously and whisper, "What does that mean? What Coven?" The Coven of the Half-Fae stands silently around us. The Enchantress levels her eyes directly at me but offers no assistance.

"What does that mean?" I shout. Aiden reaches for my arm, but I wrench it away from him. "How does that help me find out what happened to Leo? How does that help me find what I need to find?" The Enchantress continues to stare at me, unmoving. The anger bubbles up inside of me.

"Some all-powerful coven!" I shriek. Aiden tries to speak, but I lash out. "No, I'm not going to let them walk all over me!" I move up to the Enchantress, unafraid. "Give me something to work with!" She stands still. "Tell me what happened to Leo! Tell me!"

She looks at me calmly. "We have given you the answers you need."

I practically scream in frustration.

"You both are welcome to stay here and rest as long as you need. One of our own will show you to a resting place. But be gone once you have slept. The people will be restless with outsiders in our midst. They will not harm you, but you mustn't antagonize them. The protection won't last forever."

"No…" I hate how choked up my voice sounds. "You can't just leave me with this."

The Enchantress dares to lay a hand on my shoulder. "Child, this is your story, not ours. We are only supporting players. We cannot help you any further."

With that, the eight of them slowly begin to fade around us—almost as if they had never been there to begin with, only ghosts or shadows of a memory. And I am left here in the middle of the cave with a pounding heart and more questions than I have answers.

CHAPTER NINETEEN

I barely pay attention as a young woman escorts us to a large, round hut just on the edge of the oasis. The colors and the brightness I saw on our way seem to mock me now with their cheeriness. The constant staring of the people milling about the oasis is getting on my nerves, and it's taking all of my energy not to explode and hit somebody. *Anybody.* We pass by many little houses and huts on our way down a sand-covered path before arriving at a small cave with a wooden door. The young woman ushers us in the door, and I hear a squeak as she rushes away after she closes the door.

She's afraid of us. Like all the others.

I look around the place, trying to calm down. Up a couple of stone stairs, two beds sit on a raised platform on top of soft woven rugs. I itch to just curl up on one of them; it's been so long since I've lain on something plush and comfy. A soft waterfall tumbles off the far-left wall into a large pool. I walk over and graze my hand across the water's surface and then plunge my hand in fully when I realize it's warm. *A warm bath, a clean bed... at least the Coven knows how to treat their guests.*

"What the hell was that?" Aiden's voice grumbles behind me. I hadn't realized his irritation while I was wrestling with my own.

I roll my eyes and stand to face him. "It was bullshit. That's what it was. All prophecies are."

Aiden moves to me and grabs my arm. I look up at him in alarm. "I'm not talking about the damn prophecy; I'm talking about you going off on those mages."

I jerk my arm away from him and storm over to one of the beds, stripping out of my weapons and bags. *How dare he?* "First of all, don't grab me, or I swear by the Lady I'll take your hand off." I throw my dagger down violently. "Second of all, you heard them. They twisted all of my questions, didn't answer a *single thing*, and then went off about some second Coven of history-makers."

"You were disrespectful, Grace," Aiden continues to argue. "We need them to get us home, you know."

I scoff even though I know he is probably right. I pull off my jacket and let it fall to the floor. "I am here to find answers about Leo. Nothing more, nothing less. If they knew about me like they said, they knew why I was there. They know more. They were just choosing to withhold it."

"Look, I get that you're mortal, and you don't understand how things work around here, but maybe pissing off the people who were offering us a brief moment of protection from the demons wasn't the best idea," he said sternly. "That's all I'm saying."

I whip around and get up close to Aiden. "I don't know about you, but I was doing just fine without their so-called help."

"What about everything we just talked about? How you were ready to just give up? Hell, I found you fighting off three demons on your own, half-dead in the woods of the Lower Realm!" Aiden shouts. "How is that doing well?"

I scream back, "Well, whose fault is it that I had to go alone in the first place?"

"Yours! You always jump in without thinking! This place is dangerous, Grace! Your amulet will not protect you from most things down here! You are not Fae! Stop acting like you're invincible!"

I shove Aiden. "How dare you! You have no idea what I had to work through to get to where I am right now. Just because I am not Fae does not mean I am not strong."

Aiden throws his hands up. "That's not what I said, Grace."

"That's what you meant, though. Isn't it? Look at the pathetic little mortal girl! She's no match for the Upper Realm and us powerful Fae! Well, guess what, Aiden? I got myself here! I navigated that Lady-damned land on my own! I did the research, I trained my ass off, I got supplies off the black market, and I found a way to fake magic to travel undetected. I did that! That was me!"

I jab my finger into his chest. "I don't need you here. I have never needed you here. You wouldn't leave me the *hell* alone. You chose to come with me, and you can choose to get the hell out of here now."

"What makes you think I'm *still* gonna let you go gallivanting across the Lower and Upper Realms alone?"

"Oh, honey, you don't have a choice. Get out. Now." I push him again hard toward the entrance.

He grabs my upper arms, and I struggle in his grasp. Aiden lashes out, "I have no qualms about still turning you in, Grace, if you push me out again." I freeze. He freezes too, almost in shock of his own words. But I know better.

My foot flies out and kicks him between his legs hard. He drops me and falls to the ground. I curse inwardly as I realize my dagger is too far away to kill him. Aiden looks up with pained eyes. "Grace," he stutters out.

"You'll have to find me first," I interrupt him dangerously. I storm over to his bed, grab his backpack, and throw his bag hard out of the cave. "And trust me, you won't. You will chase me over every single damn House, but you will never find me again, I swear by the Lady."

"Grace, I didn't mean it." Aiden tries to protest, but I am not hearing it.

"Of course you did. You're Fae," I spit. "Fae always look out for their own self-interests. And you want me and my kind trapped in a depleted realm while you and yours live your lives without fear or consequence."

"Grace..." he sounds almost pleading.

I wrench him up by his arm and shove him of out the cave. "Get out."

He stands and stares at me for a moment. I glare at him unwavering. Eventually, he turns around and disappears outside where he fades from view. "I'll be back, Grace," he says quietly.

Good riddance.

***

How dare he. How dare he say... those things...

I wish I could say I forgot about him instantly. I wish I could say I jumped immediately into the warm pool and then went directly to sleep.

But as much as I wish to be, I am not that heartless. I can't stop worrying about Aiden. It takes nearly a half-hour for me to calm down from fighting. But slowly, cursing him and his whole kind turns into wondering if he is headed back to the border. I wonder whether he will encounter any demons on his way. I wonder if he's going to survive. We had each other's backs out there. Eventually, even that turns into *I shouldn't have kicked him out.*

As much as I hate to admit it, I've enjoyed Aiden's company. He has a certain charm about him that drives me absolutely insane but is also kind of… nice. Our verbal spars have always been productive in one way or another. He's an incredibly intelligent man. He could have turned me in back when he first found me, could have killed me even. But he chose to help me. He chose to come with me and offer something I could have never replicated—an intimate knowledge of the inner workings of the Upper Realm.

He's been an invaluable resource to me. And… maybe if I close my eyes and forget that he's Fae for a minute, I could even admit to him being a friend.

I shake my head and stand from my crouched position in the corner. I sit on the end of my bed and lie back against my satchel as a pillow, staring up at the ceiling. Eventually, I feel myself begin to grow tired. I close my eyes and after a moment's hesitation, I fire off a quick prayer to the Lady. *Hey… can you watch over him… just for tonight? Just keep him alive.*

With that, I drift off into another uneasy sleep.

CHAPTER TWENTY

If only I had known what was coming for me, I never would have closed my eyes.

Leo stood at the entrance to the mine. His eyes were furrowed in concentration and worry, but his body stood strong and confident. His mission was so clear, yet so destructive in its nature.

Black obsidian. The very substance he had sworn to protect, he now must destroy in its entirety. He knew the Fae would find out eventually, if not immediately. He would be on the run from them until they caught up to him. He would be dead within the day.

Grace... his sweet Grace still waited for him at home. Such a special little girl. She never did have any idea what potential she had. He always had known. He had lifted her up for so long, pushing her forward, pushing her to try new things and learn as much as she could. He couldn't let her down.

So, he moved forward with his plan.

He had placed multiple charges of explosives over the course of the last hour in key positions in the framework of the mine. He had made sure the workers were out of the mine *and off to lunch.* He held the detonator in his hand now, ready to press down and blow the damn place to the Lower Realm.

"Hey!" a shout came from behind him. He spun around rapidly as a group of Fae soldiers began to approach him. "What do you think you're doing?"

If he failed to detonate the dynamite, he would be taken away, the Fae would continue to mine the obsidian, and what he knew would not save his family. He took one look at the soldiers, and he charged headlong into the mine.

The Fae soldiers shouted after him, but Leo kept running. Deeper, deeper. They chased him, but he didn't stop. Deeper and deeper into the mine, he ran. As he heard them catching up, casting frantic spells after him to try to immobilize him, he closed his eyes and begged the Lady to take him in. He begged Her to protect his Grace.

Then he hit the button.

The mine blew instantly. The falling rock collided with Leo's body, breaking bones and crushing flesh. His body caved in, and he crumbled into dust under the blood-stained stone...

I fly out of my bed and sprint forward blindly. The bile bubbles up in my throat. *The blood... So much blood...* I reach the outer edge of the cave and promptly vomit all over the dirt. I stumble and hit the ground on my knees hard. "Leo," I choke out into the night. I bend over on all fours and cough up more gunk from my throat.

The cold stings my face as I collapse onto my back. I sob wildly, and the harsh wind freezes my tears against my cheeks. I am so cold. *What happened to the sunshine? Is it snowing?* I take in a breath and scream without abandon into the night. I scream and I scream and I scream. I scream until I can't draw breath, and then I scream hoarsely. *Leo... Leo...*

LEO! Darkness prickles around my eyes and I welcome it with open arms. I tumble down into unconsciousness.

***

"Grace!"

I hear a vague voice call out to me. I can't place it, but it sounds worried. I feel so heavy… heavy enough to sink into the earth beneath me. Is there earth beneath me, or am I floating? It's so cold.

"Grace!" A blurry oblong shape appears in front of my head, and I struggle to focus on it. I groan softly, mentally pushing the figure away. I want to be alone.

Suddenly, I am roughly pulled upward. My body slides from the snow and against a solid mass. Aiden's chest. I recognize the voice mumbling above me as Aiden's now. It's so slick and warm. If only I could feel anything.

I can't feel anything. How am I still alive?

Two burning hot fingers press to the side of my neck. I cry out, or at least I manage a whimper, as I weakly struggle against his hold. *It hurts, it hurts, make him stop.* Aiden breathes a sigh of relief above me. "Damn it, Grace." He roughly gathers my limbs and lifts me up. We head toward the cave as my head lolls against Aiden's shoulder.

Once inside, Aiden sets me down on the cave floor. I'm still so cold. He begins urgently pulling at my clothes, pulling them away from my skin and off my body. I am too weak to protest. He can see me naked. It doesn't matter. Nothing matters. *Leo.*

Aiden swears loudly, ripping the last of the fabric off my body. I vaguely wonder whether he's looking at me. Does he see anything worthwhile? Does he see anything better than

CHAPTER TWENTY · 185

I do when I look in the mirror? Am I pretty to him? *Why does it matter so much?* His hands slide under my legs and back, and I'm in the air again. His hands feel incredibly hot against my skin.

Suddenly, Aiden throws me.

I hit the water. White-hot pain rushes through me as I slide down into the dark depths of the pool. I'm on fire. I can't breathe. I struggle and thrash, trying to move to the top. I can't move. My limbs won't work. *Is this how I end?*

The Fae will always destroy... never forget.

No... no... not my Aiden. Aiden is kind and good, and he wouldn't let me die a slow death from the cold. No... he knows I want to die quickly, even if it's painful. How he knows... I don't know, but he wouldn't leave me to suffer. Oh, that sweet man. If only I had gotten to know him sooner, gotten to thank him for his help.

I wish it wasn't already too late.

I'm coming, Leo. Your sister is coming home.

An arm grabs me and pulls me up to the surface. My head breaks the water, but I still can't breathe. It's too hot. I'm boiling alive; my skin is bubbling and blistering. *The Fae will always destroy.*

"Grace!" Aiden screams in my ear. "Breathe, Grace. Come on, Grace, just breathe." I want to scream at him. Why is he asking me to breathe? He wants me dead. He left me to boil. But then why is he in the water?

Aiden's hand thumps against my back hard. Suddenly, I cough up water, and my lungs are clear. Gasping for breath, my body convulses in the water. His arms tighten around my body, and I'm cradled against his chest.

"Shh shh shh... come on, Grace. It's alright. Just breathe."

The water is starting to cool down to just hot, and only then do I realize it wasn't boiling before. I'm hypothermic, or very close. I tremble against Aiden's bare chest, and my head spins. "That's right," Aiden's voice breaks through my consciousness. "That's it, just relax, you're gonna be fine."

As much as I want to tell him *No, things are not going to be alright*, I can't help but revel in the comfort he is offering at the moment.

He rubs my arms with firm, steady hands, trying to get some more warmth into me. I'm hyperaware of the fact I am naked in front of him, against him. "I'm sorry for throwing you," he murmurs. "I had to get you warm quickly… I dove in right after you."

I raise my hand weakly to stop his protests. "Don't…" My voice sounds feeble and gravelly.

He covers my mouth quickly. "Don't speak, Grace. Don't strain yourself…"

I begin to panic when he covers my mouth. I feel the dust and rubble fill my lungs again, slowly suffocating me. I buck up in the water and fight against him, screaming as best I can against his hand. My throat burns with the strain.

Aiden quickly removes his hand. "Grace! Grace, calm down! I'm not gonna hurt you!" He grabs me, but I'm entirely blind by the memories of my nightmare. I punch and kick violently against him.

He suddenly traps my arms and legs in a holding spell. My limbs freeze, and I cry out in fear. Trembling in the water, I shut my eyes incredibly tightly, waiting for the final blow to strike.

But the blow doesn't come.

Instead, a hand touches my head softly and hesitantly. I'm shaking so much; his hand vibrates lightly against my head. Suddenly, there's a heady, heavy warmth radiating from his hand. It combs gently over my forehead and my hair, smoothing down the wet locks with focused care. Aiden speaks quietly, I would suppose not to startle me.

"Grace... It's me... It's alright, Grace... I promise I'm not going to hurt you..."

I whimper against the holding spell. "Please..." I beg. "Please take it off."

Immediately the spell drops, and I can move my limbs again. I nearly slip under the water in relief.

"I'm not going to hurt you, Grace... I'm sorry I scared you. Forgive me." Aiden seems to be afraid I won't forgive him, but I'm not sure why. I nod groggily. He holds me up in the water for a while, alternating between rubbing my arms and stroking my head. I warm up gradually, but the haziness doesn't leave my head. He eventually pulls me into his chest and lifts me up and out of the pool. He carries me to my bed where he pushes my stuff aside and sets me down.

He wraps me carefully in a towel before turning to his bag. He pulls out a loose shirt and a pair of pants for me. "Put these on. They'll be warmer than anything you have." He turns around respectfully. "I won't look."

I stand up shakily and pull the clothes on. "It wouldn't matter," I say quietly. "You've already seen everything."

I swear I hear him mutter, "Not everything." But I brush it off. My legs are still a little shaky, so I quickly sit back down on the edge of the bed. Aiden was right. The clothes are toasty warm, keeping away the shivers that threatened to topple me at any moment. "Thank you," I whisper.

Aiden brushes off the thanks as he kneels below me. His fingers lightly brush against my forehead. "I don't think you have a concussion."

I nod slowly. "Good…" I can feel my eyes flickering in exhaustion. Aiden sighs and gently ushers me into bed, pulling the covers over my body.

"Rest. We'll talk when you wake up, alright?"

I don't even remember if I answered him before I was lost to the world.

CHAPTER TWENTY-ONE

The sickness came on the same as it always does.

I'm trapped inside a swirling dark mass of power. The strands intertwine around my limbs and my neck. I can feel it tightening around every part of me, tugging and pulling, threatening to wrench me apart. Inside of the whirlwind, I'm being bombarded with horrifying images that force me to my knees and rip screams from my lungs.

Leo's body broken and bloodied under the collapsed mine.

David caught by the Fae authorities… his head expands until it explodes into a rainstorm of skin, bone, and blood.

My mother moaning and sobbing as her skin distorts and slowly begins to melt off her face.

Lisden burns in a raging inferno.

There are so many faces, so much blood and gore; I can't escape it. I feel the tendrils of magic tighten further and further. I scream and scream as they pull at me and shake me violently.

"Grace!"

A voice echoes faintly in my ear. I try to turn my head to hear it, but the magic holds me tightly in its grasp. I hear my name shouted over and over again, starting at a whisper until it builds to a roar.

"*Grace!*"

At the moment I hear the voice directly in my ear, my body lurches, and I surge forward awake. Arms catch me almost immediately and force me into Aiden's chest. I can't breathe; I'm thrashing around against him, screaming at the top of my lungs. I cling to him and grab at his shirt, desperately looking for something to remind me I'm awake.

"Grace, baby, come on." Aiden presses my head tightly to his chest and holds me fast. He begins to rock us back and forth, trying desperately to get me to calm down. "Grace, you're awake. It's over now. You're alright. You're awake; it's okay. Come on, angel." Eventually, the words penetrate my body, and I stop screaming. My chest heaves while I struggle to catch my breath.

"There you go. That's right. Breathe, angel," Aiden murmurs above me. He presses his chin to the top of my head. I hug him as tightly as I possibly can and make myself smaller against his body. I hope he doesn't notice that. When my body stops trembling in full-body shivers, I pull away reluctantly.

I stare at my lap, and Aiden stares at me.

"I'm sorry," I whisper.

"Don't be sorry," Aiden whispers back before lightly reaching out to touch my shoulder. "What happened?"

"It's complicated," I automatically reply. Out of the corner of my eye, I see Aiden nod slowly. All I can hear is the sound of my own heartbeat. He's really not going to push me to answer him. He'll sit here quietly with me as long as I need without asking any questions.

That alone drives me to answer. "Ever since I was a kid… I don't know, it started when I was eight or nine. Whenever

I was thrust into a high-stress situation, I have this surge of continuous nightmares. It's always the same; I'm trapped in a black mass of power, and I can't escape. I start to see… all these… people and places, and I can't get away from it. I get physically trapped. No one could wake me up. It had to run its course."

I sigh and slowly get up to walk. Just to get away. "I'm surprised you were able to wake me. No one has since… Since Leo." The room is silent for a while.

Then Aiden gets up and moves toward me. He sits down at the edge of the pool and beckons for me to do the same. "Let me fix your hair. It's not dried all the way, and you look cold." His voice is so gentle. Hesitantly, I sit down in front of him. He motions for me to turn around. As I do, his hands begin to gently untangle my curls. The heat coming off of him siphons the water from my hair, warming my scalp. I want to melt into the touch.

"My brother used to do this," I blurt out.

His fingers still. "Really?"

"Well, without the magic…" I stumble over my words. "He would… sit with me in front of the fire… And comb out my curls… like this." I catch Aiden nod out of the corner of my eye as I continue, "My hair was always too unruly for me or my mother to brush out. Neither of us had the patience for it." I chuckle. Aiden's baritone chuckle joins mine. "But he didn't mind. He said I should… keep it at mid-length. He said any longer, and he would stop."

Aiden chuckles, and I smile softly.

"Tell me about him."

I turn around slowly. I meet Aiden's eyes and sigh quietly.

The words come slowly. I barely know where to begin. Then all of a sudden, I'm pouring out everything I remember.

I tell him about our childhood together. How Leo would always tease me and push me around, but then comfort me when I slipped and skinned my knee, pressing a kiss to my forehead even at six years old.

I tell him how when I started playing the violin, Leo elected to stay home and help homeschool me. I tell him about my very first performance in front of a paying audience, how I was terrified, and how Leo pushed me to take the stage. When it was over, he clapped the loudest, whistling for me and embarrassing my mother greatly.

I tell him of Leo's soldier days and how he trained so hard to be the top of his class. How every mission he brought me back a present to remember him by while he was off on his next adventure. I told him about the seashell bracelet I had cradled in my hands the day I found out Leo died and how I couldn't take it off for nearly six months. Ice cream for breakfast on the day of the Summer Solstice and pancakes for the Winter Solstice and dancing through the city streets as kids for the Spring Solstice Festival. Leo was always the better dancer of the two of us.

Eventually, Aiden pulls me into a soft hug.

I tell him about the day Leo left with the Fae. How I was so ashamed of crying so much, and Leo just laughed and placed his hand on top of my head, swearing he would come back to me. He promised to bring me seashells from the Fae seashore.

The last thing he ever said to me was how much he loved me.

I'm so overwhelmed with emotion; I've never properly grieved for my brother. I've always put my mother first, her sadness first. I've been so numb for so long; it's all coming out now. The tears pour down my face in continuous streams.

I struggle against Aiden's hold, turning my head as far as I can away from his gaze.

He doesn't let me get very far, though. He forcibly pulls me closer, picking me up and turning me around to face him. I wrap my legs around his torso, and he cradles me with one hand at the back of my head. He begins to rock my body, and the tears come faster. *He feels so good.* The hand in my hair begins scratching lightly at my scalp. It's soothing, light enough to be comforting and firm enough to give me something to cling to.

I cling to him. I can't care less in the moment that I still hate the Fae for taking my brother away, that I still can't come to terms with how I feel about Aiden. I still hate the way he smirks at me and the way he always has to boss me around, but right now, I need to feel safe. I want to feel safe.

He begins to sing softly in my ear, an old Fae lullaby I vaguely recognize. I have shaky memories of my brother singing to me when I would wake up from a nightmare. I wonder if it's a song all Fae sing to their children. I have no energy to protest the song choice. I welcome it by sinking further into his embrace. In return, he pulls the blanket up tighter around me.

"Hush now," he whispers gently, continuing to rock me. "You want to tell me what happened earlier tonight? When I found you?" I shake my head violently, and he shifts his hand back to soothingly stroke my head. "Shh, alright… alright… you don't have to say anything. Just relax…"

I close my eyes and give back into the gentle sway of his body cradling mine. "There's a good girl…" I hate how much I preen at his praise. I whimper into his neck. "I'll protect you."

I continue to cry into him until I'm hiccupping softly. All the while, Aiden continues to hold me. He rocks me, rubs my back, strokes my hair, and cradles me in such a way that is more comfortable than any embrace I've ever been in.

As I calm down, I feel the urge to speak, to tell him, to tell someone. "I dreamed... a memory..." I whisper. Instead of confusion, Aiden looks somber.

"I've always heard the Lower Realm opens up your worst demons," he replies finally. "I should have warned you about nightmares..."

"It wasn't a nightmare," I interrupt. Now I see the confusion in his eyes. "It wasn't my memory... it... it was my brother's..." I sob in my throat. "The moments before his death..."

Aiden pulls me impossibly tighter into him and shushed me again. "You watched him die?" he asks incredulously. I nod slowly.

"Ohhh," he lets out a breath. "Angel... I'm so sorry."

Surprisingly... I don't want to protest anymore when he calls me angel.

"C'mere..." I turn into his chest and cry again, softer this time. I weep for Leo. I weep for his soul in heaven somewhere. I weep for my poor mother in the mortal realm whose children both abandoned her in some way. And for the first time, I cry for myself. I cry for the little girl who wanted so much to be like her older brother and for the young woman who swore to take blind revenge on the Fae who took him from her.

I cry because I have no idea what comes next.

And Aiden. Aiden holds me protectively. He presses his lips to the side of my head and holds there fast. I can't touch enough of him at the same time. My hands clutch at his skin reflexively, and he doesn't seem to mind. At one point, he takes my hand and holds it in between us over his heart, letting me feel his heartbeat. I move my ear to meet it, and he shifts to accommodate.

I begin to drift off, safe and warm against his chest. Just before I lose consciousness, I jar slightly when he lifts me. He carries me over to a bed and sets me down. Desperately, I clutch at his hand. "Don't... don't go..." I slur. My eyes flicker.

I vaguely see him smile at me and tap my head. "You're in my bed, silly."

I realize a second later that he's right. His clothes are strewn across the end of it, and the other bed has my bag and weapons sitting on top. I blush deeply at my stupidity.

Aiden takes off his shirt before climbing into bed next to me. He flips the covers over both of us, and I unconsciously lean a little closer to him. As he moves closer to me, our eyes meet hesitantly. We both stop. I'm frozen. I don't know whether to inch forward or whether I should let him. I don't know whether I should even want to move closer. We stare at each other for a few moments.

Then, without warning, he rolls over onto his other side away from me. "Good night, Grace," he says quietly.

I'm taken aback by the abrupt change in his mood. I reach out softly to touch his bare back, but my hand stalls right before I reach his skin. I don't know how to ask him for what I want. I chicken out and roll onto my side with my back to him. To my horror, silent tears begin to fall down my cheeks. *Stop it, you stupid girl. Why are you crying now? Because he doesn't want to hug you now? He's been holding you all night. Get over yourself!* I sniffle once and quickly wipe my face. Closing my eyes, I resign myself to a sleepless night.

Arms wrap around me from behind, and one slides under my head. It's thick and strong beneath me, cradling my head like something precious. "Hey," Aiden whispers. "I'm messing with you, silly girl. Trying to make you smile." His fingers brush across my cheeks. "Don't cry anymore, Grace. It's okay. If you really want me to, I can hold you. But you're gonna have to tell me, okay?"

I sniffle lightly and nuzzle his arm. "Oh no no no," Aiden catches my chin lightly in his hands and turns it so I'm glancing at him over my shoulder. "You're gonna have to ask. I'm not gonna have you hurt me in the morning because I took advantage. You're a force to be reckoned with, angel." His playful smirk makes me think things just might be alright. *Or at least close enough.*

I blush and ask quietly, "Will you stay… closer?"

He chuckles. "Close enough." He tightens his grip on me, and I sink into the warmth.

"Sleep, Grace. I'll be here."

And I do.

The most peaceful sleep I've had in ages.

CHAPTER TWENTY-TWO

―

I wake the next morning surrounded in a pleasant warmth that I just want to sink into and stay in forever. I sleepily rub my cheek against the smooth pillow and burrow down into the blankets around me. The warmth grows more insistent at my back. I lean back into it. Something oddly uncomfortable pokes me in the back.

Only then do I realize that the "pillow" I've been nuzzling is Aiden's arm.

I stiffen almost immediately as I recognize exactly what is poking me. I blush a deep red and try to shift away. But as soon as I move, Aiden shifts with me, pulling me closer and tightening his arms around me in his sleep. I stifle an exasperated groan.

As I try to blink the sleep out of my eyes, I begin to take stock of where I am. *One: I'm curled up in Aiden's arms, practically cuddling like a lovesick fool. Two: Aiden's morning wood is definitely pressed up against my back. The logical conclusion is... ?*

I have no experience with men. I don't know how to deal with attraction or desire or feelings in general. David and I tried some sort of relationship thing for about two months until we realized we were much better suited as friends rather than partners. I read some things in my lifetime, of course, but books can get you only so far in matters of the heart. Perhaps not even halfway. I don't know what to do here.

Slowly, I rotate my body to face Aiden. He stirs but does not wake. I reach up and touch his face lightly. I trace it slowly with my thumb: the dimples in his cheeks, the curve of his eyebrows, and the thin lines of his lips. *By the Lady, he's beautiful.* I like how peaceful he looks when he's asleep. Like he's not worried, not afraid of anything that could happen in the near future. I wonder if my lines ever smooth out when I'm asleep.

He stirs. I remove my hand quickly and duck back down, closing my eyes and leaning against his chest to feign sleep. *Coward.* I feel him turn slightly and yawn and then freeze in place. I suspect he's noticed me. His hand moves down and cautiously brushes over my hair. I wonder if I make him nervous too. He combs over my curls once, twice, three times. Then his lips brush my forehead ever so slightly, and I can't help but shiver.

Unfortunately—*unfortunately?*—my movements startle him, and he pulls away immediately, shifting me off of him so I'm lying on the cool sheets without him. I hear him move away to sit at the edge of the bed. *Well, so much for a quiet morning.* I roll over onto my other side and feign a yawn and a stretch. "Morning," I mumble, trying to sound sleepy.

He turns back to look at me. "Morning," he says with a soft smile. "Did you sleep alright?"

I nod.

"Good. Do we have a plan?" he asks as he sits up, reaching for his shirt. I can't help but ogle him out of the corner of my eye.

I sigh in frustration and reluctantly climb out of bed. *So much for a slow morning.* "We have to find our way back to the border. Get back to the Middle Realm. Figure out where to go from there." I stumble over to the other bed with the last remaining sleepiness draining from my eyes to rummage through my bag. "Hurry up and finish and then get out so I can change."

Aiden raises an eyebrow. "You're embarrassed to change in front of me?"

I scoff. "No," I reply. "I just don't want you looking at me naked and fantasizing for the rest of the day," I finish boldly.

He chuckles. "Suuuuure, angel." He slings on his pack and strides toward the cave entrance. "Whatever helps you sleep at night."

I chuckle and try to avoid the slightest sting at his dismissal. *Does he not find me attractive?* I quickly shake the thought from my head. *Yeah, Grace, cause the one time he saw you naked was when you were half-dead. Wait until he sees you in a much better context. Wait, what?* Sighing, I quickly change. No use for these thoughts this early in the morning.

"Grace?" I hear Aiden's panicked shout from outside.

My head whips shortly to the cave's entrance. "Grace, don't come out here!" Aiden shouts.

"Aiden, what's wrong?" I sling my bag over my shoulder and rush over to the entrance. I can't see Aiden at all. I walk as far to the left as I can, peering around the side of the cave entrance. My breath leaves me in a rush. Aiden stands incredibly tiny against the backdrop of an army of ogre-like creatures towering over the barren landscape. Their tusks protruded from their mouths like trees shooting up out of the ground and just as long. Battle axes stand five stories tall charged with black lightning that crackles around the blades in long, menacing sparks. The Half-Fae run around like rats underneath their feet, some rushing to their homes to be safe and others into position to fight.

At that point I realized the magic surrounding us could only be so strong.

I charge outside in a rush. "Are you insane?" I scream back at Aiden. "You want me to leave you to take care of these alone?"

"Grace, get back inside! We got this!" With a war cry, Aiden charges at the ogres and leaps, the earth underneath him rising under him to propel him to chest level. The Half-Fae rush to his aid. My eyes widen as the swirls of magic cast by them rush up to meet the ogres and blast them. The air is vibrating with the amount of power being used right now. But it's not enough to faze them. Dark magic is being sent in waves through the oasis, taking out trees, and exploding the earth.

I hear the cry of a young child as I see her mother go flying into the air with another blast. Without a moment's hesitation, I charge toward the boy and catch him, flipping him over my body and underneath me as a tree comes crashing down right where he stood. I look down at his face to check for injuries, and the horror in his eyes stabs me in the heart. I flash back to my first claustrophobia attack as a child and Leo looking down at my terrified face.

What has this child had to endure just from the simple fact he was born not fully Fae? *Am I this child's comfort in this moment?*

Shoving the child into my chest, I wrestle to my feet and take off toward the village. I spin past more rock explosions and duck under dark waves. I deposit the child into a neighbor's waiting arms and shove them not-so-gracefully inside a wooden home. Though I don't know how that will hold if the ogres get any closer to the village.

I turn back to the battle and swear loudly. I watch in horror as the ogres surround Aiden, blocking him from my view. From tiny cracks in their formation, I see swirls of red, brown, and purple magic flying in and out. Several ogres stumble back, and one or two go down, but the rest seem intent on tearing Aiden apart. It takes me only two seconds to know I have no intention of following Aiden's orders no matter how honorable his aims were.

I fall to my knees and thrust my hands into my packs, searching for something, anything that might get us out of this mess. My hands close around two items: my grappling gun and one of the few vials I had picked up at that market back in Faraday.

Yes, miss, this is one of the most potent explosive potions I have in my supply. Combined magic of a fire elemental mage and mages skilled in force field generation and energy conversion. Our own army guys use some of this stuff. But it'll cost you dearly.

It may have cost a pretty copper, but it just might save us now. Scrambling to my feet, I sprint full-on toward Aiden and the fight. I scream at the top of my lungs at Aiden, who I can only hope is still alive and coherent in that mass of ogres. "*Get down!*" The Half-Fae look at me like I'm crazy, but I scream louder with more purpose, "*Get down now!*" They hit the ground immediately. I have no time to contemplate how easily they trusted me in battle. I stop just below the ogre's feet and fire a single shot with the grappling gun into the air. It connects and adheres itself to the top of one of the demons' bald heads. He shrieks in pain. By the time the others turn to acknowledge the new presence, I am being slingshot straight to the sky.

My body soars at top speed, and I shake with the force. I let go at the top, allowing my momentum to carry me a few feet higher. I shout one more time, praying to the Lady that Aiden hears me. "Be ready!" *Hopefully, he gets what that means.* I throw the black vial down violently and hurl my body backward over the ogre's head again, tumbling down his body.

The earth shakes with the intensity of the explosion. An orb of fire erupts from inside the circle of demons, and I shout triumphantly as it consumes most of them in a blaze. I tumble rapidly toward the earth, and I admit, I did close my eyes about halfway. I wasn't sure if Aiden heard me, so I'm not sure if he's alive. If he didn't, well, I'm going to be meeting my brother in the afterlife.

Then a force field surrounds me in a glowing sphere, and I nearly cry in relief.

I hit the ground and bounce like a ball inside the orb. Aiden appears beside me, reaching through the barrier and ripping me out with a quick jerk. "What the *hell* were you thinking, Grace?"

"No time!" I shout. "Attack now!" I shout at everyone behind me. The Half-Fae see what I'm getting at, and they focus a concentrated magical strike against the ogres again. I knew the magic I used wasn't strong enough to destroy the demons, but it may have weakened them just enough to be defeated by the Half-Fae. Aiden adds his own stream of magic to the thread, and it isn't long before a colossal blast strikes the ogres. Squealing and howling in pain, the demons retreat back into the forest.

Aiden and I stumble back into each other, holding each other up. The Half-Fae cheer behind us. I'm too exhausted to celebrate. *That was too close. How do they manage every day?* I can't help but see that child's face, cowering against my body as the trees and the earth flew up around us.

I hear a throat clear behind us. We turn to see the Enchantress placing a hand on both our heads. "Thank you for your assistance," she says softly. "You have helped us to live another day. You have our eternal gratitude."

"What happens now?" Aiden asks quietly.

"We will rebuild. We always do. We strengthen the barrier. And we carry on." Her eyes pierce my heart. "We must always carry on, no matter what the damage."

Don't tell me to move on from Leo. I can't.

"I will send you to the border," she continues. "Be careful. I do not know whether there will be demons where you are dropped. You must return to where you belong." Her tone conveys some sort of stronger meaning, but I have no chance to question it before we are awash in white mist yet again.

We land on our feet a few hundred yards from the border wall. I see the tunnel plain as day, and I let out a whoop. I cringe as I hear the cry of demons moving toward our location. I grab Aiden's arm and pull him alongside me, helping him run the last hundred yards to the wall. I glance behind us as I shove Aiden to his knees in front of the crawlspace.

"Go!" I shout and watch anxiously as the demons close in behind us. It won't be long before they reach us, seconds maybe. Aiden moves to throw up a forcefield around me. I stop him and push his head down. "No, you idiot, move! There's no time!" He finally listens to me and moves into the hole quickly. As soon as his feet disappear, I crouch down and dart into the tunnel after him.

My feet slide through just as the first demon reaches his hand through to grab me. The border shocks him and causes him to disintegrate, sending a shower of black ash over my legs and feet. Aiden pulls me through and out of the tunnel into the light, and I collapse on my back, heaving. He falls beside me and does the same.

Staring up at the sky, I can't believe we survived. I *survived*. I'm a mortal woman without any magical power or instinct or training, and I came out of the fucking demon realm alive. How many people can say that?

I tentatively reach out my hand to Aiden's. I tell myself it's to check on him to make sure he's okay. When my skin brushes his, I feel his fingers automatically curl to meet mine. Our hands intertwine. I look at Aiden out of the corner of my eye, and I can see that through his short breaths, he's smiling at me. I can't help but smile back.

I slowly sit up and look down at Aiden. "You doing alright?"

He stretches. "Yep," he groans. "Just gonna… stay down here for a while."

CHAPTER TWENTY-THREE

As we lie together on the damp ground, the sun begins to rise on another day in Lorraine. I squint a little as the sunbeams shine down on us and into my eyes. *Ugh... can't we have just a few more minutes of rest?* But the brighter the sun gets, the more I can't hide behind my eyelids anymore. "We've gotta figure out where we're headed next," I say softly to Aiden. I boldly reach out and rub Aiden's head lightly, trying not to stress him out too much.

"What do you have in mind?" he answers quietly.

I think for a minute. "Something's missing..." I climb to my feet and begin to pace around Aiden's prone body. "First of all, I think we just need to completely disregard whatever that damn prophecy was; it clearly had nothing to do with Leo."

"But, Grace," Aiden pushes himself up to a seated position with a grimace. "Look... whether it applies to you or not, I think we heard the prophecy Xavier mentioned."

"Absolutely not. No way. Why tell us? We have nothing to do with Upper Realm politics. Why us?"

"Grace..."

"I mean, okay, I suppose you're a soldier, but you're not right at the top! Why was there a necessity for the Coven to bring up a prophecy?"

Then it hits me.

"Unless…" The wheels in my head are spinning out of control. "Unless Leo was involved somehow."

"How do you figure that?" Aiden asks.

"Think about it. The Coven specifically made it clear they had given me everything I needed. We have the origin story of the Houses, the prophecy, and with what you and I found out from Xavier…" I clap my hands suddenly and move quickly toward Aiden. "Black obsidian." I grip Aiden's hands excitedly. "That's the only thing that would bind it all together. It's what the nobles are looking for, what the prophecy would have been revealed through, and it's what Leo sacrificed himself to destroy."

"It's the only thing that would fit," Aiden agrees.

"Fuck, I wish I knew what he knew," I swear in frustration.

"Is there anyone he would have told about how things were going in the Upper Realm? Any friends there or anyone he would have written to?"

I shake my head. "No, he went up there with some older gentlemen—no one he knew. And he only wrote home to us." A flash of a face dances before my eyes. "David."

Aiden looks at me, confused. "David?"

"His best friend David! Our friend. It's a long shot, but if Leo told anyone, it would have been David." I grab Aiden's hand, pulling him to his feet, and yanking him along, I take off toward Lorraine. "Come on!"

***

Out of the corner of my eye, I watch Aiden on the bench where I left him from the ticket counter. Despite being exhausted, his eyes are curious. They dart around the station, trying to take in the atmosphere and the people. I can tell he's people-watching, straining his ears to catch bits and pieces of conversations. When I walk over, he shifts slightly to try to hide it, but I know better. It's hard to not look guilty after a bout of curiousness.

"Doing a little research?" I can't help but jibe. He blushes, and I grin triumphantly. "You know, I could tell you pretty much anything you would want to know."

He groans as he sits up. "Yeah, I know. But I want to figure out things for myself. This place… it's nothing like I have ever heard about. I mean, when you mentioned that stuff about the food shortage when we first met, it was the first time I'd ever heard about it." He chuckles to himself. "And I'm supposed to be serving the people. But… you know, the Fae don't really need too much civilian help… it makes you wonder…" He trails off.

I understand what he's saying. I've wondered the same thing myself. If the Fae had bothered to check down here once or twice or paid attention to communication from their puppet government, maybe we could be in the same prosperous position they are. It would at least strengthen the relationship between the two.

"Come on," I whisper, standing and offering my hand to Aiden. "Let me show you what flying feels like here."

As soon as the train car begins to rumble and roll down the track, picking up speed, Aiden falls in love with it.

"By the Lady, Grace!" he shouts as he watches the scenery fly by. "How fast does this go?" I grin at his antics. The people are around us are looking at him like he's crazy, but everyone seems too tired to address it. I don't think they suspect him as Fae; I pulled the edges of his hair down over his ears and bought him a hat with a few coppers I had left to cover his face. He's never been exposed to such technology. Only the House of Darkness has the technology of rapid transportation like we do, and from what I've read, it isn't the nicest place to travel to.

Aiden eventually runs out of excitement and returns to his seat, falling asleep while leaning against the windowsill. Fine by me, it gives me a little time to think about how I'm going to get in touch with David. More importantly, I'm trying to figure out how to get in touch with David without alerting my mom or my uncle that I'm in town. My mission isn't over yet, and it would do no good for them to see me when anything could still happen.

Although, for the first time in the entire course of this expedition, I feel like I will actually succeed and make it home.

When the train rolls into Lisden, I gently shake Aiden awake and lead him forward out of the car. My foot hits the pavement, and I take a deep breath of the familiar thick smoke. I see Aiden furrow his brow and break into a small coughing fit. I reach over and pat him on the back until he regains his breath.

"Sorry about that," I say loudly over the din of the train station as I pull him toward the exit. "I forget people who've never been to this city before take a while to adjust to the air."

"Yeah," Aiden coughs again. "What the hell is all this?"

"Smoke from the factories. You get used to it after a while." I shrug.

"What is this place?"

I turn back over my shoulder and give him a small smile. "Welcome to Lisden. My home." *My home.* The words taste foreign and yet familiar on my tongue.

I grew up here; my childhood was spent gallivanting through these streets, and yet I don't know if I ever admitted to myself that this was home. The city might be a mess and rundown, and the people might be poor and struggling, but I'd take this place over the Upper and Lower Realms any day.

I don't waste any time in navigating us through the city to the old gym. I manage to head off Billy from asking too many questions about why I haven't been in recently and get him to send word to David to meet me here. When I turn around back to Aiden, I find he's disappeared into another room. I wander through the building until I find him at the combat ring, watching a couple of guys finish up a sparring match. I move up behind him.

"What? Are you surprised mortals can fight?" I quip.

Aiden chuckles. "They're decent, sure."

I roll my eyes at him. "Those two? Matt and Sam? Some of the best around here. I think they're third- and fourth-ranked in the ring. I learned a lot from them."

He crosses his arms as he watches the two men shake hands and climb out of the ring to put up their swords. The guys wave to me as they exit the room. "Who's the top around here?"

I smirk. "Me."

Aiden's head swivels. "You?"

"Me."

"You serious?"

"Absolutely," I say smugly. "You can check the board if you don't believe me. I have the most wins, and I started learning years after most people. Billy calls me little firestarter cause

CHAPTER TWENTY-THREE · 211

of how fast I picked it up. Started all kinds of rivalries in that very ring. They respect me, but they hate me for it."

Aiden's eyes sparkle. "Get in the ring with me."

I laugh. "Absolutely not."

"You afraid you're going to lose?" he smirks. *Ah, he's going to play that game, huh. Alright, Aiden, I'll bite.*

"No magic," I add.

"No magic," he agrees.

I pretend to think about it for a few seconds more before strutting past him, knocking his shoulder. He chuckles as I reply, "Choose your weapon."

He falls in line behind me as I cross to the practice swords. I waste no time in selecting my old favorite, one I used so much the handle has worn down enough to exactly fit my grip. No one else dares to touch it. I hop into the ring and do a few stretches while Aiden spends an oddly long time testing weapons. He picks each one up to feel the weight and tests the nimbleness of it. I have to admire his decision-making process.

"You backing out on me?" I call over.

He smirks and finally moves over to the ring, sword in hand. "Not in the slightest, angel."

Rolling my eyes at his antics, I crick my neck and slide into what I like to think is my warrior mode. My features even out and even narrow into sheer determination. My hand grips the blade with practiced ease, and I hold my head high. Aiden's eyes change too, becoming more calculated. I can see the muscles in his arms tighten as he raises his blade, and I resist the urge to stare.

This is going to get interesting.

I don't have another second to think before Aiden makes the first move at me. When our swords collide, the force of it resonates through my arm. *He's not playing around.* He strikes another series of blows in rapid succession. I counter every one, moving and turning to change the angle and stay upright. Aiden's on the offensive, *smart move.* I imagine he guesses if he doesn't keep me on the defensive, I have a solid chance of taking him down. He doesn't hesitate in his movements. Each swing of the sword is calculated. He's obviously been trained very well.

But so have I.

Finally, he hesitates for a millisecond. His blade shifts just enough to the right, and I swirl past it as it whooshes by my arm. Then, finally, I'm on the offensive. I attack with fervor, slashing and stabbing forward as I try to push him into the corner of the ring. Aiden's just as strong with defense, however, and all too aware of my strategy. He counters me with forceful strikes. We move in circles around each other, switching off who has the upper hand rapidly and endlessly.

After what feels like ages, I manage to catch his blade at just the right angle, knocking the sword out of his hand. I spin my sword and point it at his chest. "It's over for you, Aiden," I grin wickedly.

To my surprise, he only smirks back. "Not yet, angel." Before I can blink, he kicks high and catches my sword, sending it flying across the room. It clatters against the wall before hitting the ground with a resounding thump. My jaw drops, and let me tell you, I am pissed.

"Oh, is *this* how you want this to go?" I growl and put my fists up.

He laughs as he matches my stance. "Bring it on, darling."

I lunge for him. In hindsight, probably not the best idea. He catches me with ease and throws my body backward onto the ground. I hit the mat with a grunt. Aiden just laughs and laughs. I jump to my feet and make another attempt. He catches my wrist and pulls me closer to him, our faces landing mere inches from each other. He grins and then flips me downward to the mat again. This time, he comes down with me. Before I know it, he is straddling my body, pinning my wrists down.

Oh, screw this. While he's chuckling, I push up on him hard, bucking up into his stomach. His breath rushes out with an "oof." That little bit of give and a little force from my leg grants me enough momentum to flip us over. I land on top of his chest, and I pin his wrists instead. "Ha," I pant.

Then I catch Aiden's face. He's staring at me. And *by the Lady,* he is way too close to me. His warm breath puffs against my face, and our eyes lock. I can hear my heartbeat ringing in my ears. I feel too hot. This is too much. This is…

"Grace? What the hell?" David's voice chimes in. I jerk up to see my friend's shocked and pissed off face as he moves over to the ring.

Shit.

"David!" I scramble off of Aiden and jump to my feet. I don't even know how to get out of this.

"Grace?" David's eyes glint somewhere between confusion and borderline anger. "What the hell is going on? Who is he?"

"Who is who?" I cringe at my own response.

"Him!" His finger jabs at Aiden, scrambling to get up.

"Uh…" I stutter. I can't find the words to even begin to explain; I am so flustered.

My friend holds his hands up and backs away slowly. "Look, I'll be outside when you get your head together. But you are gonna explain…" He looks up at Aiden and gestures in his direction. "All of that."

I just nod and let him go. Hopefully by the time I step outside, I'll have come up with a feasible cover story. And I'll have figured out how to look Aiden in the eye again.

CHAPTER TWENTY-FOUR

When Aiden and I make it outside to meet David, he's leaning up against the wall by the alley. He shakes his head when he sees me and holds his arms out. I move into them and accept his tight hug. "Grace Richardson, you about gave me a heart attack." David pulls me away from his body and holds me at arm's length, inspecting me for any damages. "When Billy's message got to me, I was sure it had to be a mistake." He gives me a boyish smile. "But here you are, and in one piece!"

I smile back at him fondly. "Did you expect any different?"

He chuckles and then gives a slightly menacing glare over my shoulder. "So. Are you going to explain that?" he says, looking pointedly at Aiden.

I glance around and then grab both David's and Aiden's arms, pulling them further into the alleyway. Once we're sufficiently out of sight and out of earshot, I turn to David again. "Alright, David, this is Aiden. Aiden, this is my friend David." Aiden holds out his hand; David reluctantly takes it. "He's a soldier like my brother."

"From where?" David knows something's up.

"Look, don't flip out, but…"

"I knew it!" He claps his hands and starts to pace. "I knew it, Grace, you little disaster, what have you done?"

"You didn't even let me finish!"

"Oh, I could tell as soon as I saw you on top of him!" he shouts. I unwillingly blush. "He's Fae, isn't he?" David hisses.

"Yes," I answer simply as Aiden reveals the points in his ears.

"I can't believe, Grace, that you have the *gall,* the *nerve* to bring a Fae man with you. They killed Leo! Or did you forget that on your little escapade?"

My mind goes blank. I see red.

Suddenly, David's up against the wall, and my hands feel rough fabric and surprisingly smooth skin. He chokes.

"How dare you," I whisper. I can't think. "How *dare* you!" I scream in his face. My hands are holding him up, choking him, but it's not me. It's not really me. "I loved Leo! I loved him more than you! *He was everything I had!*" I keep screaming at him as if that will shake him out of his anger of me, as if that could get him to give Aiden a chance.

I'm being wrenched backward by a pair of strong hands, and all I can think about is trying to get back to pummeling this man who claims I have forgotten my purpose. "You don't know *anything* about what I've done," I shout. "*Anything!*"

I am aware of Aiden's voice behind me telling me to quiet down, to calm down. David slides off the wall to the ground, coughing and heaving. I feel my body fall backward. Aiden catches me, and only then do I become fully coherent.

By the Lady, what have I done?

I shudder against Aiden's chest, and he grips me tightly. David slowly stands up, staring at me with a new sense of fear in his eyes. My heart seizes. "David…"

"Why did you call me here?" he interrupts me, his voice strained.

"I needed you," I beg.

"What do you need me for? You've got this guy," he scoffs.

"David..."

"What do you need, Grace?" David snaps at me. "So help me, I will leave you high and dry if you don't answer the question right *Lady-damned* now."

"Fine!" I shout quickly to stop him from leaving. "Look... all I need to know is whether or not Leo ever wrote you a letter about black obsidian."

"Black obsidian?" David repeats. "What the hell are you looking for with black obsidian?"

"You know of it?" I breathe heavily.

"Leo never contacted me about it, but yes, I'm aware of it. What do you know of it?"

"It's connected with his death. The mine he was guarding, the Fae were mining black obsidian, or attempting to at least. Leo... Leo blew it up," I trail off. With a gulp, I continue. "Please, I need to know what you know."

If David is shocked by this, he doesn't show it. He glares at Aiden for a moment before he speaks. "There's been some activity in the House of Darkness sector recently. A lot of questions being passed around through various channels about if anyone has caught any word or any sight of this substance. They're even involving us now to see if we have it on the mortal side of the border. Everyone involved has been put on high alert."

"The House of Darkness?" Aiden interjects incredulously. "You're sure?"

"Yes, I'm sure," David snaps.

"We need to get back to the Upper Realm then," I stop both of them. "David, we need to be on one of your transports."

"I am not letting a Fae man know how we do business down here, Grace, and that is final!"

"He's not going to say anything; what reason would he have?" I suddenly flash back to Aiden's story about his friend who died by the black-market runners. I actually have no idea whether he would say something or not. I couldn't ask him to set aside his personal vendetta for the sake of this mission; I've dragged him all over the Realms enough to warrant him to be a little selfish. I look to Aiden in concern.

His little nod back at me reassures me.

"If we absolutely have to, we can blindfold him," I offer to David, pleading. "Please, David. I gotta see this through. For Leo."

David stares at me for a minute. The anger falls away just enough that I can see a hint of something sad in his eyes. He nods swiftly. "For Leo." He turns to leave. "Meet me at the darkest part of the morning on the edge of the city. But after this, Grace, I'm done. Don't expect any more help from me."

***

I wish I had never come back to Lisden.

Somehow in the span of an hour, I've managed to straddle a Fae man, strangle my best friend, and break David's trust. I've never fucked up this royally in my entire life. The whole interaction with David is just a blur, but in my heart of hearts, I know his last comment meant our friendship from here is over.

I can't say I blame him. I showed up out of the blue with a Fae man on my arm with barely an adequate explanation and no context. I didn't even get to tell him how Aiden saved my life. Though I don't know if it would have made a difference. He's just as prejudiced toward the Fae as I am. *Was.* I don't think I blame the entire race anymore. I can't say that with Aiden beside me. I don't hate him. He's… different.

When David leaves us, I take Aiden's hand and lead him just past downtown to the abandoned hotel. We make our way through a cleared path of debris up to the back stairs and onto the roof. I breathe in deeply and let out a long sigh. *It hasn't changed a bit since I left.* "This is my favorite place in the whole city," I glance over my shoulder. "It's got a good view."

Aiden peers over the edge of the building. "Do you live here?"

I chuckle. "No, I do have a home."

"Where's that?"

"Down on 10th Street. Closer to the heart of downtown."

"You gonna take me there too?"

I bite my lip softly. I stretch out on one of the lounge chairs. "I can't take you to my apartment."

Aiden settles in another chair next to me. "Why not?"

"I can't let my mother know I'm in town."

His eyebrows rise. "You're not going to tell your mother you're home?"

I sigh. "I can't. She doesn't know where I've been. Do you really think she would have let me go if I had told her? Not a chance." I stare up at the sky. "I could still die trying to do this, Aiden. If I'm coming back at all… I have to come back for good."

"What about your dad?"

"I never knew my father," I reply softly. "He left when I was born. I don't even know his name."

Aiden's hand brushes mine. "I'm sorry."

I look over at him and smile lightly. "Don't be. With any luck, I'll be home soon."

Our fingers intertwine slowly. "Are you ready to be home?" he asks.

It takes me a while to answer him as we watch the sun begin to set over Lisden. "I don't know, Aiden. I honestly don't know. Everything feels… different now."

"How so?" he probes softly.

"I can't explain it," I whisper. "I have seen so much in the Upper Realm that… all of this… it doesn't feel right. It's never felt right. But now that I've seen what you and your people have, how can I come back to this… and be okay? How can I be okay again… knowing what the Fae have taken from us… and from me?"

Aiden is quiet for a long time after I speak. I almost regret speaking so plainly, but then he squeezes my hand. "When I go home… I'm going to find a way to help your world. I promise."

I squeeze his hand back. "Thank you. I appreciate that very much." He smiles softly, and I lean my head on his shoulder very softly. He doesn't ask me to move, so I relax just a little bit more. We look out over the city as night falls. And once again, I only try to forget.

CHAPTER TWENTY-FIVE

David guides us to the border under the cover of night while I keep an arm and a close eye on the blindfolded Aiden beside me. We take the same wagon with the same guide and hop the same train as before. Only this time, David does not say a word more than necessary. His silence cuts me deeply. I never intended to choke him. Or to break his heart. I lost control, and I will be regretting it for the rest of my life.

When we reach the barrier, I slip the blindfold off of Aiden and push him through the barrier quickly. I stand alone with David. "David… I'm sorry," I beg softly. "I don't want this to end like this. Please forgive me."

David sighs and frowns. His jaw tightens, and he looks at me with piercing eyes before finally speaking in a low tone. "There's a man in the House of Darkness. He goes by Mahlin. He's the highest ranking official of the black market on the Upper Realm side that we know of. I've met him once. He may know something about what you're looking for. Search the alleyways. He's always prowling around in alleyways; he says it's his natural habitat."

"I'll find him," I promise.

"Let me know if you find anything out."

"I will." We look at each other silently. Neither of us seems to know what to say.

"You need to go," he finally says. I nod and reach out to hug him, but he backs away from me. My heart breaks. I turn around and take a swig of the border potion before stepping through the barrier. *Back into the Upper Realm I go.*

***

I can feel Aiden's eyes on me as we travel silently toward Faraday once again. I barely speak. I wouldn't know what to say. I feel uncomfortable with the whole situation. My experience dragging Aiden through my home world felt nothing like traipsing around Aiden's. There's much less pain stored up on this ground than what I left behind in Lisden. David, my mom, Leo. I just want it all to stop.

I'll keep on my mission until I know everything about what Leo died for. Then maybe I'll be able to go home and face the people I care about. But I can't stop thinking, *Here in a land I don't belong in, I wish I could hide out for at least a little longer.*

Aiden rents two horses from another merchant in town looking to get them to a stable just outside of Craine, the main city of the House of Darkness. Aiden and I, we just ride. We stop for meals once or twice, but I barely remember sleeping. It takes two days to reach the House of Darkness from the border. I try to lose my cares in the wind as we fly over the countryside. All I get is whiplash, a sore butt, and some sort of wistfulness for what little time I have left on this side of the world. *Figures.*

This is what I get for trying to figure out emotions.

We end up dropping the horses at a stable just outside of the city and walking the rest of the way on foot. When we reach Craine, I feel like I have stumbled upon a city of ghosts in beggars' clothes and demons with businessmen's suits. From the hilltop, I can see a distinction between the two classes as clear as day, just like Lisden. The Fae on the streets are either deathly pale and thin with haunted eyes or stately and grand wrapped up in the finest of silks. "Is this it?" I ask Aiden quietly.

"Yes," he breathes in my ear.

Aiden leads me away from the edge, and we hop a monorail headed for the city center. I stand and lean against the side windows, trying to catch a glimpse of what this place is made of. Skyscrapers of glass, more impressive than the ones in Lisden, whip by the rails as we speed along. Their sharp angles contrast from the dull color and lifelessness they project out over the city. Small figures below us hover in between, crouched low and leaning in deep, dark alleys. Had I not had the knowledge of how black-market deals worked under the cover of the alleyways, I would not have noticed the shadowy figures who occasionally stand and interact with other shadows. Such an odd way to conduct business when a fixed eye from a certain vantage point such as this would blow the whole operation.

Aiden guides me off the monorail platform when we reach the city center. As we traipse down the stairs together, I have this uneasy feeling settle deep in my stomach, something like being followed. "Is this how the House of Darkness always feels?" I ask hesitantly in a hushed voice.

Aiden replies in kind, "Pretty much. I've only been here once for... a conference."

"Didn't go well?"

"You could say that." Aiden keeps rotating his head as we walk, watching for any sign of something amiss. "The heir lord and I don't get along too well."

"How does that work?" I continue while keeping my ears perked. "Do you meet with nobles often?"

Aiden coughs. "Yes, essentially. I'm kind of the... go-to guy for that."

"You're of higher rank than I thought then."

He nods absentmindedly beside me. "So... what's the plan?"

I look around the square as we come up on it. "I'm not sure yet... What is with this place? I thought this was one of the richest cities in the Upper Realm. It... it doesn't look right."

"It is one of the richest cities in the Upper Realm," Aiden replies dryly. "Doesn't mean the wealth trickles down. What does trickle down goes almost entirely toward importing food. The House of Darkness is one of the least fertile locations in the Upper Realm. They have to import nearly everything just to sustain themselves. They've got enough in the treasury to keep it together and working." Aiden's jaw locks. "They just don't use it," he forces out.

I nod slowly in understanding, glancing around at the people huddled in different corners of the square. My heart goes out to them. Even my city isn't this poor. Beggars are far and few, and small daily jobs have always been made available for those who need it. Maybe that's a unique thing about mortal society that the Fae haven't caught onto yet. What kind of place leaves their people to starve while they sit high in their tower?

Um, the same people who live contently inserting a puppet government over the mortal realm, letting the people grow weaker even though they have all the technology and resources to assist. They won't bother to take a look and see that we might have something to offer them as well? Those people?

Sigh.

I turn to Aiden, shaking my head slightly to quiet my own thoughts. "We need to split up."

Aiden sputters. "Excuse me? You just got finished telling me how creepy this place feels to you."

"I know," I reply. "But we need information. The best place to get that is the black market." I ignore Aiden's pointed glare. "Trust me, no black-market trader worth half a copper coin would ever talk to two people at the same time. Too many risks. A group of more than two in the shadows is way more spottable. We have to split up if we want to get any answers." I lay my hand on his arm reassuringly. "We can meet back here in two hours with whatever information we have."

"Not a chance, Grace. You can go into the alley alone, but I'm following you."

I sigh in frustration. "Fine, but you need to leave me and then follow from a distance. You need to stay out of sight and out of earshot from me. Observe from somewhere you can jump in if necessary but not make out the conversation. These guys are probably trained just like you are, if not better."

He sighs and, to my surprise, puts his hand on my shoulder and squeezes. "Fine. Be careful, Grace." I nod once in response. He turns and disappears around the corner.

I let out the breath I was holding. I wasn't lying to Aiden when I told him it was better for us to split up. Technically, it is. But my reasoning for separation wasn't complete. I look around the square carefully before slipping down the alleyway behind me.

I feel horrible for the way I left David. That wasn't fair to either of us, and I know it was primarily my fault. I chuckle dryly to myself. *David may disagree with you. Besides, he did accuse you of losing your focus.* But I have to imagine what it must have looked like to him. Me back home in the mortal world, back at the gym, straddling a Fae man? Yeah, I probably looked like a real nutcase.

My heart unwillingly clenches at the thought of being on top of Aiden.

Ugh, forget this. Gotta stay focused.

That's why I'm going to send David a message. The least I can do is tell him about that additional entrance on the coast. Maybe he'll be able to connect with the people there and open up a whole new line of black-market trade. I don't want to fail David. I don't want to end things like that with him, not after everything he's done for me and for my brother.

I wander through the alleyways aimlessly until I end up deep in the heart of the city. As I pass by an old rusty fountain with a black marble base, swirling with green marble ravens, I sense a presence nearby. I hear a soft sound from the nearest alleyway, something like a shuffle and then a kick of a pebble. When I peer down the street, a man's shadow awaits me. *Him.* Something just tells me this man is the one I'm looking for. I close my eyes before bravely pressing forward. *For David.*

CHAPTER TWENTY-SIX

"Mahlin?" I call down the alleyway in a quiet but firm voice. I am met with silence. I consider risking a second call, but the figure shifts into the light. A short, stocky sort of shadow stands impossibly still behind the outline of a doorframe. If he hadn't inclined his head ever so slightly, I never would have recognized his acknowledgment. "Are you Mahlin?" I speak out, a little quieter this time.

"Depends on who's asking," a gruff voice chimes back.

I press forward with caution. "A woman looking to send a message to the Middle Realm," I reply. "A woman who is willing to pay quite handsomely for it."

I hear shuffling come from the alleyway moving closer into the faint light affixed to the wall. A man with a scruffy face steps into the dimness and crosses his arms, looking me up and down. I inwardly cringe at his sweeping and insistent gaze. "How much?" he says shortly.

"Three silver."

He nods in approval. "What is the message? And who to?"

"Do you know the runner, David, from the city of Lisden?"

He nods again. "I'm familiar with the name. My contacts from the House of the Day talk about his efficiency frequently. He's one of the best they have on the other side."

"I need you to take a message to him that there is another gateway."

Mahlin stops short. "Excuse me?"

"Another gateway into the Upper Realm. A more lucrative one on the coast. There's a gateway to the House of War by ocean."

Scoffing, he turns his head and begins to walk off. "I'm not delivering your message. Not for any price."

"Excuse me?" I glare.

"No, you listen, little girl." Mahlin turns abruptly and moves menacingly toward me. "I'm not about to remove a runner we need closer to the middle cities and move him to an unsung gateway we already have plenty of business from and have managed to keep a secret from the Middle Realm for hundreds of years. So you can just take your message and go f—"

"Mahlin," a new suave voice chimes in from the alley. "Treat the lady with some respect." My heart seizes. *Who the hell is that?*

"Boss, she's just some…"

"Uh, uh, uh," the new voice tsks. "There are ways to decline without being rude. Your breeding is showing." Mahlin growls, and the voice chuckles low. "Leave me alone with the nice lady." His condescension is thick, but Mahlin obeys without a question. Striding back into the darkness, he disappears through a door at the other end of the alley and leaves me alone with the mysterious male voice.

I wait for the man to step into the light, but he seems to favor the shadows. Instead, he shifts so I can see the faintest of outlines. "Hello, gorgeous," the voice slides over me with a shiver. "What brings you down to this part of town?"

I square my shoulders. "I believe you are already aware of why I am here."

A low chuckle echoes between the buildings. "Perhaps. But I would like to hear it from you. Why are you here seeking out the most... dangerous of contacts?"

"I was unaware that I had anything to fear from a supplier," I reply, struggling to keep my voice even.

Another chuckle. "Oh, Mahlin? That particular supplier has killed more people than you've probably met in your tiny little life." Despite talking about something so shocking, the man's voice seems more teasing, almost prideful. A shiver creeps down my spine.

Clearing my throat, I move closer to the voice on the edge of the dim light. "If you don't mind, sir, I would prefer to see who I am speaking with."

Silence. Then I hear a body shift, grazing against the building wall. Slow, steady, echoing steps click against the pavement, striding closer to me. As the man steps into the light, my breath rushes out of my body.

By the Lady.

The man oozes darkness with enough swagger to make him both beautiful and dangerous. His dark hair hangs low over his eyes where I detect a hint of red. When he looks up, I realize they are a glowing amber that adds to his shady appearance. He's well-dressed for hiding out in an alley; dark red and black leather cover him from head to toe. The soft smirk crossing his lips seems more menacing than mischievous. I can't help but take a small step back.

"Like what you see?" he growls playfully. *He's toying with me.* I don't answer, to which he chuckles. "The name's Faolan," he holds out a hand for me to shake, and I hesitantly take it. His grip is firm, slowly tightening and crushing my hand. Then suddenly, his grip goes light, his thumb trailing softly along my skin. He moves it in soft caresses, unnerving me. "And your name, my dear?" He continues to grip my hand and assert dominance.

I don't play that game.

"Ana," I lie.

"Ana…" the name rolls off his tongue. Faolan smirks. "Such a plain name for such a… powerful woman."

"Excuse me?" I stutter out.

"I watched the way you carried yourself with my associate," Faolan purrs. "You speak with such passion and authority. You don't take no for an answer very easily. Do you?"

I choose not to respond. He chuckles. "No… you want to work your way around the nos." Letting my hand drop, he reaches over and tucks a curl behind my ear. "What business do you have in the Middle Realm?

I jerk backward. "That is none of your concern."

Faolan laughs. "Yes, I could use a woman like you in my ranks."

"Your ranks?"

He steps back with a sweeping bow. "I run the black market, darling."

My eyes widen. *By the Lady… this is the man.* David and Leo used to tell me stories about the origins of the black market, based out of the House of Darkness by a dark man with power unimaginable and greed to match. And I'm standing in front of that legend. *By the Lady…*

"Stick with me," he continues, "and I can bring you wealth, power, and maybe more if you're willing." He raises his eyebrows suggestively.

I square up my shoulders in preparation for a fight. My hand slides back to my brother's dagger. "I have no interest," I say firmly, "in joining your operation. I find it useful, but I have no interest in being a part of it."

Faolan laughs. "Just an offer, dear. No need for alarm." He looks pointedly at the weapon in my hand. "Though I would love to spar with you. What's your magic like, darling?"

"Stronger than yours," I fire back.

He bursts out laughing, nearly doubling over. "Oh, darling, I highly, highly doubt it."

I back away slowly toward town. "I'm going to leave now. Do I need to be worried about you following me?" I ask bluntly.

"I don't care enough to follow you, Miss Ana," Faolan replies. "Though I cannot ensure your message will reach its intended destination." He shrugs. "Gotta keep my business running smoothly. Letting too many mortals help on the coastal side might cause them to want to travel over onto our side. That would be… chaotic. You understand that. Right?"

I nod slowly and start to back away. "See you around, Miss… Ana." Faolan seems to literally fade into the darkness. Uncomfortable with whether he's actually disappeared or whether he's only hovering, waiting to see what I do next, I turn tail and run out of the alley.

CHAPTER TWENTY-SEVEN

I rush back through the city streets until I find the last square where Aiden and I separated. He rejoins me soon after. "I lost you somewhere in the back half of the city," he scolds. "Thank the Lady you're alright. Did you find anything out?"

"No," I try to hide my blush. I didn't even think to ask about the black obsidian. I was too busy trying to figure out how to fix my relationship with David. "I'm sorry," I apologize genuinely. "I couldn't get a word out of anyone."

"That's too bad. What happens now?"

My fingers flutter lightly against my sides as I try to come up with another plan. Then it hits me.

"We need to infiltrate one of the Houses."

Aiden's jaw drops. He looks at me incredulously. "You want to do what?"

I hold my hands up defensively. "Hear me out, okay? I think the best way to figure out what the nobility is up to is to go undercover, straight into the belly of the beast itself. I want to pose as a servant. I bet they hear everything that's going on. And if not, I'm a decently sneaky person," I smirk. "I'll figure it out." The more I talk this plan out, the more I like it.

Aiden chuckles nervously, interrupting my thoughts. My eyes narrow slightly. "Um… what are you thinking about, Aiden?" I ask cautiously.

"Well…" he starts and then pauses again. He rubs the back of his neck, and my suspicion increases.

"Spit it out, Aiden," I demand.

He chuckles again. "Well… I can solve our problem about getting into a House."

"Look, I'm sure you're talented and all with your military clearance, but I'm sure you can't get me into a palace library." I turn away from him.

"Actually, I can."

I whip around. "Excuse me?"

"Remember I told you that… my past was a little complicated?"

"Yes, yes, I remember. What does that have to do with anything?"

"I'm the second heir to the House of the Sun."

…

"*What*?"

Aiden holds up his hands to try to calm me. "Grace, you gotta hear me out…"

"Like hell I will!" I leap to my feet in one clean jump. "You've been a noble this entire time, and you never thought to mention it once?" I storm away from him.

He tries to follow me. "Grace, you have to listen to me."

"Why? Clearly, I can't trust a thing you say." He grabs my arm and spins me around forcibly. I struggle against him. "Let go!"

"Not until you listen," his voice grows softer, more pleading. I struggle more. "Grace, I don't tell people I meet that I'm a noble. I hate people treating me differently because of it. I swear to you, I've been trying to get away from my heritage. That's one of the reasons I joined the army, Grace; only a handful of people know."

I tear away my arm from him, but I don't walk away. "I'm listening," I finally reply.

Aiden takes both of my hands in his, and I resist the urge to pull away. "Look," he starts, eyebrows furrowed. "I know you don't have the best trust in Fae in general, but please... I'm telling the truth. And I didn't hide it from you maliciously. Remember how I saved your life in the Lower Realm. Remember how I've been by your side this entire time, learning the same things as you, fighting for the same things as you, and not once have I fought you on your comments about the Fae." He shakes his head. "I know something is up. I've sensed it. There are rumors running through the army, but never anything concrete. All the information you have is the best information I have.

"I will not betray you, Grace," he finishes.

I look down at my feet. *Damn it all to hell... he knows me too well.* With six words, he assuaged my worst fears. Don't get me wrong, I'm still pissed, and I'm not sure what to do with that feeling and him. But... for now...

"You can get me into the House of the Sun?"

"Yes. And I'll be with you every step," Aiden answers immediately.

I nod swiftly. "Alright. I'm in."

***

As we ride toward the House of the Sun, Aiden starts to tell me stories from his childhood. As we trot beside each other, he tells me about the first time he got on a horse at the age of four, how it nearly took off with him much to his mother's horror. "But I remember that split second of feeling like I was flying. I was hooked," he grins. "I begged to ride again, but they wouldn't let me start until I was six. Too afraid I'd get hurt."

He tells me about learning magic from Xavier and how quickly he took to it. How he used to spend as much time as he could in the palace's arena, firing spells at practice dummies. How much he loved to spar with whoever came by to visit, whether by magic or by the sword. He tells me about his older brother, Nicholas II, named after his father, who he was close to when he was younger but soon grew apart from as his brother was groomed to be the heir to the throne.

I watch his eyes grow emotional when he tells me the story of how he was finally able to leave the House of the Sun to join the army. His father promised him a chance to get out of the nobleman's life if he proved himself worthy within the next two years. He tells me how he trained and practiced, and on his eighteenth birthday, he displayed his prowess in a grand spectacle fight against the most highly ranked members of the army. On that day, his father begrudgingly granted him his freedom. He joined the traveling army that day and hasn't been back home but twice in the last four years.

There's something amazing about… watching him light up. The energy is so brilliant, and I can feel my anger at his lie start to fade away. Aiden's not this stark nobleman with a political agenda. He's a boyish warrior with a thirst for adventure and a gift for persuasion and teasing me. The more I watch him smile, the more I get this both exhilarating and sinking feeling that it is very possible I can't be angry with him for long.

The ride gets tiring as the night closes in. Aiden suggests we stop at a village at the House of Earth, and I agree. However, when we arrive at the inn, we run into a bit of a roadblock.

"What do you mean twenty silver?" Aiden demands incredulously.

"You heard me. You want the last room, you appear to be fairly well off," the innkeeper glances over Aiden, "and it's my damn inn."

"Twenty silver coins is ridiculous for one night in one room in a village like this!"

"Excuse me, a village like this?"

I try to butt in. "He didn't mean it like that-"

Aiden interrupts me. "Can we at least negotiate?" I'm taken aback a bit by his willingness to talk over me.

"I don't negotiate with out-of-towners!" the innkeeper snapped furiously.

"We'll barter with you," I plead.

"Grace," Aiden turns to me sternly. "Let me handle this."

My jaw drops as he turns away. *Excuse me? Did he just dismiss me?*

Aiden and the innkeeper continue to argue over top of me. *Idiots.* By the Lady, I hate when I get drowned out, especially by men. I feel an eye roll coming on. I turn my head away from the conversation. The inn doesn't seem busy at all. Only two lone men sit at the bar, sipping on some whiskey. There's no life in this place.

Then I spot it.

A carved violin... lying up against the hearth, long since forgotten with a clear inch of dust along the wood. It's old, but beautiful. Aiden doesn't notice as I break away from his side and stride to the violin. I pick it up and blow gently.

The dust flies off in one soft, misty cloud. My fingers trail the wood and the strings with such care. I pluck each string lightly, surprised to find it in tune. Maybe it's a Fae thing—an instrument that never goes out of tune. How convenient.

I turn around. "How about I play?" I call over to the innkeeper. "One night of music to attract a crowd. You get more business, and we get that last room."

I am ignored. The men continue to argue.

I growl softly in my throat. *I don't have time for this. If they won't listen to my words, I will make them listen to me.*

The violin swings onto my shoulder. My fingers curve around the neck and over the strings. The bow sits lightly in my grasp, pressing to the string in anticipation of the first note. I look up at Aiden, who still can't be bothered to acknowledge me.

Idiots. Watch this. Watch me, Leo. I glance skyward.

The violin cries out like a siren, my finger slowly sliding up along the string until I reach the first note of an old Fae folk song. Vibrato: my finger vibrates, sticking the note and giving it body. Then my bow begins to move.

The bartender stops wiping the counter. The sleepy gentleman at the bar turns his head. What few people remain at the dinner tables stop their conversations. Aiden turns to me, eyes wide. I smirk.

And I play.

The beginning moves slow in long, broad strokes of my bow. Then my hand begins to fly across the fingerboard. I lean with the music, exactly as I remember from my performances back home. I walk forward as I play, moving toward the people. They look on in fascination. I hear footsteps coming toward the door, and my smile only grows.

I hop up on the bar and let loose. The melody trickles from my fingertips like glitter. I let the violin sing with high-pitched squeals of the highest string and staccato scales up and down all four strings. I watch the door out of the corner of my eye as the Fae begin to trickle in. I can feel them straining to hear like the music could cure them of all ailments.

Good to know I can still dazzle.

I lock eyes with Aiden; he still stands and stares at me in awe. He's captivated by me. I let a genuine smile spread across my lips, and I drop low onto the bottom string. My fingers play the same sequence over and over again, a refrain that draws the Fae closer to me. The suspense builds as I keep trained on Aiden, daring him to look at anyone else but me. I move forward slowly.

I watch his sharp intake of breath as I jump off the bar. Time slows. I'm flying.

I hit the ground and burst into another melody. The room goes up in cheers. I laugh and spin around the inn with ease. The song finishes with a flourish against the backdrop of the fireplace. The Fae break out into excited chatter around me, crying out "encore," "more," and "another round" as they take residence in the tiny inn.

Turning to the innkeeper, who is smiling for the first time all night, I say haughtily, "Here's my proposition. Give us your last room, room and board for the night and tomorrow morning, and I'll play this bar until midnight as payment."

He laughs at me. "You've got yourself a deal, young lady. Play on!"

The Fae cheer.

I feel powerful. I stand back up on a table and set my bow to the string again.

Hours later, I've attracted quite the crowd. The Fae sit around and eat and drink in great amounts, swapping stories and cheering me on. As I break out into a dance song, the clapping begins in earnest. I begin to jig as I play, my feet jumping and leaping across the floor. As I drop to the low strings again, I grow bolder. I plop myself right in the lap of an attractive young man, teasing him with my eyes and my music. I play the flirtatious girl, drawing him in and then flying off his lap just as quickly. I turn to Aiden, and he looks murderous.

Oops.

He moves toward me, his anger slowly turning into something more devious. I back up, spinning away from him as I play. He's not giving up, though; he continues to come for me slowly but surely. *Oh, by the Lady, I need a plan.*

I hop up onto the bar to escape. My hands play from memory, but my brain is trained on the man behind me whose eyes swear I'm going to regret that last ploy. He still continues to pursue me! I jump and dance around his hands as he reaches for me over and over again. The patrons think it's hilarious and cheer Aiden on more. *Traitors.*

I reach the end of the bar at the height of the song, and he smirks wildly. Suddenly, he sweeps my legs out from under me as I play and catches me in his arms. We spin in circles on the floor. I falter for only a moment before grinning and leaning back so I'm half hanging out of his arms. He supports my back underneath as I play upside down. I trust him not to drop me.

For the first moment since I arrived in this realm, I'm enjoying myself.

As I finish the final notes, Aiden sweeps me up and sets me on his shoulders. I thrust my violin into the sky, victorious.

When the clock strikes midnight, I set the violin gently down on the bar and collapse onto a bar stool wearily. Aiden sits next to me with a soft hand on my back. The innkeeper wipes off the last glasses of the night as the few remaining stragglers sleepily make their way to the exit. "You've more than paid for your room, young lady; that was some spectacular music," he says to me.

"Thank you," I respond politely.

"Your room is on the second floor: third door on the left."

"Thank you," Aiden answers this time. "We'll be going now." He helps me up and pulls me toward the stairs. We stumble up them together.

When Aiden pushes open the door to the room, the first thing I notice is the purple haze shining in from the window. The moonlight shines down and illuminates the thatched roofs of the tiny huts around us. They reveal untold stories beneath us: an elderly couple sitting on a front stoop, a young couple tenderly kissing each other goodnight on another, and a mother rocking her tiny newborn baby on another still. I wonder if my city looks like that at midnight. I don't know why I'd never noticed it before. *Some things never change. Fae or mortal, life goes on.*

The second thing I notice is the bed. The very... very tiny bed.

·········

"You can take the bed," Aiden starts.

I shake my head rapidly and groan in exhaustion. "Aiden... just... I don't care. I honestly don't care. I'm so tired right now, I can barely see straight. We've shared a bed before. Unless you're uncomfortable..."

"No," he answers quickly. "I'm not."

An awkward silence follows. We stand there looking at each other in complete silence. I finally get tired of it and look at him pointedly. "You need to climb in first so I can see where I fit."

Flustered, he moves to the bed and lies down on it. There's a small space for me to curl up comfortably pressed right up against his chest. I summon whatever remaining courage I can find through my exhaustion and lie down next to him. His arm wraps around my waist and pulls me lightly into him, resting above my hips.

"Are you comfortable?" Aiden asks quietly.

I nod quickly, and my head knocks against his. "I'm so sorry. Are you alright?" I try to turn around to check if he's bleeding, but the movement is only pressing us up against each other more. He fumbles to give me space, and I fumble to look at him.

Suddenly, we're pressed chest to chest, our noses almost touching.

I stare at him. He looks back at me with a peculiar expression. *What is this feeling?* I don't recognize the swirling in my stomach. *Am I nervous?* I hesitantly reach out and touch his temple lightly where my head flew into it. "Are you okay?" I repeat quietly. He nods very slowly.

I must be imagining it, but I swear our faces are leaning closer to each other. His eyes begin to close.

Oh no...

I flip over onto my other side suddenly, and I feel his forehead press against the back of my head, his lips grazing my hair. "Good night, Aiden." I cringe at how shaky my voice sounds.

He sighs softly in my ear. "Good night, Grace." His arms loosen around my waist and no longer hold me tightly against him. I almost regret the loss.

By the Lady, Grace, what have you gotten yourself into?

CHAPTER TWENTY-EIGHT

―

When we arrive at the House of the Sun the next morning, I can already see Aiden's attitude changing. Even from behind him on my horse, I watch his shoulders relax, and the whoop he lets out as we ride through the town is a pretty good indication he's excited to be home. I can't imagine what it would be like to be away from home for so long. Though I'm starting to get a good idea.

When we reach the castle, I can't help but grin. Its bright yellow walls shine with the morning sun. The reaction to our presence is almost automatic. Several gardeners light up as we ride by and wave at Aiden. A maid sweeping the front stoop gasps and darts inside. A moment later, I hear a joyful cry as we hop down off our horses. "Aiden!" A woman runs out of the castle and down to Aiden, throwing her arms around him.

He laughs as he wraps his arms around her tightly. "Hi, Mom."

"You're home! My sweet boy, you're home!" She kisses both of his cheeks. I can't help but feel a soft pang in my heart for my own mother.

"My son," a new voice comes from the doorway. I look up and swiftly kneel. I really don't know if this is what I'm supposed to do, but I feel it is necessary given his status. The High Lord and another younger, taller man behind him come to join the two in the courtyard. "Welcome home." The father places a firm hand on Aiden's shoulder.

"Good to see you again, little brother." Nicholas reaches forward, and Aiden meets his hand with a firm clasp. The mother then pulls both brothers into a squeezing hug.

"Oh, I'm so happy both my boys are here again together!" she exclaims. "Nick, call someone to set up your brother's room."

"Actually, Mom," Aiden interrupts. "Make that two rooms." He looks down at me and smiles. I smile back a little. As if seeing me for the first time, Aiden's mother's expression changes to one of surprise and then excitement—I assume at her son bringing home a girl. The thought unfortunately makes me blush. Aiden then walks over to me, reaching down and pulling me to my feet. He steers me directly to his father.

"Aiden," I hiss under my breath.

I hear a soft chuckle before I'm staring up at the High Lord of the House of the Sun. "Dad," Aiden begins grandly. "This is Grace. Grace Fairmain. I met her a few months ago during my service in the House of the Day, and she has since become one of my dearest friends." I try very hard not to blush. "I have brought her home with me to perform for us during the Winter Solstice celebration. She is the most incredible violinist I have ever had the opportunity to hear play. You will not be disappointed by her talent."

The High Lord nods. "The trio we have requested to play at the ball shall be canceled at once."

"With all due respect, sir," I suddenly interrupt. Horrified by my own boldness, I immediately bow my head. "I am sorry for speaking so boldly, High Lord. I only request that the band be allowed to keep their performance, sir. I can play as their accompanist. I need not be paid." I dare to raise my head slightly to look at him. "As a budding musician, I remember how difficult it was to keep food on the table when the season was slow. I would not wish it on another."

Out of the corner of my eye, I can see Aiden watching me carefully. I'm sure he can tell I didn't pull that story from nowhere. The High Lord looks at me with a budding respect in his eyes. "Very well, Miss Grace. But I would like to hear you play first."

I nod my head respectfully. "I would be honored to play for you, High Lord."

He nods and snaps his fingers once. "Winnie!" A woman appears beside him, startling me. "Bring one of our violins to the Great Hall. I wish to hear our young musician play in the room she shall be performing in a few days' time." He then turns to Aiden with a wry grin. "Well, son, won't you bring your guest inside? Or have you forgotten your manners after being away for so long?"

Aiden chuckles and puts a soft hand at my back. "Come inside, Grace. You're going to love it."

When we step inside, I can't take it all in fast enough. The entry soars up all the way to the highest tower, sunlight pouring in from the glass windows all down the shaft. Purple tile mixed with patches of red sweep across a floor that is wider than my entire family apartment. A grand staircase marked with yellow steps winds its way to the second floor. We stride forward under it toward a large hall with the heavy wooden doors swung wide open to greet us.

I stop in the doorway, entirely awestruck until Aiden nudges me forward, gently reminding me people are behind me. The Great Hall is the most spectacular room I have ever stepped into, and that includes the luxury ballrooms I played in back home and even the library in the House of Peace. It's a golden ballroom, complete with a star-filled sky of a ceiling. The marble floor shines like light reflected off a mirror. Golden chandeliers hanging down from the ceiling complete the excessive, yet so beautiful atmosphere.

"It sure is something. Isn't it?" Aiden breathes to me. I can't do anything but nod.

The attendant arrives through a side doorway with a violin. I turn to High Lord Nicholas, and he gives me a slight nod. "Well, Miss Grace, we would like to hear a little bit of what you can do, if you wouldn't mind."

"It would be an honor to play for you, High Lord," I reply with a slight bow of my head. I quickly check that the instrument is tuned before playing a simple and beautiful Winter Solstice hymn that many of my clients used to request specifically for their parties. Light and airy, the bow floats over the high-pitched notes like a bird riding the wind.

When it is over, they applaud me vigorously, and I smile widely. The High Lady reaches out to me, laying her hand over mine. "Grace, that was beautiful! How long have you been playing?"

"Since I was five, ma'am."

"Wasn't that wonderful, Nicholas?"

High Lord Nicholas strokes his chin and nods in agreement. "You have an incredible talent, young lady. You are welcome to perform for us any time. You will be compensated handsomely for your company."

I bow my head in respect. "Thank you, sir. Your kind words mean a lot to me." I glance up at Aiden, who grins from ear to ear. I can't help but grin back.

"Margaret!" High Lord Nicholas calls. An older woman appears in the doorway with a broom. "Take our young guest up to the third floor and find her a guest room where she can freshen up. Feel free to explore the castle as much as you would like before you join us for dinner."

"Yes, High Lord," she replies plainly before motioning to me. "Come on, dear, let's find you somewhere comfortable." I give Aiden a small wave before rushing to catch up with the housekeeper. Behind me, I hear the noble family begin to ask Aiden about his recent journeys. I smile to myself as I hear Aiden's excited voice ring out above all the others.

I trail behind Margaret for several turns of the staircase before she ushers me down a long hallway. "Next door on the right!" she calls out to me. I stop abruptly in front of it. With a quick glint of a key, the housekeeper turns the knob and swings the door open to let me in.

I am surprised to find a fairly luxurious guest room, especially for a young peasant musician like I've made myself out to be. It's larger than the main room of my family's apartment. A large four-post bed sits against the wall in front of an ornate tapestry that covers the entire wall. It is laden with plush and pristinely white sheets and more pillows than I have ever seen on a bed in my life.

A golden vanity sits against the other wall with a cushioned stool; it's like what I imagined a lady would sit at and do her makeup in the morning. By the bay window, I see a comfortable chair for reading by a warm fireplace. I have a whole sitting room, and as I look to my left, an entire bathroom as well.

I turn to Margaret. "Are you sure this is for me?"

Margaret smiles. "You came as a guest of Lord Aiden. The High Lord said you were to be given fair accommodations. Is the room to your liking, miss?"

I trail my hand lightly across the wooden frame of the bed. "Yes, ma'am…" I reply softly in awe.

"You have free rein of the castle, except for the fourth floor, which is the noble family's private quarters. Please enjoy your stay here." With that, Margaret turns around and closes my door behind her. I spin around the room slowly and sigh. *I could get used to this.*

CHAPTER TWENTY-NINE

I immediately run into the bathroom and nearly whoop in delight. Marble and precious stones cover the walls and floor in a magnificent array of color and luxury. A porcelain bath stands in the middle of the grand room, and I don't hesitate in stripping off my clothes and flipping on the faucet. I peruse an array of soaps and oils before pouring a vanilla-and-rose soap into the tub as it fills with warm water.

I moan as I sink into the bath. It feels so good to wash off the trials of travel. There's something comforting about taking a nice hot bath at the end of a long journey. As I lounge languidly in the tub, my mind wanders to the man downstairs. I wonder if Aiden likes being back home. I wonder if he brings girls home very often.

Not that I'm like… a girl he's bringing home, per se, I'm just a friend. Just… a friend.

Although, it couldn't hurt to act like someone he values, even just for a little while. Maybe I could start with dressing right for dinner. *Mmm… if only I had something nicer to wear. Well, I'll just have to dress up what I have.*

After soaking for an hour, I reluctantly climb out of the tub. The tile feels warm under my feet, and I bask in front of the mirror in the steam for a while. I chuckle to myself as I stare at my reflection. It's silly to be prancing around like this, acting all foolish and giddy over a hot bath, a large bedroom, and a hopeless man.

Yet, after everything I've been through in the last few weeks, maybe I deserve a chance to be a little foolish. I've spent so much time trying to take care of everything, trying to make sure everyone else around me was alright. It has been forever since I looked after myself, pampered myself, let myself relax.

This is my time. Even just for a few hours.

When I walk back out into the bedroom, I notice a folded parcel of fabric on the end of the bed and the door slightly ajar. I move to close the door as I pull a towel tighter around me. Then I glance to the bundle, noticing a small note beside it. *Something nice for dinner, High Lady Caroline.* I smile at the kind gesture. I imagine it's something old of hers; the High Lady and I appear to be about the same size. Or maybe she had it sent for me. Either way, I couldn't be more grateful to have something nice to go with how I'm feeling in this palace right now.

I spread out the dress onto the bed, a soft lilac one with a floor-length hem. The fabric is so soft. It slides against my skin smoothly as I pull it over my head. I turn to the vanity and take a sharp breath when I see myself. The more I stay in Fae clothing, the more I see myself as a Fae. I mean, seriously, all I need is the magic, and I could pass for one. I might be clueless about everyday affairs, but I'm practically Fae with this whole getup and everything I have learned so far.

I take a brief look in the mirror and down to my amulet I laid out on the bed. I don't feel as in danger as I did at the beginning of all of this. The amulet has protected me from a lot so far, but for now, it isn't needed. But I can't just leave it out in the open. After taking a look around the room for a good hiding place, I stash it in the very back of the long drawer in the vanity.

As my hair dries, I decide to slip out of my room to explore. I wander down the hallway and back to the staircase. I walk down one floor and then stroll down that corridor in search of something interesting. I can't get over how extravagant this palace is. Statues and paintings of inestimable value line the walls. I'm almost afraid to reach out and touch something. I pass by a handful of closed doors, which I assume are other guest rooms like mine.

After a little while, I come across a door that simply says *Library* in beautiful gilded lettering. *Finally, something to do.* Seeing as the one Fae library I've been in already blew my mind, I hope this one is just as spectacular.

I am not disappointed when I step inside. A large wall of windows brings in an incredible amount of light even as the sun begins to set. It casts a yellow-orange glow over the cozy room. Although simply furnished, the large library feels grandiose with the sheer number of books on the floor-to-ceiling bookshelves. They round the walls and wind around the corner of the L-shaped room. I'm in awe of the volume.

I finally manage to make myself move inside. It takes me another few minutes to get the courage to pull a book off a shelf. Once I'm convinced I'm not going to damage anything old or expensive, I settle into a chair to read in front of the fireplace. It's been a long time since I've had the freedom to just sit down and read a book for pleasure's sake. I soon get lost in the story. Only when the clock chimes five do I realize I'm going to be late for dinner. I leap out of my chair and dart down the stairs to the dining hall.

***

Dinner is a delicious affair with more food than I have ever seen at a table in my life. Platters of meat pies and mashed potatoes, cornbread and fruit tarts line the tablecloth, and I try not to feast too quickly. The conversation bounces between Aiden telling his parents stories about his military career and me talking about my "experiences" as a traveling musician. I'm able to weave stories from the mortal world with a Fae context, making me sound way more impressive than I actually am.

You're just a really good liar, Grace.

After dinner, Aiden takes my hand and leads me from the dining hall. "Come on, I want to show you something." Back up the staircase we go, winding around until we reach the fourth level. We rush by a dozen rooms before he pulls me into one of the towers. I'm greeted by a simple but elegant music chamber with a piano, a few chairs, and a selection of string and wind instruments.

I blush. "So, this is what you wanted to show me."

"Absolutely," Aiden smirks. "I thought it would be your favorite room."

"I'd say that's about right," I laugh. I run my fingers softly over the piano keys. "Did you spend any time in here as a kid?"

"I took piano lessons and singing lessons in this very room."

I burst out laughing. "You took singing lessons?"

Aiden feigns incredulity. "I'll have you know I am a wonderful singer."

I can't believe how much I'm giggling. I don't giggle.

"I wanna hear you sing," I tease.

To my surprise, he sits down at the piano and plays a couple chords that I recognize from a folk song. *By the Lady, is he actually going to...* "Only if you play with me," he says sincerely. "Do you know this song? It's got a real pretty violin part."

I bite my lip. He's looking at me again with that little smile that threatens to knock me over every time I see it behind the smirk. I slowly cross over behind him and pick up a violin. "I know it."

"Good." He plays the same two chords again before pausing for me to begin. I tap my foot once, twice, and then launch into the sliding melody. A moment later, he plays along underneath with the first verse. It moves fast and free, taking on a very backwoods tone. His voice rings out strongly above it all. *Damn, he wasn't lying.* Aiden sings with the confidence of a professional, but with the soul of someone who's just singing for the joy of it.

He keeps glancing over his shoulder with mischievous eyes and wiggling eyebrows as he sings. He's hamming it up to make me laugh. I only chuckle and keep playing, occasionally joining in to sing a harmony. I lose track of time. My feet go from tapping to moving around the piano to keep up with the dancing notes.

When the song ends, I set the violin carefully back down on its stand. "You do have a very nice voice, Aiden." I tap his shoulder lightly.

"Thank you, angel," he smiles at me. "You were right. You are a prodigy."

I blush fiercely. "Thanks." We look at each other quietly for a while before I drop my eyes.

"I hate to do this to you, but my father wanted me to meet him for a drink right around now. I'm gonna have to bow out."

Aiden stands. "Feel free to do whatever you want; you've got free run of the palace."

"Except the fourth floor?" I smile.

Aiden chuckles. "Except the fourth floor."

I stand with him. "Thank you." We stare at each other again awkwardly. The air is charged again like last night at the inn. I don't know whether to move or to stand still. I feel like I'm waiting for something to happen. I just don't know what it is. I want *something* to happen.

Then it does.

Aiden reaches out and lightly brushes a strand of hair behind my ear. He smiles softly, that secret smile I love. He leans in and brushes a kiss across my cheek. Then he turns around and disappears from view.

And I'm left breathless

By the Lady...

CHAPTER THIRTY

The next few days fly by. Aiden takes me down into the towns and the villages all over the House of the Sun. We wander together through the market square where he introduces me to his people. They receive him well, like an old friend being welcomed home for a visit. He has me try every delicacy at the finest inns, to my delight. One afternoon, he takes me out on a boat on the lake. We swap stories from our childhood and share laughs and tears. When we return to the palace after our long days, we spend nights together in the music room mindlessly chatting or playing music or in the library researching black obsidian—unfortunately, without much luck.

Aiden makes no mention of the kiss *because that's just my luck now, isn't it?* But for the first time, I feel my heart opening up to another person. I never thought I would find that, not since Leo. I feel full, almost satisfied. But without fully understanding Leo's death, I worry this happiness, this feeling I feel, is all only temporary. I wonder how long before I succumb to my need for revenge. For justice.

It's the day before the solstice, and I'm getting lost in another warrior's tale from the library. When the clock strikes five, I finish my page and hop to my feet. I'm almost late for dinner. In the process, I trip over the foot of my chair, falling to the rug. As I sputter against the fabric, I burst out into a quiet fit of giggles and roll over onto my back to stare up at the ceiling. *You take one step into a castle, and suddenly you let your guard down about everything!* my inner self scolds. Sighing, I roll over.

My hand strikes an uneven groove just below my fingertips.

I wrinkle my forehead and feel over the rug again. *There's that spot again.* I've always been fascinated by edges and smooth textures, so I'm not surprised I picked up on something so small. Curious, I flip over the edge of the rug.

In one section of the stone tiles, there's a carving, a stamp of the House of the Sun's crest. I trace its design absently. As I start to pull my hand away, I squint and peer down at a tiny, tiny implant in the center of the sun. I run my finger over it slowly and feel a slight indentation when I do.

Suddenly, the entire facade spins. The rug, the fireplace, and me on it rotates toward the wall. I scramble to my feet, eyes wide. *By the Lady, a revolving platform.* The floor turns rapidly as I try to keep my balance. Within seconds, I am inside an unfamiliar room.

The fireplace illuminates the stone walls. I see another luxurious rug leading to a large meeting-style table sitting in the center of the room. The table looks worn and well used, and the carvings on its legs are ornate and old-world. I imagine it might have been in the family for generations. When I get my bearings, I move to the table. A bunch of papers are strewn across the wood surface, and I recognize this must be some sort of private discussion space—a place to conduct business far away from the eyes of others in the castle. I know

I shouldn't pry into what could be private affairs, but I can't help but take a quick peek.

What I find, I wish I hadn't.

The documents on the table aren't private affairs; they are foreign ones.

I need to find Aiden. I rush to the rug on hands and knees and rediscover the indentation in the crest. With a quick press, I trigger the mechanics and the room spins around again. I flee the library and head straight for the dining room.

***

Unfortunately for me, the meal has already begun, and I cannot pull Aiden aside without alerting his family. All throughout dinner, I can't focus. Aiden is so animated talking with his brother that he doesn't notice my pleading eyes or grim face. He is too far away across the table for a well-placed kick, so I have to fake a smile and make small talk until I have a chance to pull him aside.

"Aiden," I hiss as we finally leave the table and walk into the hallway.

He turns to me with a big smile and wraps his arms around my waist in a surprisingly familiar gesture. "Hello, Grace."

As much as I want to bask in his smile, I am on a mission. "Aiden." I look up at him purposefully and cringe as I see his smile smooth out to a concerned grimace. He beckons toward the stairs, and I take his hand to pull him upstairs. I feel his father's eyes on us as we leave.

I pull Aiden to the library and steer him to the center of the rug. When I hit the button to spin the room, I hear Aiden's gasp of shock. Obviously, he's never discovered this room before. At least I know now he couldn't possibly be involved, which makes what I have to show him about a million times worse.

I pull him to the table. "Look," I say simply. I hate how his face transitions from stoic to absolutely gobsmacked. He scans over the papers, moving painfully slowly.

"Grace," Aiden speaks hesitantly as he reads. "What am I looking at, what…?"

"I don't know, Aiden. I don't know, but… there are documents on the mine, research on black obsidian, everything. There're inventory reports of various towns between here and the House of Darkness. Harvest reports, treasury estimates, among other things." I slide another set of papers over to him hesitantly. "And this, this is correspondence between the House of the Sun and the House of Darkness."

Aiden scans the letters with fervor. "By the Lady, what in hell's name is this? Are you telling me my father has been corresponding with the House of Darkness on this issue for six years?"

"Yes, but why is that an issue?" I ask, confused.

"You don't get it, Grace," Aiden's hands slide into his hair and tug. "The House of Darkness doesn't work with us."

"What do you mean? Don't you trade?"

"Somewhat, but they primarily exchange with the Alliance of the Lily. Not us."

I can't process all this information at once. "Alliance of the… what are you talking about?"

"Oh…" he groans in frustration. "Right, sorry. The Alliance of the Lily is one of the two alliances between the Houses. It's a trade alliance, a war alliance; it's been this way ever since the founding of the Upper Realm. There's a little bit of interalliance trade between them and us in the Alliance of the Rose, but there's not a lot of interaction." He pulls more documents in front of him. "I don't get why there's suddenly all this contact between us and the House of Darkness. And it's got something to do with the black obsidian."

I can tell Aiden's starting to get flustered as he explains things while trying to read. I lay my hand on his arm to comfort him. Then I glance over the papers over his shoulder again.

Something catches my eye, and suddenly everything clicks.

I stumble back violently, gripping the edge of the table and scratching it with my nails. Aiden grabs me to catch me. "Grace? Are you alright?" He pulls me up and closer to him, looking over me. I can only shake my head. His eyes narrow in concern. "Grace?"

I fly out of his hold and push everything out of the way. Papers scatter to the floor. I know I'm gonna have to pick things up and straighten them out so it looks like we were never here, but at this moment, I don't care. I pull sheets from various piles and lay them out one by one in a line. Aiden peers over my shoulder.

I can't help but speak, trying to speed up the process. "The Alliances…" I say slowly. "The Alliances are fracturing." I move my hand over one of the damning pages. "This here… shows records of the House of Darkness building up their army. Right? We've seen more black-market trade. Weapons manufacturing has increased while food importation has decreased. That's where the money's going."

I move my hand to another page. "This is a letter from the House of Water to the House of the Sun detailing their concern over growing unrest in the regions to their south. Are they a part of the Alliance of the Rose?" Aiden nods slowly.

I continue. "A cousin to the noble family came back from a visit to a friend in the House of Darkness, and the people there are restless. They're getting stirred up about the lack of food coming into their country. More people are joining the army in order to feed their families."

My words come out in a rush as my chest heaves. "This… is a contract drawn up by the House of Darkness and the House of Fire. On the surface, it is a trade deal promised to bring the two countries closer together. But if you read the fine print…" I scan the page for the signatures before thrusting my finger forward to the paper. "Your father signed the page as a witness," I say carefully. "He's been involved with them since the beginning." As Aiden looks over the last page, I sigh deeply. "And that… is a copy of a contract for a three-way alliance—the House of the Sun, the House of Darkness, and the House of Fire. Your brother also signed as a witness."

When I turn around to catch Aiden's gaze, the anguish in his eyes knocks me down. *By the Lady, this must be impossible for him.*

"Grace… is… is this right?" he stammers shakily. I want to reach out to him, comfort him somehow. "Are… are my father and brother involved in this?"

My heart breaks as I am forced to slowly nod my head. "I am so sorry, Aiden." This time, I do rush to him when he falls to his knees on the hard-stone floor. "Aiden!" I cry as I catch his torso before he falls any more forward.

I turn his face toward mine, and I am crushed when I see tears in his eyes. "No, no, Aiden," I breathe as I frantically try to brush them from his eyes. My hands glide over his face helplessly, trying to soothe him somehow through touch. "Aiden, please don't cry. We can fix this, we can…" I stop speaking because I can tell it isn't helping. I don't even know what I'm saying.

"Grace, what the hell is this?" Aiden suddenly leaps to his feet and I tumble forward onto my face. "What the *hell* is this?" He grips his hair in frustration. "This undermines both Alliances. There has never been any cross-alliances in the entirety of the Upper Realm's history!"

"I know," I whisper helplessly. "I know!"

"I have to confront them," Aiden storms toward the fireplace. "How do you spin this room back?"

"No, Aiden, no!" I stand in his way. He tries to push me aside, but I hold fast. "This is part of it. Don't you get it? The mining in the House of the Day run by the House of the Sun? The increased black-market trade? The prophecy? This is all tied together." I push against his arms. "I don't know how much yet or why, but you have to see that it is. We can keep an eye on things, Aiden. You can keep an eye on things. If things go south, we can stop it from the inside!"

I plead with him, "If you let them know what we know now… I'm going to end up dead."

Aiden's eyes seem to come out of his rage. "What do you mean?"

"They can't touch you, Aiden. You're of the noble family. Your father would never let them kill you. But me, in connection to you… I would surely die."

His face falls, and he moves my hands off his arms, holding them instead. "I can't let this go, Grace."

"You don't have to. We don't have to." I squeeze his hands tightly. "We just have to wait. Please… wait with me."

He freezes. For a moment, I think I've lost him. But his arms soon wrap around me, strong and tight. We hold each other as best as we can. Standing there in that room with shreds of conspiracy scattered around us, we make a silent pact to stick this out until the end. No matter what that end comes to.

CHAPTER THIRTY-ONE

On the morning of the Winter Solstice, I come downstairs to the castle in a bustle. Servants are moving things rapidly across hallways, and the Great Hall is flooded with people trying to straighten out the final details. As I reach the bottom of the stairs, the entire working population seems to disappear out of sight, retreating into side rooms or off the first floor altogether. I walk to Aiden by the entryway and furrow my eyebrows in confusion.

He smiles at me. I've gotten used to his eyes on mine, and I no longer feel like running whenever he looks at me. What that means, I don't know. He pushes me lightly behind the doorway. "Stay there, angel. You'll have a good view of the procession from here."

"Now, remind me why I can't come outside with you."

"As a lowly musician," Aiden smirks, "you are not allowed outside for the procession. You're supposed to be getting ready anyway."

I punch him in the arm. "Your people are out there. Why can't I be?"

"Technically, for a short period of time, you are under the employ of the House of the Sun. Servants are not supposed to be outside during the ceremony. Many of them watch from the windows, but I got you the best spot." I glare at him. He ruffles my hair. "Hang in there." He then disappears out the door.

Rolling my eyes good-naturedly, I peer out from behind the column and watch Aiden's back as he joins his family on the stairs. Around the courtyard, a crowd of people from the surrounding towns has gathered to welcome the incoming nobles. With a raise of the High Lord's hand, the noise dies down. The castle is silent for a few brief seconds. Then the courtyard begins to vibrate, the rumbling echoing off the entryway and bouncing through the entire first floor. The crowd of people erupts into cheers. Two by two, a caravan of carriages makes its way up the spiraling pathway and into the courtyard.

The Twelve Houses have arrived.

From the very beginning, you can tell the process is ceremonial. First, the High Lord of the House of the Sun moves down—step by step down the stairs—to greet the caravan with grand hands. The procession winds around the grand circle, and every other carriage stops in a specific formation while the others progress off to a hidden place in the back of the castle. I assume those contain whatever attendants each House brought with them.

Then the noble families step out.

A hush comes over the crowd for a moment. I hold my breath, for what I'm not sure. Then, the High Lords each thrust their hands into the sky in perfect sync. Tendrils of colored light corresponding to the House Colors shoot up into the air and form the points of a twelve-pointed star. My eyes widen in awe. It's an incredible display of strength and magic. I can see why the crowd falls silent and then erupts into raucous cheering.

I tuck behind the column quickly as the nobility moves toward the door. Aiden winks at me as he comes in and mouths *Good luck* to me as he strides into the Great Hall with the rest of his family. I nod in acknowledgment and stay hidden to watch people file in.

When I was researching for my trip up here, I did a brief reading over some charts about the noble families who head the different Houses. Aiden tried to bring me up to speed on names so I could be ready for today, but we kept getting distracted. Seeing them all in person for the first time, I can barely pull all the information together to match a name to a face. Luckily, the House of the Sun's herald is posted just outside the door to announce the nobles.

First, the House of the Moon: High Lord Daniel Marseilles with his wife, Lily, and daughter, Luna. The House of the Day brings High Lord Michael and his eldest son, Jason, future heir. Only High Lord Alexander is here to represent the House of the Evening; his wife and children usually stay home to celebrate the solstice at their House with their own big festival. The House of Light follows with the entire Blake family: High Lord Aaron, High Lady Maria, and the twin Ladies, Alena and Aurora.

The House of Darkness sweeps into the room in a huff, capes swirling behind them. High Lord Carron strides in confidently with the twins, one Lord and one Lady. As the crowd builds inside, the herald's voice begins to get drowned out by the ambient noise. I don't remember their names, but the Lord looks oddly familiar to me, like I've seen him somewhere before. Then there's my favorite, High Lady Morgana and her daughter, Aira. The High Lady of the House of Wind rules without a husband and does a damn good job of it, from what Aiden said. She's the only matriarch of the Twelve Houses. How I would love to meet her.

The House of Fire brings High Lord Thomas Halden and his oldest son. The House of Water is next, dressed in the most colorful and stylish arrays of fabrics and jewels. I remember Aiden told me that High Lord Dylan and his son, Tristan, share the same flair for fashion design. High Lord Adam Jameson, High Lady Haley, and Lord Demetrius trail in behind them in representation of the House of Earth. The House of Peace brought their entire family, including the two younger daughters. High Lord Gabriel leads them in while High Lady Sarah, Lady Seraphina, and Lady Kiara struggle to keep track of the whirlwind that is Lady Lara. And finally, *finally*, the elusive House of War brings up the rear with the presence of High Lord Brandon and Lord Duncan, rarely seen outside of their territory.

Feeling exhausted after watching the procession into the Great Hall, I push myself off the wall and rush down the hallway to a side door to prepare for my performance. The band is waiting for me just outside the entryway. "Where have you been?" the lyrist asks me. I pretend to misunderstand the question and shrug. With a secret grin, I swing my violin onto my shoulder and throw open the door.

The nobles barely acknowledge our presence; they are too busy exchanging pleasantries and mindless conversation. The Winter Solstice banquet and ball isn't a time to discuss business. That's what the day after is for if people choose to stay. But they won't have to worry about trying to think of something kind or polite enough to say for too much longer. Although I originally told High Lord Nicholas I wanted to accompany the band, I know I will inevitably stand out in my own right.

No one can resist the strains of a well-played fiddle.

I see Aiden on the side of the room, talking animatedly to Tristan from the House of Water. He glances over at me, however, and gives me a tiny, imperceptible wink. *Good to know he's paying attention.* I can already see his body language changing, turning toward me in anticipation of the music. *He's sweet,* my treacherous mind betrays.

I glance at the band standing behind me. With a brief nod, I whip around and thrust my bow into the air definitively before slicing it down and attacking the violin strings with vigor. The room goes silent instantly as I play. Through narrow determined eyes, I catch the surprise on many of the nobles' faces. With a smirk, I open the celebration with the same song I played for my mother before I left home. Something fun to wake people up and get this party started.

The ballroom immediately shifts. Gone are the political pleasantries and forced smiles. Instead, I see people begin to open up. I see genuine smiles and a few tapping feet. I spot the musicians out of the corner of my eye begin to respond to the audience responding to them. I grin and slowly bring up the tempo. I hear clapping from the back of the room and whistling from the sides. When we switch over to traditional Winter Solstice songs, the nobles begin to join us in song.

For the finale, I play a spinning thriller that involves a little pageantry. After all, pageantry is my specialty. I move forward off the area where the band and I are staged. I hear a couple of quiet exclamations from the musicians, but I ignore them. I know exactly what I'm doing. I dance directly into the crowd amid startled breaths and eventual clapping. I play right up next to the House of Peace's daughters, and the littlest dances around me with joyous laughter. I grin and crouch down to her level temporarily, my fingers flying across the strings. She stares at my hand in fascination, and I do a couple notes of finger plucking to make her eyes widen further. Then in a leap to my feet, I spin off again amidst impressed applause.

Weaving in and out of people, my feet dance as quickly as my fingers do. However, I feel something just behind me as I step back to do another turn. When given the choice to trip and potentially fall to the ground or to pull off something tricky and hope it works, I choose the latter. I do a backward flying leap, landing on one leg and spinning as gracefully as any traditional dancer.

But I am not prepared for what I see when I make my way back around.

My violin held out and my other leg behind me in a straight line, I complete the spin and nearly stop playing all together… when I see Faolan in front of me.

By the Lady… I'm so fucked.

I manage to skip over a couple notes but force myself to continue the song and try to hide the horror on my face. Unfortunately, it is essentially already too late. Two seconds after I leaped over his foot, Faolan's eyes flash in recognition. They narrow at me, and a horrifying, knowing smirk crosses his lips. Gazes locked, it's a struggle of wills. I try not to break the stare. My muscles tense up even as my bow glides over the violin. I'm ready to fucking run if he decides to give me away as someone else.

He may not know my real identity, but from that look in eyes, I can tell he realizes something is up.

Either way, this is bad.

But... to my surprise, Faolan doesn't do anything to expose me. Instead, he drops down into a low bow, almost in apology for impeding my performance. But his eyes sear into me, and I can tell this isn't over. He's going to do his best to talk to me later. And I'd better let him, or he will expose me right on the spot in front of everyone. I can't have that. As the song finishes, my head and heart are racing. I need to find Aiden now.

But I don't have that chance. Immediately following the finale, the Fae nobility begin to file into the banquet hall for dinner. I am ushered in the opposite direction where I am to eat dinner in the informal dining room with the household and the musicians I just performed with. I won't be able to join the ball until after dinner. Throughout the meal, I can barely eat. Winter Solstice-time always brought my favorite meals back home even when times were rough. But I can't focus on eating when my cover is about to be blown. I pick at my food in nervous circles.

When we are finally allowed to return to the ballroom, I am the first one out of the dining room. I rush back inside and immediately skid as I realize that without the proper height, I am searching for Aiden blindly in a large crowd. And that crowd just got larger as wealthy Fae from the House of the Sun have joined the ball.

Wonderful.

I take a deep breath. *Alright, Grace, let's do this logically. Leo always said when you're searching for someone, start on the outside and work your way in.* I squeeze through a group of Fae to the far wall and begin to make my way down the room.

Suddenly, a rough hand catches my arm and pulls me backward through the crowd. I struggle violently, trying not to cause a scene. But no one gives me and my captor a second glance. I'm thrown against a column with unnecessary force, and the breath rushes out of me in a whoosh. I look up furiously at the man who dragged me, and although I'm startled by his face, in all honesty, I am not that surprised.

"Was the force necessary?" I spit out.

"Oh, I think it was, *Ana*," Faolan hisses at me. I glare at him, and his eyes match mine in intensity. "You have two minutes to explain yourself before I tell everyone in this room you're a liar and a dealer on the black market."

"I would think you of all people would understand the benefits of giving a false name when trying to send a message to someone on the black market," I reply coolly.

"That may be, Miss Grace, if that is actually your name, but I do not tolerate people lying to me." Faolan slowly creeps forward, making the space between us uncomfortably close. "Now, I've been going over your story in my head a thousand times since you played that little violin of yours, and something just doesn't add up, little girl."

He stalks even closer, his hot breath brushing my face. "How would you know someone, a runner no less, on the mortal side of the border? Have you been sneaking down to the border to hook up with somebody? A forbidden romance, perhaps? Now, see, my men may not know how to ask the right questions, but I think you owe me an answer. Or I'll give away your little secret right here, right now, in this packed ballroom. There are more guards here than you can possibly imagine. You'll be caught in minutes."

"Is there a problem here?" I nearly collapse against the column in relief when Aiden's arm reaches in between Faolan and me and pushes him backward slightly. "Is there a reason you're assaulting my friend, Lord Faolan?"

Faolan's lip curls up, and his eyes flash again in recognition. "Lord Aiden…" the name slides over his lips like honey. "Is this one yours?"

"You could say that," Aiden says lightly, his eyes glinting dangerously in contrast.

Faolan chuckles almost as if it was the answer he had been waiting for. "So, you're fucking her? Is that what this is?" His eyes look up and down me sleazily. "I have to say I approve of your choice. You know, I just might like a turn with her. You willing to try something a little… kinky?" He rakes over me hungrily.

Aiden's fists clench at his sides, twitching slightly like he's straining not to haul off and punch this guy. "I would suggest you walk away, Faolan," Aiden says through gritted teeth. "Before this turns into the Summer Solstice of '37."

Faolan grins maniacally and gives another one of his signature bows. "My apologies, Lord Aiden." He glances over to me. "Miss *Grace*." He mouths *We'll talk later* before disappearing into the crowd.

Aiden turns to me with concern in his eyes. "Are you alright?" he asks. He places his hands on my shoulders and inspects me carefully.

I cover his hands with my own. "Yes, Aiden, I'm fine."

"What business did Faolan have with you?"

I sigh and shake my head. "Don't ask."

"Grace…" Aiden warns.

"Drop it," I pull away softly. "Please. I promise I'll tell you later, just not now."

He nods slowly and moves to take my hand. "Alright… on one condition." He smiles at me. "Dance with me."

My eyes widen. "Woah woah woah, wait. No, I'm terrible at dancing," I gush.

He smirks at me, and before I know it, the protectiveness of the column is away, and I'm in the crowd with Aiden's arm around my waist. "I have seen you dance around with your violin as gracefully as any of the ladies here. Let go. Relax, and just enjoy."

"I'm going to step on your toes," I try to protest.

Aiden laughs. He suddenly spins me around with him, and I instinctively grab onto his shoulder and his hand. He smirks. "I told you, you know how."

"Okay, I know how, yes. Do I want to in front of everyone? No!"

His smile eventually makes me begrudgingly give in. I follow his lead, spinning around the ballroom floor in carefully coordinated steps. I feel myself begin to loosen up as we move along.

"Is this what you wanted?" I sass weakly.

Aiden smiles. "Yes, angel. Just like this." I am lost in his eyes.

When the song ends, he lets go of me, bowing low. I drop down into a sweeping bow myself. He grins and offers me his hand again for another dance. I can't help but follow him into another whirl.

CHAPTER THIRTY-TWO

After many, many more dances, I excuse myself and step out into the hallway for a breather. Aiden persuaded me to stay out on the dance floor much longer than I should have. My feet are killing me. I take a seat on the staircase, removing my shoes and rubbing my feet.

To my surprise, I don't appear to be the only one outside of the festivities. I hear hushed voices coming from around the corner. Curious, I stand up and creep over to listen from behind the wall. I see High Lord Carron of the House of Darkness towering menacingly over the High Lord of the House of Fire, even with the latter's tall stature.

Their words stop me cold in my tracks.

"I don't understand why the man wanted mortals in the first place," High Lord Thomas snarks, sipping delicately from his wine.

"Much easier to explain away most problems, Tom," Carron replies. "I applaud Nick for his thought process. I would have done the same thing myself. Think about it. Deadlines not being met? Blame it on mortal interference. First to die if something goes wrong. Gives us some time to move operations before people get suspicious." He chuckles. "Besides, it's much cheaper to throw some flowers and a parade their way down in the Middle Realm to satisfy them, and we don't owe them answers or anything."

I know I didn't overhear much. I know I should have kept my mouth shut. No one could hear them but me. But inexplicably, at that moment…

I. Just. Snap.

"How dare you…." I growl low under my breath as I step out from behind the wall.

High Lord Carron turns slightly, angling his eyes toward me. "Excuse me, miss?"

"I said…" I grit my teeth. "How dare you."

"Young lady, I demand that you…"

"Oh, you demand, do you?" I shout at him. "*You demand*?"

The whole hall stops cold, and my anger rings out among the silence. "Is that all that our lives are worth to you?" I knock the High Lord's drink from his hand with a quick slap. The glass shatters against the tile. Guests have migrated from the ballroom to see what's going on, filing in like a wall behind us. "Throw some flowers their way, and they'll be satisfied? A couple of gold medals, and suddenly families will be satisfied with the deaths of their sons? You think that's worth it?"

I get up in the High Lord's face and fly at him. "I know families who went off the rails when their husbands and sons came home from your world *dead*! My brother's friend, Chris, was a part of the House of Darkness Regiment 35. He was one of the only ones to be sent to your army. He came home blown up in a body bag! All the pieces were there, and your fucking soldiers gave them no warning! At least the rest of my brother's friends came home in shrouded caskets and with *military respect*! Chris's father killed himself, and his mother is now a prostitute on the corner trying to fucking survive! *And you call that satisfying!*"

I circle him quickly and violently. It infuriates me more how his eyes stay trained on me, and he shows no sign of remorse. "My brother, Leo, served your realm with passion and dedication. He was one of the best mercenary soldiers across *both* realms, hands down, highly recommended by everyone he encountered. And you Fae," I spit out, "killed him! You killed him!" I shriek.

I take a step, stumbling backward. "You killed him..." I breathe as I stumble back into Aiden who's pushed his way to the front of the pack. Aiden catches me shakily, pushing me back onto my feet.

"Grace..." he whispers in my ear. I'm confused as to why I hear fear in his voice.

Then I see it.

Carron's eyes are glinting maliciously. A small smirk crosses his lips, and only then do I realize just how miserably I have fucked up.

"My dear," Carron's voice slides over me like knives. "I find it curious as to how you know so much about the Middle Realm and... mortal affairs." My heartbeat skips. *By the Lady... No...* "In fact, I find it curious how you seem to personally know a few mortal soldiers and their families."

"I..." I start my sentence, but I realize I have no way to defend or explain any of my actions. The Fae nobles around me are starting to realize it too; they're whispering to each other.

"Well, Miss Grace," the High Lord says with a smile. "Would you like to explain to us how you know so many mortals personally? Seeing as it is against Fae law for any

Fae within our borders to cross over into mortal territory for *any* reason unless they are a soldier. Are you a soldier?"

"I..."

"You're not a soldier. Are you, Miss Grace? In fact, I don't even think you're a Fae woman after all. You don't have any powers. Do you? I haven't seen you cast a single charm since I first laid eyes on you." He grins wickedly. "You're a mortal girl... aren't you, Grace?"

Everything is silent. When I don't answer, the room erupts. "Guards!" I hear multiple voices call out.

I glance around wildly. "No... no, no, no, wait..." But it's far too late for me to protest.

"Run!" Aiden hisses in my ear and shoves me forward. I push through the crowd and rush out a side door, the entire Fae nobility screaming after me.

***

I have no idea where to go, but I have no time to think. I race down a hallway, flying past servants and maids and slamming people into walls as I try to get by. I hear the echoes of heavy footsteps chasing behind me. There's no time to hesitate. I can't get caught. *By the Lady, I'm done for.* I pick up the pace and make another sharp turn.

I dart into the kitchen and duck platters, dodging chefs and piping hot flames. I look around wildly for an exit to the outside, but I can't find one. Suddenly, Aiden appears by my side and pulls me away from the room. I don't hesitate in following him. "What were you thinking?" he shouts at me as we run. I don't have the mind or the breath to answer.

He shakes his head as if dismissing the question and pushes me toward a small side door. "Come on. We'll sneak you out the servants' quarters."

But when we reach the room, it's clear the nobles have thought of this already. A handful of guards wait for us from across the Twelve Houses. If I wasn't so terrified of what was going to happen next, I would take pride in the fact that I, a mere mortal girl, have the attention of the military authorities of all Twelve Houses simultaneously. Aiden tries to push me back through the door, but the guards chasing me finally catch up and surround us on the other side.

"Shit," Aiden hisses. His eyes are still searching for a way out of this, but I know it's already too late.

High Lord Carron strides through the throng of guards with Aiden's father not too far behind. "Well, well, well… What do we have here?" he drawls in sheer delight. "You're helping your friend escape, Lord Aiden? An accused criminal? I do believe that according to law, that puts you in league with her." He smirks.

"I will not let you put a hand on her!" Aiden fires back passionately.

He chuckles. "You don't have a choice." He waves his hand. "Seize them." Within seconds, they have both of us restrained. "Bring them back to the Great Hall," Carron says as his cloak swishes behind him when he turns away. "There, we will decide their fate."

The guards wrench our arms backward and push us forward roughly out of the kitchen. I contemplate struggling, but I can tell the effort would be in vain. Aiden seems to have the same idea as he stumbles stoically behind me. They're being a bit more careful with him since he's nobility, but they have no problem causing me to crash into walls or trip over rugs and scrape my knees.

The Great Hall suddenly becomes a courtroom with the large throne-like chairs from the dining room brought in to accommodate the twelve High Lords. Aiden and I are shoved forward into the center of the room by the guards, and they surround us to prevent our escape. I look sideways to Aiden, and the corners of his lips turn up slightly as he tries to reassure me with his eyes.

"Grace," High Lord Carron's voice booms. I stand up straighter and more defiantly. "You are here in direct violation of Realm law created thousands of years ago to protect the Three Realms from excessive interaction."

I chuckle softly. Carron's eyes narrow. "Is there something funny about that, Grace, if that is your real name?"

"Well, sir," I look over to Aiden before continuing. "I would say that your kind has been interfering in the Middle Realm for centuries with your puppet governments that run our world. So, my transgression only counters one incident of many, many of your own." The High Lords rumble.

High Lord Nicholas speaks out to me, "Think for a minute, Grace. Are you going to be so flippant to the people who are deciding your fate?"

I laugh again with a sarcastic air. "You're going to kill me either way. What I say now has very little meaning in the grand scheme of things. Does it?

I can tell I'm throwing off the nobility.

"I demand you show us some respect, or we'll make your death excruciatingly more painful," High Lord Thomas of the House of Fire lashes out. I level my eyes at him but say nothing further. "How did you get into the Upper Realm? Where did you enter from?"

"That is not a question I will answer for you, so I wouldn't bother asking," I reply simply.

"Oh, we will force it out of you, Miss Grace," Lord Carron growls. "Nicholas."

Nicholas stands from his throne and stares at me intently. "I am sorry for this, Miss Grace." He stares directly into my eyes, and I am suddenly unable to look away. I counter him with an intense stare. The silence is deafening.

He furrows his eyebrows and breaks the stare. I can move again. "I can't get into her mind," he says breathlessly. There's an uproar from the High Lords, and even I'm surprised. I turn to Aiden in confusion to find that his expression reflects mine.

"What do you mean you can't get into her mind?" Carron is furious.

"She has some sort of block up. Her defenses are incredibly strong. I have no way of getting into her thoughts." Lord Nicholas trails off as he moves back to his chair. I straighten up triumphantly, smirking at Lord Carron.

"Then search your son!"

"I taught my son to withstand the pull," Nicholas replies. "I will have the same result with him."

"Faolan!" Carron snaps. "Go to Aiden."

Faolan looks at me as he trails over to my partner. I see something odd behind his eyes. It's not disdain... it's almost disappointment, perhaps resignation. He pulls Aiden to his feet and holds him fast.

"You will explain why you are here, or my son will do some damage to your little confidant here," Carron growls. Nicholas exclaims in protest, but there is no need. I'm not going to risk Aiden's wellbeing for mine.

"I will not tell you how I got here," I shout. "But I will tell you why I am here." I stride forward, and the guards quickly grab my arms. I lean forward in struggle against them. "My name is Grace; that I did not lie about. I am here to find what happened to my brother, Leo, who was killed while in active duty in the Upper Realm in the employ of the House of the Sun."

"You did not receive anything from us concerning your brother?" Nicholas asks, his voice full of concern. "We tend to make it very public about the lives of the mercenaries who serve with us." I see High Lord Carron's eyes flash in recognition and lean over to Nicholas hastily.

I scoff quietly. "With all due respect, High Lord, my mother and I did not even receive a body. We had to bury an empty coffin. No flowers were sent. There was no ceremony. The delegation came and left without so much as an explanation. There were no medals, and no one made any offer to cover the funeral costs. We ran ourselves into the ground trying to make sure my brother had the full honors he deserved, and even then, we came up short. I struggled to pay the rent on our apartment for a year afterward along with everything else."

I stare at Aiden's father intently. "You would understand then... why I had to take matters into my own hands."

"So, you chose to break Fae law for your family?" a new voice from the High Lady of the House of Wind rings out over the Great Hall.

"Yes, ma'am," I answer plainly.

"How can we punish her for that?" she continues, turning to her fellow rulers. "How can we honestly punish her for searching for her brother? I would have done the same thing in her shoes. Let's take her back to the border and leave it at that."

I like her.

"Absolutely ridiculous!" Lord Carron chimes in. "She broke sacred law!"

"That law hasn't been rewritten since this realm was created!" the High Lady argues.

"It doesn't matter! She has to pay!" Thomas chimes in. A heated debate breaks out among the High Fae. I look over at Aiden. The pride in his eyes at my testimony lifts my heart just a tiny bit. I smile softly. He smiles back at me. *By the Lady, Aiden, I am so sorry for pulling you into this.*

Carron speaks out definitively on the matter. His voice rings out over the din. "As in accordance with high capital traitors," he smirks. "I believe these two must be subjected to a magical duel of the heirs."

"A duel of the heirs?" High Lord Gabriel stands up in alarm. "That hasn't been held for almost three hundred years. Do you really think this is the time?"

"Why not?" Carron says with a sly smile.

"They're just children!" High Lord Nicholas fires back.

"They are both fully capable adults with full knowledge of what they were doing. Why are you worried, Lord Nicholas? Your son is capable of holding his own in a fight, is he not?" The former High Lord falls silent. "All in favor?" Carron stands slowly. His eyes bore into me. I don't see the count of hands, but it must have been the majority because the guards begin to pull both Aiden and me away. I do not break eye contact with the High Lord Carron, however. Defiant to the very end.

CHAPTER THIRTY-THREE

The Fae guards march me and Aiden up the stairs to Aiden's room, pushing us forward when we slow for even a second. One of them pulls open the door roughly, and the other two shove us in unceremoniously. The door slams shut behind us, the lock clicks shut, and I can hear the guards positioning themselves in front of the door. *They're really going to guard us all night.*

I slowly turn to look at Aiden. His eyes look stormy, and for the first time in a while, I see his frustration directed at me. I move over and sit on the end of his bed in an attempt to put some distance between us. I'm waiting for the fallout to hit, and sure enough, in the next minute it does.

"What were you thinking?" he starts slowly, his low voice pushing through gritted teeth.

"Aiden…"

"No, what were you thinking, Grace?" he faces me abruptly. "Did you lose your *head* in there? What the hell possessed you to go off like that? You've exposed yourself! You've exposed everything!"

"Aiden, it… I just… I couldn't take it anymore!"

"You managed to get this far without breaking character! Everyone believed you! Hell, I almost believed you! Now you're going to die!" He storms up to me and gets in my face, sending me reeling back. "Do you get that, Grace? Tomorrow, you are going to die!"

I breathe heavily as he leans toward me, and eventually, my swirling emotions give me no choice but to burst into tears. I curl in on myself and bury my head in my hands. I hate breaking down in front of him; I hate crying in general. But I can't help the fear and panic coursing through my veins. For the first time, I'm beginning to realize just how dire of a situation I put myself in by speaking out for my brother. And now my worst fears are coming true.

I am going to die.

As I cry, I try to reassure myself with the thought of being with Leo again. *I'll see you soon, big brother.*

"No…" I hear Aiden breathe. "No, wait, Grace. I'm sorry." He sits down beside me and pulls me into a hug. I throw my arms around his neck and hug him close as I cry. "It's gonna be okay, Grace. I promise. I'll keep fighting for you as long as I can hold out. Maybe we can…" I hit him softly once on the back to make him stop talking. I don't want to hear him lie to me.

He holds me loosely against him. "Don't cry, Grace," he whispers softly. He pulls my head back from his shoulder and wipes at my tears with his fingers. "Look at me."

"I am so sorry," I choke out hoarsely.

"What are you sorry for, Grace?"

"I'm sorry for dragging you into this whole thing."

He chuckles and rubs slightly against my back. "Silly girl… You tried to kick me out in the first place, remember? Multiple times, I might add." He nudges me, and I can't help but smile through the tears. "I chose to come along with you. I chose to follow you."

He cups my cheek. "And Grace, I don't regret a single thing." He strokes lightly over my head and whispers, full of emotion in a soft chuckle, "You are the greatest adventure I've ever attempted to follow."

We stare into each other's eyes intently. I am overwhelmed with the desire to show him that he means something to me too. "I could never have made it here without you," I whisper as I subconsciously shift closer to him.

"Oh yes, you could have..." Aiden leans in.

Our faces inch closer, and I bravely close the gap between us.

When our lips collide, everything is lost to me. I grip Aiden tightly to me as I kiss him passionately. We hold on to each other and kiss like it is the last time we will ever draw breath. *And it very well might be for me.* His lips taste like coming home, that feeling you get when you breathe in the familiar scent of safety and comfort. I can't get enough of it. Breathing doesn't matter; this is a matter of life or death. If I don't keep kissing him, I swear by the Lady I will die.

He flips us over on the bed, leaning over top of me and capturing my lips again with his own. I fumble for the edge of his shirt, yanking it over his head. I freeze. I wasn't anticipating going this far with him, especially not now. But looking at the fire in his eyes, I have never felt more ready.

Aiden smirks down at me, the hunger in his stare growing. His voice grows deep, "Don't hide from me, Grace." *Damn mind reader.* His fingertips slide under the edge of my shirt, tracing along the skin just beneath it. With a flick of his wrist, my top disappears.

"Hey! No magic," I growl.

He laughs and then runs his hands over my chest. I forget to protest. He lowers his lips to my neck, and I squirm beneath him, desperate for friction. My fingers tangle in his hair, pulling on it slightly. I feel Aiden smirk as he grazes my skin lightly with his teeth. His lips travel down my body, kissing and teasing. As he fumbles with my pants, he kisses along the edge of my waist. With a swift tug and a frantic toss, his fingers finally reach my skin.

I am lost.

When he crawls up my body once again, we are joined together for the first time. He moves slowly, but deliberately, consuming me. The heat is almost unbearable. With every movement, he awakens something inside me. We roll around the bed, colliding with each other, body and soul, over and over again. Then I am broken in his arms, and yet somehow, I am made whole again.

I moan softly against his neck as he presses a soft kiss to my shoulder and rolls off of me. He wraps an arm around my waist and pulls me lightly against his side. I fall bonelessly into his chest. Fingers lightly trail over my curls and over my bare back. They draw soft strokes in careful lines. He draws the cool sheets over us. I'm so lethargic; all I can do is softly whimper. He smiles gently at me. "You're so beautiful," he whispers.

I curl into his body and close my eyes, drifting off slowly.

I feel him press a light kiss to my hair and whisper lightly, "I am," he chuckles lightly, "utterly and hopelessly in love with you, Grace."

I want to reply to him. I want to tell him I'm terrified of the morning. I want to tell him I need him too. I want to say so many things.

But my exhaustion is taking over, and all I can manage is a whimper. He shushes me and presses me closer to him. "Sleep, angel." I obey and slip down into sleep.

CHAPTER THIRTY-FOUR

―

I wish we could have stayed like that forever, Aiden and me, pressed up against one another and wrapped in each other's arms without the rest of the world interfering with us. It feels so cruel that we only have one night together, and not even an entire night at that. I feel like our relationship grew so fast in the span of the last few days. And now… I'll never know how things would have been.

When my eyes open softly with the breaking of dawn, I almost forget where I am. It is easy to think we're back at the inn in the House of Earth in that tiny bed; that's how wrapped up we are. A whole bed, and we're essentially taking up one person's width. I look up at Aiden's closed eyes and lightly reach up to drag a thumb over his cheek.

He opens his eyes only moments later. We stare at each other in silence. His hand slides to meet mine against his face while the other meets my back to pull me closer. There's a moment of peace. He kisses my forehead as I kiss his shoulder. We lie in the inklings of light, belonging only to each other.

Then it all breaks down.

Aiden's bedroom door is torn open with such force I am surprised it doesn't get ripped off the hinges. Armed soldiers storm in along with Aiden's father and High Lord Carron. I shriek in surprise and pull the sheets higher over my body, covering my nakedness. I watch both High Lords' eyes flash in recognition. Aiden's father looks pained, while High Lord Carron just looks smug. *Bastard.*

"Get up, girl," one of the men hisses at me, reaching for my arm. Aiden immediately flips us, pinning me underneath him to protect me from grabbing hands. "Lord, you need to…"

"No!" Aiden shouts at him, tightening his arms to shield me. "You have absolutely no right to barge in here like that."

"Actually, we do," Carron sneers. "You're both convicted criminals at this moment. Especially her."

"Please," Aiden pleads. "Can you please give her a minute to get dressed?" Carron seems to contemplate this question with a long, drawn-out pause that has everyone holding their breath.

"Give me one good reason I should let you," he said.

"Please… I'm begging you. She's still a person. Fae or mortal. She's still a person!"

Carron stares at the two of us on the bed. I try to avoid his eyes. He finally nods. "Grab her a robe from the closet," he snaps at one of the guards. A moment later, the guard tosses one of Aiden's robes at me. Aiden keeps hovering over my body until I slip the robe on under the blanket. Then, he kisses my forehead once and slowly moves off.

I am swiftly pulled from the bed and forced away from Aiden. The last thing I see is his concerned face as the remaining guards snap at him to get ready. I am pushed down the hallway, down a flight of stairs to my original guest room, and forced inside.

Once inside, I see Margaret, the housekeeper, waiting for me by the window. "You have ten minutes," the guard says ominously before slamming the door behind me. I look up at Margaret in confusion. She smiles sadly at me with a hint of sympathy in her eyes.

"You should get ready," she says softly. She gestures to my belongings, which have clearly been searched and strewn all over the bed. They've taken the magical items I purchased as well as the pieces I bought off the black market. They've left my weapons, so I suppose that is a blessing.

I waste no time in getting changed back into the outfit I wore on my very first day in the Upper Realm. Today, just as then, it's time to be a warrior. I rush to the vanity and praise the Lady that they never found my amulet. It is still curled up in the back corner where I stashed it. As I slip it on, I sheath my swords into the holsters at my back, and my brother's dagger slides into my belt with ease. I feel like I did when I was about to enter the Upper Realm for the first time—wired and determined. I take one last long look in the mirror. I want to remember what I looked like, who I became in this world before I meet my fate.

I level my eyes at Margaret and nod once to her. I swear she nods back at me in recognition before calling for the guards. They open the door and stride in, reaching for me. I push their arms away to their shock. "You don't need to push me," I say simply. I turn to the door. "I'll walk out."

I stride forward with ease. The guards flank me on either side, just waiting for me to make a run for it. But they won't get the chance to grab me again. I have no reason to run now. I am headed directly for my death, and if I am to die today, I will die with dignity.

And I will take down as many of the heirs as I can with me. I may not be able to kill them, but I can humiliate them and make the whole realm question their strength.

I am steered down roughly to the grounds of the castle. Past the courtyard, past the gardens, and all the way down to a wide arena. Seating boxes and benches spiral down toward a massive field in the center of the pit. The nobility is gathered all around on the hill above the arena.

They are setting up for a show.

The Fae stare at me intensely as I am pushed past them. I make sure to look at each and every High Lord in the eyes as I am rushed by them. They will remember who they are killing by sending me into that arena. I will make them remember my face forever. When we reach the base of the hill, I see several tunnels that lead directly into the pit. The soldiers shove me forward through an entrance to one of them. They stand at the end and wave me toward the arena. "Go inside," one of the men snaps. "Now."

With a smug curl to my lips, I bow low to the soldiers. Against their wishes, I take my sweet time walking down the tunnel. The duel of the heirs can't start until I arrive. I may not be in control, but I can at least take back my entrance. I can take back my dignity and my pride. I keep moving forward so I don't anger the guards, but I do not speed up for them. I can hear muttering behind me, but I just block it out.

I cannot be tamed, and I will not surrender.

When I reach the end of the tunnel, I see the twelve heirs waiting for me, scattered across the field. I can't see Aiden at all. I imagine the nobles put us on opposite sides, hoping for a quick fight. They won't get one. Not today.

I see the herald step out onto the edge of the field and hold his hands up to the arena.

I watch his hands go down to start the fight.

I hear Aiden shout from across the arena. "*Grace!*" I hone in on his voice.

And the duel begins.

CHAPTER THIRTY-FIVE

I knew Aiden wouldn't be able to protect me. I was fully aware he couldn't fight off twelve heirs by himself. Eventually, his strength would run out, and they would subdue him before turning on me. Me, they had permission and were even encouraged to kill.

But the heirs made three mistakes when the signal went up.

One: they divided themselves between Aiden and me. If they had focused on Aiden all at once first, they would have taken him down quickly, and I would have been an easy kill. But they didn't.

Two: No one took my amulet from me when I stepped on this field.

Three: The Twelve Houses underestimated me.

It takes way too long for the heirs to realize I am temporarily immune to the magic they throw at me. I can feel the magic around the amulet taking a significant hit every time a spell collides with me, but it only wavers and does not break. Tristan is the closest to me, and unfortunately for him, he's not the most skilled at fighting. A few slashes, and a knock to the head, and he's on the ground. I see Aiden take down the twin women from the House of Light.

Swords are slashing, spells are flying, and I can't catch my breath. This was designed to be an unfair fight, but this is ridiculous. Some of these nobles fight like soldiers, but others have absolutely no training at all. Those tend to hang back. That at least gives me the opportunity to focus on the people who actually pose me a threat.

One of the heirs, Luna, approaches me with an odd calm that doesn't match the situation. I have seconds to figure out if she's a threat or not. She smiles softly at me. "Hey, I'm sorry I have to fight you," she surprises me by speaking. "You seem like a nice person, and I understand what you did for your brother."

"Thank you," I answer tentatively. "You could… not fight me, you know. You could help me?"

"You're right!" She sounds way too excited. "Why not?" She stands next to me and holds her hands up, summoning a light purple magic. I'm entirely thrown. *An ally can't hurt, I guess.*

Suddenly, Luna tumbles to the ground with a loud crunch. When her body falls, I whip around to see Faolan, sword drawn and hilt right above where her head had been. I scoff in disgust. "You'll take out your own teammate?" I spit at him.

He only smirks. "I am only out here for myself, Miss Grace. Besides, my father and I have a bet." He spins his sword. "If I'm the one to kill you, he'll give me command of the army for the year. I've got some delicious plans, darling, and I can't have you messing them up. Now can I?"

"You can't touch me with magic, you realize?"

"Oh, I can," he smiles wickedly. "That amulet won't hold forever. But I've been dying to spar with you ever since I met you."

"Let's dance then," I banter.

Faolan growls. "Right back at ya, darling."

When our swords collide, we generate sparks. Clash after clash, we rotate around each other. Every slash he throws at me, I parry, and every stab I try to slip past him, he blocks me with ease. We're certainly evenly matched, so much so that we almost look like a staged fight shown to trainees to demonstrate the best techniques.

Faolan clearly agrees with me as he speaks to me with heaving breath. "Damn, Grace, where'd you learn to fight?"

I smirk slightly through my fatigue. "My brother taught me. He was the best I knew."

Faolan smirks back. "Bet he didn't teach you not to get distracted by your opponent." Quicker than I can react, his left arm shoots out and wraps around my waist. He yanks me against him and presses his sword blade to my throat. He chuckles low in my ear. "I guess this is where we say goodbye, darling. I had so wished to get to know you a little better."

Breathing heavily, I have to think fast. The idea hits me like a bolt of lightning, and I laugh. "What makes you think this is the end for me, Faolan?" I glance over my shoulder back at him with a playful, flirtatious smile.

He looks at me with confusion, which gives me just the edge I need.

I push against his sword arm to give myself more room, which I knew he was anticipating. But he wasn't anticipating was my foot to kick up and backward straight into his crotch. The breath rushes out of him as he groans in pain. His sword arm drops just enough as he doubles over. I lash out with my sword, cutting his arm and spinning out of his hold. I slam the hilt into the side of his head, much like he did to that poor noble girl.

He doubles over on the ground, disoriented and gasping for air. I smirk wickedly and hold him at sword point. "There's no harm in admitting defeat, Faolan. You were a worthy opponent," I mock him.

He tries to growl at me. "You'll regret this."

"Not likely," I reply before walking right up to him and finally knocking him out. I stare at him on the ground in satisfaction before I sprint off to help Aiden.

Aiden sees me out of the corner of his eye and begins to run to meet me. We lock eyes, and in the next instant, we're pressed back to back, fighting people off around us. Aiden weaves spells to deflect them away from us. I spin in intense sword combat with whoever comes my way. Together, we're pushing them away. *By the Lady, we might actually win this.*

But I was too hasty in my exclamation. Several of the people I've taken down have been revived either by time or by others, and I can tell Aiden's energy is starting to fade. Faolan steps back in front of me, red eyes burning with anger and hatred. He flies at me with everything he has, locking me in another intense battle.

Unfortunately, that means I'm not covering Aiden as well as I need to be. Duncan from the House of War slashes at Aiden's arm, and he goes down. The heir from the House of the Earth immediately seizes the opportunity to trap him in a force field.

I watch Aiden banging on the forcefield, screaming silently and begging them to spare me. His anguish tears me apart. I fell in love with him too hard and too fast, but

I can't imagine not ever having him in my life. I swear that, for him, I will go down fighting.

Faolan laughs gleefully as he turns from the forcefield to focus on me. "I'm gonna enjoy this," he chuckles. He begins to stride toward me. The other heirs follow suit, some hesitantly and others like Faolan, with glee. They close in on me.

I growl low in my throat. I am so damn tired of Fae. They think they're going to get an easy shot; they're gonna find out otherwise. I feel the anger build up inside of me like a wave of heat. My hands shake as I clutch my sword. I feel like I'm on fire.

I smell burning.

By the Lady, I smell burning.

There's an audible gasp from the heirs around me and from the crowd above. I look down at my own hands.

My hands are on fire. They're burning my sword handle straight through.

My blade clatters to the ground as the handle disintegrates.

I have no idea what the hell is happening. *My hands are on fire!* The ground begins to vibrate underneath me as I panic. The heirs start backing up slowly, except for Faolan, who stands there and stares at me in frozen horror and something that looks like sickening realization. My panic builds. I shake and vibrate with the earth, my hands buzzing with unseen energy. I feel it build and build, spiraling out of control.

Then the world explodes.

I scream with the intensity of the blast, and I raise my hands to cover my face from the wave of purple magic searing toward me. But nothing hits.

Only when I uncover my eyes do I realize the magic was moving outward all along... *from me.*

All of the heirs lie unconscious on the ground, many bloodied and bruised. Aiden's laid out flat on the ground, covering his head with his hands, but he's conscious. The forcefield surrounding him is gone. *Did I incinerate it? Is that possible?* He looks up at me with a mixture of fear and shock in his eyes.

It takes a moment to realize he's not afraid of me; he's afraid of what it could mean for me.

The crowd of Fae nobles is silent behind me. No one speaks a word. I don't dare to breathe. I look down at my hands in horror. I turn them over to my palms and then to the backs of my hands, searching for some sign. I find nothing but my own skin. Beneath my feet, a glint of purple crystal catches my eye. I reach for my neck to find that the amulet is missing. It takes several long seconds to realize that the pendant is actually shattered beneath my feet.

By the Lady… What the hell was that?

CHAPTER THIRTY-SIX

The ringing in my ears intensifies. My vision blurs until the field around me fades away. My hands vibrate again, and I fall to the ground in horror, hitting my knees hard. I can't help but scream. My voice echoes across the field.

Something foreign brushes across my shoulders. I flinch hard and tries to push against it with my shaking hands. "Grace!" a faraway voice calls out to me. I push hard, continuing to shout. "Grace…" the ringing sharply disappears, and I recognize Aiden's voice.

I can suddenly see again. Aiden's on his knees in front of me, pressing close and automatically curling around me protectively. He takes my hands and cradles them in his, squeezing tightly. When his hands are around mine, I realize the magic surge is gone and my hands are just plain trembling. Although my hands are slowing down, my whole body is going into full convulsions. Aiden wraps his non-injured arm around me, pulling me to his chest.

"Breathe, Grace, just breathe. It's gonna be alright." As he tries to call me, I can't help but notice his voice is breathy and uneven, like I'm sure mine would be if I tried to speak. I cling to him tightly, silently begging the Lady that whatever just happened isn't going to change everything I know.

My prayers were not to be answered.

The field is suddenly flooded with everyone from the stands. The Fae nobility and their personal guards sprint down into the grass, careening toward us with impressive speed. I flinch violently and curl up tightly against Aiden. He shifts arms to have his good arm free to fight if necessary.

The closer they get to us, the louder the shouting gets. Everyone wants to know what kind of a demon I am, how the hell I managed to take down everyone, and a few exclaim that I am to go free because, technically, I won. If I had any of my former sarcasm left to muster, I would scoff at that. *There's no way they'll let me go after this.* I hear questions being flung from everywhere. "How does she have magic?" "Does she have magical heritage?" "What in hell's name is going on?"

The din just gets louder and louder. I can't take it.

"I don't know!" I cry back hoarsely. To my surprise, the Fae go silent. "I don't know. Please," I beg softly to Aiden. I feel too weak to hate how pleading my voice sounds. "What's happening?" He pulls my head into his chest again.

"She must have some sort of Fae lineage," the High Lady I like says. *She's the most levelheaded of them all.* "Somewhere down the line, one of our cousins or our ancestors must have mated with a mortal." The protests start up again, this time debating whose lineage was the purest or the least pure. All of the talk is giving me a headache.

"Wait!" a strong male voice rings out over the chaos.

The lords turn to face him as the High Lord of the House of the Evening descends the stairs. I look up at him from my knelt position. He stops in front of me, and a cautious and puzzled frown crosses his face. Then his face changes drastically, and he looks like he's seen a ghost. "By the Lady…" He stumbles back and collapses to the ground.

The attention shifts off me and onto the fallen High Lord. Nobles scramble to pull him to his feet. Medics are called. He waves everyone off and pushes forward to stand over me again. "Child… what's your mother's name?"

I frown in confusion. "Amelia… Amelia Richardson."

His face grows pale, and for the first time, I see a Fae noble look weak. He clutches his heart in agony as he spins around. Some of the others move to catch him again. "What is it, by the Lady?" High Lord Nicholas begs.

High Lord Alexander breathes heavily. He manages to get back on his feet, and he turns to look down at me. "This girl… she's one of mine."

....

There is a moment of silence. Then the field explodes into chaos. Nobles left and right are shouting, clawing at me. Aiden grabs me and pulls me into his chest, trying to protect me even in his injured state. His dad and brother are shouting at him to get away from me. I am shell-shocked, and I can do nothing but hold on to him. *What does he mean, 'one of his'?*

High Lord Alexander shouts over top of the noise. "I met her mother almost twenty years ago!" My head jerks up along with everyone else's. "I met her at a bar in the mortal realm. I was a fool, about to take the throne and about to be married. I decided to travel to the Middle Realm for one last hurrah… one forbidden adventure."

In an unprecedented gesture, he kneels down to my level. His eyes are haunted as he stares into mine. "Your mother, Amelia, was one of the most incredible people I've ever met. She was beautiful and talented in every way. When I realized

I was falling in love with her, I tried to leave then and there… but she convinced me to stay one more night…"

I gulp and squeeze Aiden's hand hard.

High Lord Alexander stands slowly. His expression is grim. He folds his hands and finally addresses the crowd. "This child here is mine," he declares plainly. "She is a Faelie." He hesitates. "She is nineteen… And one year older than my oldest son. By Upper Realm universal law… she is the heir to the House of the Evening."

I can't breathe.

The world blurs out of focus, and all I can hear is my heart beating in my ears. *Half Fae. Heir to the House of the Evening. Faelie… Fae… I'm half Fae.* I am entirely separated from my body, my consciousness floating above the crowd as the congregation erupts once more. The nobles are shouting and screaming, demanding answers from Alexander, lamenting the corruption of a bloodline, condemning the Half-Fae child.

By the Lady, that's me.

I am jerked back to reality by Aiden's arms tightening around me and pulling me closer, curling himself around me. It takes me an extra second to realize that he is protecting me from the hands reaching for and tearing at me. As my hearing rushes back to me, I realize questions and insults are being hurled at me as well.

"Half-Fae bastard!"

"Ill-bred scum!"

"What have you done?"

I cringe away from their words. I chance a look up at Aiden, and his eyes are steely and determined as he shouts back at the other nobles. "Leave her alone! Get off her! Get back!" Even with an injured arm, he manages to push everyone away who comes close.

Suddenly, High Lord Alexander shouts above everyone. "*Silence, everyone!*" The arena falls silent again. "We can all squabble about this in Council in a few hours. Right now, you've all forgotten your injured children on the field." Mothers gasp in horror, and fathers bring hands to their mouths in realization of their heirs lying in a haphazard circle on the grass. Alexander nods once and then turns to an attendant nearby. "Summon every healer you can find. Bring them here at once."

Then people finally begin to move. The noble families rush to their children on the field or begin to file out of the arena, conversing quietly, as if raising their voices would anger Alexander… or perhaps me. I look up at Aiden and move up higher against him, hugging him tightly. He holds me just as tightly. "Aiden," I whisper into his ear almost desperately.

"Grace…"

Suddenly, I'm being pulled away from him. I immediately buck against the hands pulling me back. "Let go of me!" I scream. Aiden's being pulled away too by a healer with softly glowing hands, but he's struggling almost as much.

"Hey, let go of her! Grace!"

"Aiden!" I struggle harder. "Let go of me!"

"Miss Grace!" a woman's voice yells sternly from behind me. "You are hurt, and your friend is hurt too. You both need medical treatment; you can see him later."

I barely hear her as I am dragged away from my only safety. "Aiden…" I sob as I'm pulled away from his view.

The healer keeps a tight grip on me the entire walk down the stairs to the infirmary, and eventually, I stop struggling. I lose my strength to fight and sink into her arms. When we get to the room, she pushes me into a bench and heals up my cuts and bruises with a few waves of her hands.

"See, now isn't that much better?" the healer says condescendingly.

I almost growl. "Couldn't you have done that in the arena?"

"Miss, I had strict orders to separate you from the others. For your own protection."

"Protection from who?"

"With all due respect, miss, you were just discovered to be the half-breed heir to the House of the Evening, upsetting the entire noble system of government as we have known it for hundreds of years, all in the span of one duel. I would say quite a few people will be unhappy with you and your very existence."

I nod pensively. "I suppose that's a good point," I reply begrudgingly.

"Besides, your father wants to see you now."

My head whips around toward her. "Excuse me?"

She sighs and turns to wash her hands. "Your father is two doors down, miss. He would like to speak to you. I would suggest you go to him." She then turns to look at me with some sort of sympathy in her eyes. "You'll have to do it at some point. Better now than with the rest of the world looking on, hmm?"

I watch her back while she busies herself with tidying up the infirmary. I hate to admit that she's right, especially after all the stress she just put me through. But it's highly likely if I don't speak to him now, the next time I see him could be in a room full of noblemen shouting at me. *Again.* No... I have to face him now.

I slowly slide to my feet and walk out of the infirmary. Dragging my feet, I make my way down the hallway. My footsteps seem to echo along the empty corridor. When I stop in front of the door where my father is, I hesitate just before touching the knob. I don't have any idea what is waiting for me on the other side.

Summoning all of the courage I can muster, I turn the knob and push open the door.

CHAPTER THIRTY-SEVEN

I stand in front of my father for the first time. I never thought I would see this day. I had never really thought about meeting my father. I assumed he was some lowlife, some cheap bastard who couldn't bother with raising a child. Turns out I was wrong about the lowlife by a long shot. But maybe not about the bastard. I don't know whether to judge him or to wait for him to speak.

We stare at each other blankly, and it startles me even more that his expression mirrors my own. The more I look, the more I recognize myself in him. We're built the same, wiry but strong. I have his blue eyes; those piercing eyes I have always taken pride in, that people have always commented on in me. They came from a man I know absolutely nothing about. It startles me. And I really have no idea what to do next.

I gulp. "Sir."

He hesitates. "Child…"

"I'm not a child, sir," I reply simply.

He nods absentmindedly. "No… I suppose you're not…" He rubs the back of his neck in clear nervousness. "I… I am sorry…"

"Don't," I try to interrupt.

"No, Grace." I stop short when he uses my name. "Let me speak."

The man moves closer to me. I do my best not to step back. "Grace, I... regret abandoning you. I had an inkling that night something... more had happened with Amelia. I put my lorddom ahead of my duty as a father, and... I do regret what that has done to us."

My eyes narrow. "I don't believe there has ever been an us, sir."

"You have every right to say that," Alexander continues. "However, we need to discuss some things."

"I'm listening." I cross my arms.

"According to Fae law, you are the heir to my lorddom," he starts.

"You mentioned that," I snip back.

He sighs. "Unfortunately, I have not had enough time to prepare you over the course of your life as I would have liked if I had the knowledge."

"Prepare me for what?"

"To lead."

I laugh. *Who in the world does he think he's talking to?* "I have no interest in leading your House or staying in this realm another day. Once I am done here, I will be leaving for my home tomorrow."

"You don't have a choice, Grace."

I chuckle again. "Excuse me? I don't see any reason to stay."

"Even though you are now aware you are half Fae?"

I level my eyes at the High Lord. "I am a mortal. I was raised mortal, and that is who I will remain."

"But you're not, Grace. You're not just a mortal anymore. You are my daughter. You are half Fae. You have magic, Grace, and you have to be trained. You could hurt someone with the amount of uncontrollable magic you currently possess."

"What I currently possess? Don't you think it would have manifested itself before now? It was just… a fluke… a mistake," I protest.

The High Lord shakes his head. "You have noticed nothing over the course of your life? Something more… powerful. A skill that came more naturally to you than anyone else. Could you connect with people better through your words or through something you did? Our family has a propensity for empathetic magic. Did you ever feel restricted, trapped by something from within?"

My heart stops as my life flashes before my eyes. The nightmare sickness, that loss of control and emotion that happened every single time. The natural ability to play the violin and draw people in with only a few notes… *By the Lady, is that empathetic magic? Is my ability truly unnatural?* And then the fire… This is too much to process.

"Grace, you are the heir to the House of the Evening," the High Lord emphasizes again. "That cannot and will not change unless all Twelve Houses choose to rewrite ancient laws that have been in place for thousands of years. If you refuse, the seat gets left up to be feuded over by other families in the House, other families across the entire Upper Realm. The world descends into chaos. We lose all credibility in the Twelve Houses."

Alexander sighs and moves away from me. "As much as I would like to give you a genuine choice, there really isn't another way. Do you understand that, Grace?"

"No, I don't as a matter of fact," I snark. "You have a son. Don't you? Why can't he take the heirship?"

"It is the way of the Fae," he says quietly. "The oldest child is heir to the throne, regardless of the circumstances. It has been several centuries since there was a bastard child who took power, but even born out of wedlock, the first child prevails. There has never been a half-mortal child to take the throne. But the laws still apply."

I jump when the man lays a hand on my shoulder. "Ignoring your heritage won't make it go away, Grace. What if something happens in the Middle Realm? What if your magic releases itself again and you hurt someone close to you? What if you hurt your mother?" I turn my head to stare at the wall and avoid his gaze.

As much as I want to throw his soft and gentle manners back in his face, he unfortunately has a reasonable point. I do have magic now. It's a wonder I haven't hurt anyone before now. And it would absolutely destroy me if anything ever happened to my mother, or anyone else for that matter. I could not ignore that I was half Fae and if it ever came out in the Middle Realm, I would not survive to my twentieth birthday.

But could I really become a Lady? Or, for that matter, a High Lady?

By the Lady, I'm going to be a High Lady.

"Alright," I finally speak out. "I will come with you."

Alexander sighs in relief. "Thank you, my child. We will leave in the morning. And I will do everything in my power to make up for the lack of my presence in your childhood."

I shake my head quickly and stride toward him. "Don't bother. With all due respect, High Lord, I do not need you to recreate my childhood. I had a wonderful childhood with my mother and my brother. I did not know you then, and I don't know you now. I will go with you to protect my mother from my magic, and maybe, maybe to prevent the infrastructure of the Twelve Houses from crumbling. I haven't decided yet whether I care about that at all."

I stop directly in front of him. "However, I do expect you to treat me as an equal. As the heir to your House, I demand respect. Respect as your daughter, as your oldest child, and as a magical equal. I am a woman now, Father," I throw the word out at him. His eyes can't hide his shock. "I am no longer a child. Don't forget that."

With that, I leave the room and my father behind, sweeping out with more confidence than I felt.

***

I hide out in my room for the rest of the day. Margaret brings me a late lunch and something for dinner up from the kitchen, but I barely touch either. How can I eat after all I've just witnessed? How can I eat when my world has been flipped on its head? I'm surprised no one has come to attack me yet. There must be some sort of protection placed on this room. I chuckle dryly. *Or maybe they're all afraid of what I'll do to them.*

I rarely move from my bed. I just lie on top of the covers and stare mindlessly up at the ceiling. I study the cracks and the specks on its rough surface, searching for answers in its minuscule designs that I will never find.

I can't process any of this information. My brain is literally incapable of processing any of it. The worst part is the more I try to think about it, all I can think of is my sweet brother, Leo, who isn't my brother after all. There was no mention of a previous one-night stand or a previous son.

Leo is only my half-brother. After all this time, to find this out is devastating.

I just want to curl up and disappear.

Suddenly, I hear a soft knock at my door. I don't want to answer it. They can all wait. "Grace?" I hear Aiden's voice whisper through the crack. I jump to my feet and run to the door, pulling it open violently and pulling him inside quickly. I fall into his arms and hug him fiercely. *They can all wait, except him.*

Aiden brushes my hair back and hugs me tightly to his chest, his hand pressed to the back of my head. I look up at him. I can't help reaching up and touching his face with both hands, examining him for injuries. "Are... are you hurt?" To my horror, my voice sounds so much quieter and weaker than I want it to be.

"No, angel, I'm alright," he comforts and kisses the top of my forehead. "Are you hurt?"

I shake my head quietly before tucking it back into his shoulder. We stand and sway in silence for a few minutes. I can feel that he wants to talk to me about things, but I'm grateful he can read the room enough to know I just need this for a moment.

"We gotta talk, Grace," he says softly.

I sigh and pull him to the bed. I lean my back against one of the bedposts with my legs curled under me. "Alright."

"This is so dangerous, Grace."

"I know. I know," I interrupt him.

"Your brother must have known."

"I don't know how he could have known."

"Grace... you do realize what this means, right?" Aiden pleads with me, taking my hand into his.

I nod gravely. "The prophecy… I'm one of the eight. But which one am I?" The question echoes in the room.

Aiden nods with me. He pulls my hand to his lips and kisses it softly. "Do you think they know?"

I chuckle dryly. "Not yet. But they will very soon. They'll put the pieces together soon enough."

"We could run. Go back to your home in the Middle Realm."

I grab tighter onto Aiden. "No. We'll only get caught, and who knows what will happen if we are? We have to wait. Let them find out. Take them down from the inside. You're not connected to this yet. They're only going to be coming after me."

Now it's Aiden's turn to chuckle at me. "We both know I'm a part of this. The Coven made it clear both of us were involved."

"Yes," I sigh. "But we don't know which one you are either. And until then, I don't want to take any chances. You might be able to look at things from the inside. They'll know my identity soon, but not yours."

We sit silently on the bed for a while. Aiden keeps my hand loosely in his. He rubs his thumb over my skin gently. "I don't like this."

I chuckle dryly. "Do you think I do? I'm… I'm fucking Fae, Aiden." My head turns to him sharply. "No offense."

He laughs quietly. "None taken." He wraps his arm around my shoulders and pulls me into his side. I rest my head lightly against his shoulder and slowly relax into him. Closing my eyes, I let myself breathe him in deeply. His hand lightly reaches up and begins to stroke my hair. "I wish I could come with you."

Only there in his arms does the gravity of my situation really hit me. My body aches everywhere from the fight this morning. *This morning? Was it really only this morning when I thought I was about to die?* I truly wonder whether death would have been better than having my world turned on its head as violently as it has been. *I have to leave with my father tomorrow morning. With my father. To the House of the Evening. My new world... Oh, by the Lady....*

I don't realize that I'm crying until Aiden reaches down and slowly wipes away the tears from my cheeks. But they keep coming down faster. My shoulders shake with the weight of what this means for my future. "Aiden," I sob out his name once before I'm cradled in his lap again, like I was that very first night we spent in the same bed. He hushes me softly and slowly rocks my body back and forth in his arms. He plants soft kisses to my forehead, my cheeks, and my lips as I weep and try to love him back the same way he loves me.

And when he pulls me down into bed and hugs me impossibly tight, I cling to him like he is my lifeline. Because he is. We hold each other tightly until we eventually fall asleep in the early hours of the morning. I pray the aftermath of today doesn't destroy both of us.

CHAPTER THIRTY-EIGHT

As the carriage bumps over the uneven dirt path on its way up the mountain, I steel myself against the sides with my hands. The last three days have been an awkward, tumultuous journey, even more so than all the weeks I spent searching for my answers. I started out in a carriage with my father, but after about an hour of sullen silence, I climbed out and walked nearly four miles before I was granted my own carriage.

High Lord Alexander was in meetings with the Twelve Houses all night, I later found out. There were debates as to whether I could legally be allowed to rule as a Half-Fae, whether the House of the Evening could have any clout after this or whether it would have to withdraw from the Twelve Houses. To the man's credit, he was steady in his testimony. He cited the ancient laws about firstborn legacies and asked everyone if they were really willing to make such a significant change to them in order to keep me from the throne. He warned them it would disrupt all of their lorddoms; siblings would fight siblings for generations to come. And he flat out refused to withdraw.

So here we are, the carriages slowly making their way down the cobblestone streets of the palace town, Silvervale.

I feel like we're moving abnormally slowly, and when I look out the window, I can see why. I knew High Lord Alexander… *my father*, I correct myself, sent word ahead to warn his people. But I didn't expect them to all come out in droves to see their future High Lady.

By the Lady, I can't do this.

The carriage slowly comes to a stop. I'm not sure whether I'm supposed to get out or not. I hear the door to the carriage in front of me open, and a hush falls over the crowd. Alexander is stepping out to address the people. I hear him pontificating on how good it is to be home and trying to explain the situation as best he can. The people listen patiently right up until he tries to explain my existence, and then the hubbub grows quickly. So many questions, not enough answers. The crowd is restless. They demand to see me. The High Lord tries to calm them down.

"Speech! Speech! Speech!" The shouts from the crowd echoed around me.

My father holds up his hands to halt the calls, trying to gain control of the curious citizens. "My good people, my daughter has not been in our world for very long and does not yet possess the full knowledge to address her future people with…"

I can't take the noise anymore.

I stand up and whip open the carriage door. The crowd goes dead silent. "I'll speak to them," I interrupt him strongly. I stride past him while he looks at me, dumbfounded. Swinging a hand up to the baggage rack, I stand on the step on my carriage to give me a little height. Looking out over the crowd, I find a myriad of emotions. I see concern and fear, and in a few people, anger. I imagine they don't like the idea of a half-mortal brat ruling over their House.

If I want their respect, and more importantly, their begrudging agreement to my presence, I have to make my words count.

"My name is Grace Andrea Richardson," my voice rings out over the square. "As you may have noticed, I have chosen not to take the name Faelie yet. It is a decision I do not take lightly… just the same as I take my decision… to be your next High Lady seriously."

In a moment of blind inspiration, I slowly step off and walk into the crowd. They back away, parting around me. I hear quiet exclamations as I move through the people, shock and surprise that a noblewoman would actually step out into a crowd. I continue my speech. "I am not from your world. I know very little. What I do know, I learned from books and the stories of my brother, Leo Richardson, who served as a mercenary in the army of the House of the Sun. But I vow to you to learn as much as I can and acclimate to this world quickly."

I rotate to face my father. "But I want to make one thing very clear. I have no intention of forgetting my mortal heritage. I was raised as a mortal woman, and that is the precedence I am bringing to the throne of the House of the Evening. Because of this, I plan to strengthen our trading ties with the Middle Realm."

The murmurs around me increase in volume. I catch mutterings of approval and disapproval from all sides. My father looks at me, his eyes glinting with what I believe could very well be pride. I continue. "The last thing I want to do is come in here and uproot everything you know, since I would imagine my very presence here is already starting to do that." I smile softly as I hear a few chuckles from behind me. "Believe me," I sigh. "I am just as lost and confused here as you are."

I feel the tide of the crowd start to shift. The dissent and confusion are slowly turning to attention and enrapture. "But I promise you," I spin to face the crowd I'm in. "I will do everything in my power to keep us on the best path. Do not misconstrue my lack of knowledge of the Fae world as an inability to be an effective leader and fighter. Because in that regard, no one is stronger. I will do my best to prove that to you as I move into this House. Thank you." With that, I turn and walk back to the carriage.

Around me, I see the people begin to sink to the ground. I look around in shock and nearly move to help someone until I realize they're kneeling. *For me.* One by one, line by line, the people of the House of the Evening move to their knees in salute of me, the next High Lady. My father's voice rings out over the crowd. "I present to you, Grace Andrea Richardson… Faelie," he finishes hesitantly. "Lady of the House of the Evening."

***

I wish I had had the same welcome from my new home that I did from the people below the mountain.

As we approached the castle, I couldn't stop thinking about what waited on the other side. Alexander told me about my new stepmother, High Lady Elise Faelie, and her children and my new half-siblings, Neil and Analise. Neil is the heir I replaced, and the more I hear my father talk about him, the more I cringe. He's probably going to be incredibly unhappy with me. Not exactly the best way to make a first impression. Analise is ten and apparently a little bundle of energy. Maybe she'll like me.

Now, don't get me wrong, I wasn't expecting a grand entrance with warm, welcoming arms from my new family. I don't know what I was expecting. I just... I had this strange desire for them to like me. Maybe because a part of me recognized I was going to be away from my mother for a long time, and maybe I could at least have a semi-close relationship with my new family so I wouldn't feel so alone as I had for so long.

The carriages pull up to the doorway. I step out slowly and stall on the stair.

It's breathtaking. The road we're standing on extends out in a wide courtyard, and I run to the edge of it in awe. The view overlooks the towns below, all lit up in tiny fairy lights. The music playing in the taverns underneath us carries up the mountain and faintly reaches my ears. The snow cascades down the side in a beautiful wintery slope.

And the castle itself! I have to strain my neck looking up, and I still can't see the top of it. The shadowy purple exterior rises up to an impressive height adorned with intricate glass windows and giant balconies that extended over the mountainside like the courtyard. The smoothness of the stone structure is something out of a fairy tale.

"Come inside, Grace," my father says softly. "And welcome home."

Home...

As we enter, he motions over to an attendant who rushes out to the carriages to oversee the unloading process. "Feel free to explore upstairs, Grace," he says quietly. "There's a library I think you would like; it's down the hallway on the left."

"Shouldn't I meet your family first?" I asked, confused.

He sighs and walks over to me, placing his hands on my shoulders. I do my best not to flinch. "I asked them to meet me in the throne room. I need to… warn them first." He rubs a thumb over my cheek gently. "And it's not just my family, Grace… they're your family now, too."

I nod slowly. I don't know what else to say.

With a soft push, he directs me toward the stairs. "You go on and explore. Let me break it to them a little first."

Hesitantly, I climb my way up the stone staircase up to the second floor. I find the library, and admittedly, it is lovely. Although it's smaller than the library at the House of the Sun, it feels much cozier. I love the rich dark woods of the bookcases and the comfy chairs that seem to be dotted throughout the maze of shelves. I like that; it reminds me of my library back home.

But… I think as I wander over to the window seat and stare down at the valley. *That's not my home anymore. I'll never be able to travel back there. Oh, my poor mother. She'll think I'll have died. It'll break her heart all over again like Leo's death did.* I furiously blink away the few tears that have begun to leak out of my eyes. I miss Mama. I don't feel right being here in this world without her. *Maybe… maybe I can convince Father to let me go visit her just one more time, so she knows I'm okay. Or maybe I'll just sneak out again…*

"So, you're her?" an unfriendly voice appears from behind me.

I whip around. A tall, gangly boy stares at me from the doorway. "Excuse me?" I reply.

"You're that *mortal* girl," he sneers.

"Who the hell are you?" I fire back.

The boy straightens. "I'm Neil Sonra Faelie, the oldest of the *true* House of the Evening bloodline."

"Ah," I sigh quietly. "So, you're the half-brother."

"You took away everything from me," he storms into the library. I take a few steps back in reflex. "I'm the heir to the throne, not you. I've been training my entire life to take Dad's place, and you come in with your uncontrollable powers and your fucking half-mortal blood to take away what is rightfully mine."

"Look, Neil…"

He interrupts me. "No. You better watch your back, *sis*. I'm gunning for you." He reaches out and pushes my shoulders back with two fingers. I stumble slightly.

Suddenly, I can't take another second of this. *No more. No more!* I growl and shove him hard. He falls, tumbling backward and catching himself barely by a hand. "Listen to me, you pompous piece of Fae shit. I didn't ask for this!"

Before I know it, I'm screaming at him. "I didn't ask for any of this! I was perfectly happy in my little mortal world with my mother and my brother! I never needed to know any of this!" I poke him in the chest hard. "But you, Fae scum like you, took my brother from me. And then you *lied* about what happened to him. You *forced me* to come to this world and find out for myself!"

I'm backing him up into the wall by the doorway now. I savor the fear in his eyes. "*Our father,*" I spit out, "abandoned me as a child. I don't remember him at all. At least you got to grow up knowing who you were. I'm being thrown into this Lady-forsaken world with no direction, no instruction, and now I'm the heir to a fucking Fae House."

I lean in close and hiss quietly. "So, I would be very careful about who you are threatening. My uncontrollable powers might just slip and take your Lady-damned head off."

I push off of him in disgust. "Save your petty threats for some other bitch. I have bigger things to deal with than a jealous child like you."

Growling again, I say dangerously, "Get out. Now."

Neil looks hesitant. "I…"

"*Get out now! Leave me alone!*" I shriek.

He runs.

When he leaves, I collapse to my knees. This is all too much for me. I clench my fists tightly to my sides, trembling on the floor trying to contain my rage. *How dare he try to take me on right out of the gate! How dare he come after me! I didn't know a damn thing about my noble status! I wouldn't have chosen this life for myself!*

I have to get out of here.

Now.

I have to run.

I have to run.

I scramble to my feet and flee the library. I tear down the hallways of the castle, turning random corners I can't navigate and taking random forks I have no idea where they lead. My boots slam against the floor, clanging the entire way down. And all the while, I still feel trapped. I need to find a door.

A glint from a nearby room suddenly catches my eye. I skid to a stop. Leaning in the doorway cautiously, I realize it's some sort of a music room. A grand piano stands regally in the center of the room alongside a handful of orchestral instruments. And sitting near the front, on a stand, is the very thing I need to center me and clear my head. I race over without hesitation.

I pick up the violin swiftly to my shoulder, and the music emanates from it with hypnotizing lilt, speed, and rhythm.

I play, and I play, and I play, until the House of the Evening fades away around me and I can only hear notes and beats and melodies. Until the entire Upper Realm fades, and I can only feel the music coursing through my soul. Until the bow finally tumbles from my fingers, hours and hours later from exhaustion, and clangs against the tile floor, and I resign myself to a new world.

"Wow!" I hear an excited shout from the doorway. I whip around, nearly dropping the violin in surprise. Analise peeks out from the doorframe, her eyes and mouth both wide open. "You play so beautifully!" She runs into the music room eagerly. "Will you play for me? Please?"

This little girl looks up at me so expectantly and hopefully that my heart melts just a little bit. *By the Lady, she breaks my heart. How can she look at me so innocently, so purely, with no regard for where I come from or who I am?* It hits me like a train from my home realm. *She's looking to me... like... like a younger sister looks at an older one.*

Did I look at Leo like that?

Oh, but I already know the answer to that; of course I did. I trusted him to teach me and to protect me and to love me. And maybe, something in him knew I had all this power inside me, and yet he never loved me any less. If anything, he loved me more for the person I was. I looked at him like that because I knew he would never turn me away.

And when I look down at Analise, I know I can't turn her away either.

Besides, she may be my only ally in this house.

I smile softly. "Come on in." She flies in and sits on the steps at my feet, clapping her hands excitedly. "I'm Grace," I say quietly.

"I'm Analise!" She beams up at me. "Can you play that song again?"

I chuckle and put the bow back to the string, and this time... I play for her. Until she's long since fallen asleep... I play, and I play, and I play... until I finally play her awake with the sunrise.

Get ready for me, Upper Realm. I'm coming for you.

ACKNOWLEDGMENTS

When I started brainstorming for *Chasing Fae* back in January of 2018, I had no idea this would be the story that would turn into my debut novel. The past two years have been an amazing adventure of creating, drafting, revising, and marketing that I have learned so much from. Most of all, I have discovered that publishing a book takes a lot of people and a lot of spirits working together, and I am so grateful for all the support I have had through this journey. Fulfilling this dream would not have been possible without you.

Thank you first and foremost to my family and the family I have made for myself. This includes my immediate family: Morgan Hammer, Julie Hammer, and Todd Hammer; my amazing boyfriend, Daniel Sage (who made the amazing maps of the Three Realms at the front of this book); and my best friends in the whole world: Trajan Mobley, Aidan O'Halloran, Alex Washington, Cassie Wiltse, and Roger Clanton.

I want to especially thank my fantastic editor, Kristy Carter, who really saw my vision and took *Chasing Fae* to a place I didn't know it could go. I am grateful for her guidance, her notes, and most of all, her spirit and passion for my book.

Next I want to thank my extended family: my grandparents, Joan and Jack Ohlweiler, Andrew and Sharon Hammer; my Aunt Jane, Uncle Matt, and cousin Brennan; my Uncle Jack, Aunt Lisa, and cousins, Abby, Jack, and Ben; my Aunt Jill; my great-aunt and uncle Trisha and Jim Blanchard; Linell Machold, and Richard Gargett.

Thank you to my honors fraternity, the Gamma Psi Chapter of Phi Sigma Pi, for being the absolute greatest community on William and Mary's campus. I have appreciated your support and friendship so much over the last two years. Thank you to those brothers who purchased: Caleb Baker, Liberty Bassett, Caroline Cox, Lauren French, Maggie Gentry, Jessie Henry, Melaina Jacoby, Maddy Mulder, Alexa Regnier, Hana Warner, and Jasmine Wheelan. Thank you also to the William and Mary community as a whole: students, faculty, and alumni. Namely Grace Breitenbeck, Caitlin Garber, Stella Hudson, Tracy Johnson, Potter McKinney, Ryen Rasmus, and Carson Stillman.

Thank you to my boyfriend's family: Amy Sage Boyd, Cynthia Lewis, and Derek Lewis. You have been so supportive and inviting over the years I have known your son. Thank you to the multitude of family friends from my family and Daniel's who supported my writing journey: Ellen Beck, Rich Buchanan, Diane Curtis, Michelle Czajkowski, Lisa Finlayson, Sally Hilgendorff, David Jacobsen, Nadya Klinetob, Elaine Maitland, Stephanie McClung, Maureen Moore, Aarthi Natarajan, Jane Philion, Nisha Shah, Kathryn Ward, Bridget Yaple, and John Yokim.

To my friends, thank you for making my dream possible. To Molly Barresi, Elizabeth Cobb-Curtis, Prentiss Cooper, Adam Cyzner, Ashley Derrington, Kathryn Goodwin, Grace

Hasson, Stephanie Joyner, Ruth Shumway, Jenna Upton, and Laura Zielinski. You all are awesome!

To my former and current teachers and instructors, thank you for guiding me through my entire life in education. Thank you to those of you who contributed directly and to those of you who provided moral support: Matt Cosper, Philip Daileader, Chuck Edwards, Craig Estep, Betsy Fox, Sabrina Howard, Luke Ivey, Eric Koester, Christine McConaughy, Irene Pointon, Lauren Putman, Lucy Smith, Kim Smith, C.W. Stacks, Will Thomason, Tracy Vanneste, Laci Wargo, and Mike Weiss.

Thank you to my writing friends, many of whom have been with me since I started publicizing my writing journey. To Shea Ballard, Janie Begeman, Debbie Hofstetter, Michele Lugiai, Ed Maciorowski, Rashmi Menon, Judy Myers, Jessika Rucker, Kristi Casey Sanders, and Sabrina Shaw: I love you all.

Thank you so much to every IndieGoGo Contributor who made a difference in my presale campaign; many thanks particularly to Ronald Charpentier, Randy Holloway, Joe Kaiser, and Thomas Pace. Thank you also to all those who shared, liked, commented, and posted the link to my campaign to make *Chasing Fae* a reality.

Finally, thank you to Brian Bies and New Degree Press for putting their faith in me and my book. They have taught me so much about the publishing process and about myself. I am sincerely grateful to have had the opportunity to work with them and publish something that I am incredibly proud of.

To my readers: Keep dreaming. Keep creating. Keep loving. You have something amazing inside of you to share, and I promise you, all of your dreams are possible. I can't wait to see you all out there someday. Much love to you all.

AUTHOR BIO

From the time she was a child of eleven, writing her first novel between classes, Cady Hammer explored her world through her imagination. She was often teased for being in her own world, but never hesitated to invite others along on the adventure. As she grew older, Cady's studies in history and anthropology set the stage for the detailed worldbuilding that lets readers step into the story. Her stories explore the complexities of relationships crafted around the idea that love, friendship, and grief are all interwoven.

Cady runs the internationally-read website, Fluff About Fantasy, a place for young writers to learn the genre-specific craft of writing fantasy and be inspired by what they can accomplish. Find out more at https://fluffaboutfantasy.com.

www.ingramcontent.com/pod-product-compliance
Lightning Source LLC
LaVergne TN
LVHW011759060526
838200LV00053B/3632